Choose
the
SOUTHWEST

Choose
the
SOUTHWEST

Retirement Discoveries for Every Budget

by John Howells

GATEWAY
BOOKS

Copyright © 1996 by John Howells

Edited and Designed by Donna S. Lee
Cover Design by Amy Neiman
Cover Illustration © by Susan Detrich / SIS

Printed in the United States of America

Gateway Books

Distributed by Publishers Group West

Library of Congress Cataloging-in-Publication Data

Howells, John
      Choose the Southwest : retirement discoveries for every budget /
by John Howells.
            p.   cm.
      Includes index.
      ISBN 0-933469-25-X
      1. Southwest, New--Guidebooks. 2. Retirement, Places of-
-Southwest, New--Guidebooks. 3. Cost and standard of living-
-Southwest, New.   I. Title.
F785.3.H69 1996
917.904'53—dc20   96-4140
                                                                CIP

10 9 8 7 6 5 4 3 2

CONTENTS

The Southwestern States

INTRODUCTION

My last book on retirement planning, *Where to Retire*, describes and recommends 150 communities around the nation as possible retirement choices. However, many readers find that when they narrow their choices to a certain section of the country, more detailed information helps in making final decisions. Others already know where they want to retire and want to zero in on that particular area from the beginning. Because of the wide variety and large number of potential retirement locations, the amount of information on each listing in *Where to Retire* had to be kept to a minimum. Some nice places were left out because of space limitations.

So, to better inform folks who want to sharpen their focus on a particular region, a series of regional retirement guides seemed to be in order. (This eases the job of a retirement writer, for it's far easier to present more information about a location than to make painful decisions as to what must be left unsaid.)

Therefore, my wife and I started out on another odyssey of research and enjoyable travel as we visited new towns and revisited familiar places. Much of this newest research was done by towing our fifth-wheel trailer and staying several days in each town. This gives us the flavor of what it's like to live in a community, something that can't be done by studying statistics and chamber of commerce handouts. As a result, this volume contains descriptions of many new retirement locations, some places not covered in other publications, plus more in-depth information about previously discussed communities. We've evaluated over 50 different towns for your consideration and, by extension, many more places in sur-rounding localities.

What We Mean by "Southwest"

Most folks will agree, the "West" begins in Texas and ends at the Pacific Ocean. However, to sharpen our definition of "Southwest" let us agree to exclude the eastern half of Texas. Why? Because East Texas is culturally, climatically and conceptually part of the South and/or Midwest. In East Texas, we're talking swampy bayous, cotton fields, prairies, and folks who don't even own a pair of cowboy boots. In West Texas, you'll find sagebrush, dry hills, cactus-fed cattle and people who wear cowboy boots even if they're from New Jersey. For our purposes then, a north-south line through San Antonio marks the eastern-most boundary of our research.

Wait a minute; what about California? Clearly, you can't travel any farther west than California without renting a boat or donning water wings. Yet think about it; California differs from neighboring Nevada and Arizona in the same way as West Texas differs from Louisiana or Arkansas. That is, California differs culturally, geo-graphically and conceptually from Arizona and Nevada. It's true that California's eastern deserts mirror Nevada and Arizona land-scapes, but almost no one lives here. Most retirees prefer California's unique climates along the Pacific coast or the central areas of the state. These are as different from Nevada and Arizona deserts as East Texas differs from West Texas. Retirement in California is the subject of another book.

How far north does the Southwest extend? Even though the top portions of Colorado and Utah extend northward, into what some might consider the Northwestern part of the country, this book con-siders the entire states of Colorado and Utah as part of the Southwest. Their climates and geography blend with their southern neighbors and present a unified landscape of retirement possibili-ties. Folks looking for a particular lifestyle and quality of life typical of New Mexico, Arizona or Nevada might well investigate Colorado or Utah before making a choice.

One thing all Southwest areas have in common is a dry climate. Vast areas are in semi-desert or arid mountain country. Rainfall is scarce, often just a tenth of that expected in the Midwestern and Eastern states. Temperatures are dependent upon altitude here, and mountains receive more rain than low-country deserts. Higher altitudes, of course, mean more livable summers and winter snows which can vary from light to incredible, depending upon the locale.

The Southwest's low humidity turns out to be the key to its success in attracting retirees. Humidity's influence on climate can't be exaggerated. If you've ever spent time in a low-humidity location you'll know that cold days don't seem nearly as chilly, and hot days are much more bearable.

The word desert incorrectly conjures images of Sahara-like sand dunes and desolate sweeps of barren land. True, North American deserts can be like that, but rarely are. There's usually plenty of vegetation, but of a different nature. Over eons, plants and animals have adapted to living in dry country—even in places with four inches of rain per year. Trees and bushes learned to survive on little water, flourishing miraculously in a dry desert or mountain environment. The first spring storm makes the desert bloom with an unforgettable explosion of colorful flowers and a profusion of green, all of which disappear when the plants withdraw into their water-conserving mode for the summer. Some plants developed tough skins that prevent precious water from evaporating and thus stay green year-round.

Animals, too, have adapted. An amazing variety of reptiles, mammals and birds do perfectly well in the desert. Some survive the fierce summers by conserving energy during the heat of the day, then foraging and exercising in the cooler hours of the morning and evening. Other species developed patterns of migration, spending summers in higher altitudes where the weather is cool and damp, and then wintering in the pleasant warmth of the desert.

Therefore, it should come as no surprise that we humans, the most adaptable of all organisms, have also adapted to dry mountain and desert living. When living in the desert, we've learned to conserve body energy by living in air-conditioned homes, driving air-conditioned autos and by foraging at air-conditioned shopping malls. We exercise by riding bikes or playing golf in the cooler hours of the morning and evening. Midday is for naps. Instead of developing tough skins that prevent precious water from evaporating, desert dwellers develop sun-tanned skins and sip cool drinks. Forget about evaporation!

Those choosing to live at higher altitudes, or in naturally colder Southwestern climes, enjoy comfortable springs, summers and falls. There you'll appreciate shirtsleeve days, sweater evenings and sleeping under blankets at night. In August, you may play golf at noon if you please. The obvious high-altitude trade-off is a true winter season in place of the low desert's balmy, sun-filled Januarys and Februarys. So, when winter arrives, cold-weather Southwesterners enthusiastically pull on heavy clothes and strap on snowshoes or skis to enjoy their crisp, dry, winter wonderlands. Others drive an hour or so to the low desert and go swimming.

Unlike the middle United States, with its continental weather patterns, where frozen ground, ice and slush stick around all winter, Southwestern winters are livable. In all but the highest and most snow-prone areas, a Southwestern winter is an on-again-off-again affair. For example: Denver winters aren't much colder than in Sacramento, California; the key is that because of their difference in altitude, instead of Sacramento's winter rains, Denver gets snow. Denver's overnight snowfall can be dramatic, a foot deep is common, yet the snow rarely stays around for more than a day or two. It's often gone by the next afternoon. A big plus is that Denver's dry air makes cold days much more bearable than in Sacramento's humid, river-chilled atmosphere. A 50-degree, 85-percent humidity day in Sacramento will make you wish you were in Denver.

Quality of Life

Our travels have taken us through hundreds of communities, and we've checked out many, many local conditions before making the final selections for this book. However, because a town is not described here doesn't necessarily mean it wouldn't be a great place to retire. The bottom line: there is no "best" place to retire for everyone. Selecting your ideal retirement home is a highly individual decision and depends on personal lifestyle, future aspirations and, most importantly, what you consider to be an ideal quality of life.

The phrase "quality of life" means something different for every individual. When you ask New York City residents about their quality of life, you might hear them rave about the plethora of cultural events available to them. They enjoy everything from opera, jazz combos and stage plays, to world-class restaurants, museums and Fifth Avenue shopping. They'll tell you they can't imagine living without all the excitement that is characteristic of urban life. Existence would be boring without Manhattan's highly charged atmosphere of culture, entertainment and conveniences.

When you ask the same question in a small Southwestern town, "quality of life" might be defined in terms of peace and quiet, outdoor activities and low-key cultural activities. People here prize the crystal-clear quality of the air they breathe, their sense of security, safety and knowing what to expect from neighbors and community. Their quality of life is enhanced every time they're treated to the sight of a doe and her fawn grazing in a forest glade. Miles of hiking and bicycle trails, winter skiing and summer gold-panning replace opera, gourmet restaurants and museums. Hooking a trout with a fly-cast in a sparkling mountain stream substitutes for sitting in a stadium and watching the Mets lose another game.

Yet Southwestern retirement doesn't mean just outdoor activities. Many communities provide exciting cultural events and entertainment that rival those found back East—without the excitement of muggers lurking in the darkness after the performance. True, you won't see world-renowned personalities appearing in a musical, but the fact that your hair-dresser is performing in the play or your next-door neighbor works on set design makes up for the lack of professionalism. Who knows, you might decide to participate, something impossible for Manhattan theater buffs.

Southwestern Lifestyles

Because the Southwest provides such a wide range of climates and variety of cities and towns, a large number of lifestyles are possible. There's something to fit any personality or appetite, and plenty of opportunity to acquire a taste for some new hobby, skill or whatever endeavor you'd care to try. Many of the activities listed below can, of course, be enjoyed in Eastern or Midwestern settings, but not as easily and not as a regular part of your routine.

Hunting and fishing are much easier to do in Southwest environs, because most lands, forests and streams are public property. Instead of being fenced and posted with keep-out signs, most unused land belongs to the U.S. Forest Service or the Bureau of Land Management. It belongs to all of us.

River rafting is another common sport in the Southwest, simply because there are so many more whitewater rivers here, and they are much longer. Most Eastern whitewater rapids are a few miles long and can be covered in a matter of hours. Some Western rivers take days, as much as two weeks of rafting by day and camping at night. Again, since most of the land traversed belongs to the public, you can pretty much launch your boats and set up your tents wherever you darn well please.

Rock hunting and prospecting are popular hobbies in the Southwest, something not often done in the rest of the country. Again, because so much land is public, you can wander about at your pleasure. You can pan most streams for gold, you can break open rocks in search of ore or collect gemstones where you find them. Because vegetation is usually sparse, rocks and minerals are exposed for easy examination. The exciting part is, should you by chance stumble across something valuable, you can stake a claim and start mining. Don't laugh; my brother once found a silver and lead deposit and took out two million dollars from the first 85 feet of digging! However, be aware that Congress is looking to change the laws concerning mining and prospecting.

Photographers love Western ghost towns and the sensational landscapes that cannot be found elsewhere. Jewelry making is a popular avocation out West; hobbyists often use semi-precious stones they've collected in the desert and polished themselves.

Most all other social and recreational activities available to Easterners are enjoyed in the Southwest. Bridge clubs, literary groups, travel clubs, whatever you enjoyed before will entertain you here. If you can't find your niche, you can usually develop one at the local senior citizen center.

None of the Above

You may be one of those easy-to-please types whose interests are limited to television and gossiping with neighbors. We all know people who arrange their lives to fit the television schedule. Sunday is for football and 60 Minutes; Monday morning is for soap operas; Monday night is for Murphy Brown, and so on. Shopping trips to the supermarket, browsing the downtown stores and visiting neighbors have to fit into the space between programs.

While some folks would view a lifestyle like this as boring, others see it as a perfectly natural way to live; after all, this is the way they've lived all their lives. When they had jobs, they couldn't afford the luxury of staying up late to watch David Letterman, and since they worked during the daytime, Soaps were something they heard others talk about. Now, when they can do anything they care to, they choose to indulge themselves.

However, I suspect these folks won't be reading this book. For them it doesn't make sense to move away for retirement since they have everything they need right where they live. However, I would urge those who are thinking of moving to seriously consider the recreational and social facets of their new home base. Changing where you live is an opportunity to change your entire lifestyle. Your retirement can be a new beginning, not just a continuation of the same old groove (or maybe it's the same old rut).

Real Estate Prices

Throughout this book, I've tried to give the reader a flavor for housing costs and real estate prices. Aside from the probability that my estimates may soon be outdated by inflation, I've had grave doubts about the wisdom of including prices. They can be misleading in the extreme. Why? Because it's virtually impossible to truly convey an accurate picture of a housing market. It seems as if it should be a simple job: state the average sales prices in a region, and let the reader extrapolate from there. You're either prepared to pay an average price for an average home, above-average price for an above-average home, or below-average price for a below-average home. What's the problem?

Part of the problem is defining the terms "average house" and "average sales price." Suppose we agree that an average house is a 1,500-square-foot, three-bedroom, two-bath home in a safe neighborhood. That's the easy part. What's difficult is determining the average cost of that average house. You see, statistics tell how many homes were sold in a given community and how much money changed hands. Now if my junior high school math serves me correctly, we find the average sales price by dividing the total sales prices by the number of homes sold. But how many of those houses sold fit our definition of an "average house"?

Let's suppose we're looking at a community with a sudden boom in upscale housing. (That happens frequently in today's affluent retiree market.) Perhaps a large, security-gated, country-club development (the only one in the area) is selling homes at $500,000 each. At the same time, average homes in average neighborhoods aren't selling so well. Say that 20 "average" homes sell for about $120,000 each, while ten $500,000 new homes are completed and sold. That brings the average sales price to $246,666, yet we know full well that an average home costs half that amount. At first glance, it would seem this community would be out of the question for many retirees who would otherwise love living here, but could not afford a house costing over $200,000. The fact could well be that a few of these average homes sold for far less than $120,000, maybe $90,000, making this community affordable for those who are looking for something economical.

A further problem arises when an author interviews real estate brokers about values of local property. Some real estate people will quote the average "selling price" as the cost of the average home—which as we've seen may be misleading. Others, realizing that the average selling price is unrealistic, will estimate the cost of an "average" home. And others, anxious to entice buyers to the community, may exaggerate and quote lowest-offered prices as the "average prices." In this book, I've tried to steer a center course between the tilts, but I'll be the first to admit that prices quoted here are subjective. Furthermore, changing market conditions could make them obsolete before this book is ready for its second edition.

Speaking of buying property, for most of the locations in this book, you'll find one or two real estate connections, names of brokers or salespeople. Please do not take these as endorsements of any particular real estate firm, as approval of a company's integrity or efficiency. All I've done is list those professionals who assisted me in compiling information about the housing market in that particular town or city. The fact is, these real estate offices were picked at random from the telephone directory in that city. I figure that if they're willing to help me, they'll probably help you as well. I also believe that with all real estate professionals who belong to associations and are licensed, there's a good chance that one picked at random will be as good as the next. Good luck.

Private Retirement Communities

Year by year, retirement becomes more of a big business, prompting impressive corporate investment. Planned retirement communities, often of astounding size, are popping up all over the country. Arkansas, Tennessee and North Carolina lead the trend, with other states following suit. Arizona's Sun City West, for example, has 7,100 acres, with more than 15,000 homes.

Often these places are "hermetically sealed" developments; that is, to enter the property you must be a member of that development or have good reason to be there. Wanting to price property is usually a good enough reason to visit, although a few developments permit you to purchase only by invitation of other residents. Round-the-clock guards staff the gates, scrutinizing everyone who enters. Occasionally, after the project is sold out, the original developers are no longer interested in staffing the gates with expensive security guards. It then becomes the responsibility of the owners' association.

Many complexes restrict buyers to 55 and older. Youngsters may visit, but not live there. This impacts the community in two ways. Obviously, your lives will be more tranquil without gangs of kids riding bikes, playing boomboxes and knocking baseballs through your living room window. But more importantly than that, you'll enjoy a lower crime rate. Burglaries, vandalism and theft usually occur in direct proportion to the number of teenagers in the neighborhood. The other side of the coin is that many retirees prefer living in mixed-age neighborhoods; they find young children and teenagers fun to be with.

Developers look for inexpensive land for their new complexes, so they buy square miles of desert or large tracts of forested land. They can then afford to put in roads and utilities, dam up streams to create lakes and ponds, lay out a golf course or two—all at a fraction of what land alone would have cost in other parts of the country. Since local wages are generally less than in large cities, quality housing becomes relatively inexpensive.

Two caveats. First: make sure you are going to be satisfied with the physical location of your new home. Most developments we've visited are located several miles from the nearest town. Why? Because that's where the corporation found the cheapest land. This could mean a 20- or 30-mile drive into town to the supermarket or to buy a bit of hardware for the shed you are building.

Second: beware of glib promises and super-salesmanship. When a retirement project is in its initial phase, there will be a beautiful to-scale plan of the development showing the future shopping mall, clubhouses, swimming pools and all the wonderful amenities to come. An enormous supermarket and hardware store are clearly part of the plan. Believe this when you see it. Sometimes, when and if the "mall" is completed, the supermarket turns out to be a convenience store. (This doesn't happen as often with the more established developers.)

After you visit a development, check with a real estate office and the newspaper's classified section to see what resales in the development are selling for. If homes are offered at prices drastically below those of the development's sales office, you may have trouble getting your price if you later need to sell out. Also, if you like the development, you could save money by buying a resale instead of a newly-built unit.

An advantage to getting in on the beginning of a retirement complex is that it's easier to become involved socially and to make new friends with neighbors as they move in. You might, however, prefer a well-established neighborhood, where you can join existing clubs and activities instead of having to form them. Another point to keep in mind is that membership fees are involved in planned communities, either yearly or monthly. These fees can be reasonable or considerable, depending on the situation. By the way, the rule of thumb is that $100 in monthly fees is a financial commitment roughly equivalent to an additional $10,000 mortgage.

Retirees Welcome!

Many communities actively seek retirees, doing everything possible to lure them into the area. For good reason—according to a study done by the Alabama Department of Economic and Community Affairs, when 50 new retirees locate in a small community, the impact is equivalent to a $10-million industry moving in. Retirees spend money. About 90 percent of their income goes for local goods and services. They actually create jobs rather than take jobs. With half a million retirees relocating each year, we're seeing a massive redistribution of wealth, flowing from industrial metropolitan cities to rural and small-town America. A sign of the times: a McDonalds restaurant in Florida replaced the kids' playground with a shuffleboard court. The welcome mat is out for retirees!

Today's senior citizens, as a group, are more affluent than at any time in our country's history. Because of the fantastic real estate appreciation of the '70s and '80s, those who happened to buy homes when they were cheap now have tremendous equities with which to finance their retirement. (Unfortunately, we may be the last of the affluent retirees. Our children and grandchildren have to struggle to become homeowners; low down-payments and $100-a-month mortgages are faded memories.) Today's average retired couple has $225,000 in total assets. Much of this is in home equity. These unused funds, when released and used for retirement, can permit retirees to upgrade their lifestyles dramatically. When spent in a new community, this money benefits local residents. That's why so many rural towns are begging retirees to join them.

Bargain Opportunities

Local boosters too often place undue emphasis on a low cost of living and cheap real estate as prime attractions of their area. True, these items go hand in hand; that is, when you find low-cost housing, you'll also find economical living costs in general. In our travels, we've encountered real estate markets where $19,000 will buy a three-bedroom home, where carpenters will remodel for $5.00 an hour, where haircuts are still $3.50 and permanent waves $14.75. However, as I continually stress, inexpensive living isn't necessarily the same as quality living. Some low-cost areas are exceptional bargains, combining a high quality of life with welcoming neighbors and affordable living costs. Yet other low-cost areas are intensely dreary and boring, places you'd visit only at gunpoint. .

Why is the cost of living and housing so much less in some localities? Basically, you'll find two reasons for cheap real estate and low rents. The most common reason is it's an undesirable place to live. These towns steadily lose population because they have absolutely nothing going for them—no jobs, no charm. Homes sell for rock-bottom prices because eager sellers outnumber reluctant buyers. Unless you are sincerely dedicated to boredom, bad weather and cable TV, these are not places you would seek out for retirement.

The second situation deals with an unforeseen, disastrous business slump or trend that causes the job market to disintegrate. In this event, people don't necessarily want to leave and seek work elsewhere, they have to. Homes go on the real estate market at giveaway prices. There's no other choice.

Although situations like this are personal tragedies for displaced families, they open windows of opportunity for retired folks. Since working for a living and a regular weekly paycheck aren't essential for most retired couples, bargain real estate is theirs for a fraction of what similar housing would cost elsewhere. As younger folks with growing children move away, over-60 people move in and raise the ratio between retired and working people to impressive levels. The over-60 crowd becomes a majority and wields appreciable influence over local government and political processes.

We've visited a few of these towns and reported on them in earlier editions, places like Ajo and Bisbee in Arizona, where mines closed, and Colorado's Grand Junction, whose economy toppled when the oil shale industry collapsed. As you might imagine, opportunities like these don't last forever. As retirees move in and snap up the bargains, prices naturally rise. Yet they rarely rise to the level they were at before the problem occurred.

Doing Your Own Research

Magazine articles and guidebooks commonly grade retirement communities, ranking the top places from one to ten, as if they were rating major league baseball teams. With a baseball team, we can check the scores; can't argue with that. But cities and towns don't receive scores except in somebody's mind. The fact that a freelance writer likes a city and ranks it number one in his magazine article doesn't prove a thing. For all we know, maybe the writer has never even seen the place!

Favorable ratings are too often awarded on the basis of conditions that don't affect retirees. For example: good schools, high employment and a booming business climate will boost a town's rating, while horrible weather and high taxes are often ignored. Quality grammar schools and juvenile recreational programs matter less to retirees than quality senior citizen centers and safe neighborhoods. Full employment and thriving business conditions spell high prices and expensive housing. Also, cultural amenities, such as museums and operas, receive high marks in retirement analysis. Yet how many times a month will you be going to the opera? The museum? Would you rather live in a town with two golf courses and no museums or two museums and no golf courses? To find your ideal location, you're going to have to do your own ranking.

Ideally, you'll start your retirement analysis early. A great way to do this is by combining research with your vacations from work. Instead of visiting the same old place each year, try different parts of the country. Even if you are already retired, you need to do some traveling if you plan on moving somewhere else. Your travels needn't be expensive, however. Pick up some camping equipment at the next garage sale in your neighborhood. Just about anywhere you want to visit will have either state parks with campgrounds or commercial camps—places like KOA—where you can pitch a tent. Many RV parks have special spots for tent camping. Your local library will have a campground directory to help you locate a place in or near your target town.

Check out real estate prices. Look into apartment and house rentals. Are there the kinds of cultural events in town you will enjoy? A cultural event could be anything from light opera to hoisting a glass of beer at the corner tavern; the question is, will you be happy you moved there? Just looking closely, as if you truly intended to move there, will tell you a lot.

While you are there, be sure to drop in on the local senior citizens' center. Talk to the director and the members of the center to see just what services will be available should you decide to move there. A dynamic and full-service senior center could make a world of difference in your everyday life.

When investigating a town, one of your first stops should be at the local chamber of commerce office. The level of enthusiasm and retirement advice offered by the chamber staff clearly tells you something about the town's elected officials and businessmen's attitudes toward retirees. Most chamber offices love to see retirees move into their towns; they recognize the advantages of retirement money coming into the economy and the valuable contributions retirees can make to the community. These offices will do just about anything to help you get settled and to convince you that living in their town is next to paradise. However, don't be surprised if the person behind the counter isn't the least bit interested in your upcoming move. My experience has been that a few chamber of commerce offices are staffed with minimum-wage employees who seem to resent folks coming in to ask questions and interfering with the novels they are reading. When this is the case, you might guess that the level of services and senior citizen participation in local affairs could be somewhat inadequate.

Newspaper Research

Between periods of travel, you can do your research at the local library or by mail. Almost all libraries have out-of-town newspapers. The larger the library, the wider the variety. If you live in a small town where your library can't provide the newspapers you want (particularly those from another state or smaller towns some distance away), one way to obtain them is to write to the chamber of commerce in the place you are interested in and explain that you need a copy or two to make decisions about retiring there. You can also write to the newspaper office (look in the phone directory section of your library for the name of the paper). Some real estate brokers will gladly mail you copies of the local newspaper, because they know you will probably use their services when and if you decide to buy. We once had a real estate office send us a three-month subscription to the local paper to help us make up our mind.

The most important part of an out-of-town paper is the classified section. Check real estate prices, rentals and mobile home parks; compare them with your hometown newspaper and you begin to get a picture of relative costs. Contrast help-wanted ads with work-wanted ads. This tells you wage rates, should you consider working part-time, and clues you in on what kind of competition you will have for jobs. A scarcity of help-wanted ads indicates unemployment. This won't matter if you don't plan on working, but it's important if you need to work part-time.

Mobile home parks advertise monthly park rentals, giving you an idea of what that style of living costs. Should there be an under-supply of vacancies, you can expect rentals to be expensive. Comparing prices of used items such as furniture, appliances and automobiles against your local paper's classifieds also tells you a great deal about local living costs.

Display advertisements provide supermarket and department store specials to compare, particularly if national chains operate both there and in your home town. Sometimes identical specials will be priced differently from one locality to another, a further measure of costs. Ads will tell you whether large discount stores are available for shopping convenience and economy.

A newspaper's editorial page broadcasts the publisher's political stance. A paper that slants news stories to match its owner's opinions makes uncomfortable reading if you happen to be on the other side of the political fence. A publisher can profoundly influence the thinking of a community. When his newspaper is the only source of local news, the publisher's opinions are often accepted as clear truths by your neighbors. Being the only conservative in a neighborhood of liberals (or vice versa), can make you feel lonely. Particularly revealing are newspaper campaigns for or against services and spending for senior citizens.

You learn a lot about how safe a community is by the way crime is reported in the news columns. If a bicycle theft or a reckless-driving arrest makes front page headlines, rest assured the crime situation isn't too serious—assuming, of course, you aren't a bicycle thief and don't occasionally drive your Buick on the sidewalk. But if chain-saw murders, car-jackings and drive-by shootings are buried on page 27, look out!

A good newspaper will list senior citizen activities, cultural events, community college classes and other undertakings that might interest you. A paper with a large section devoted to senior citizen news reflects a high level of interest in our well-being. Look for news about retiree political-action groups; when they band together to vote, the level of services and benefits rise in proportion to their voting strength.

Libraries' out-of-town telephone books are full of valuable information. The "Yellow Pages" paint an unabridged picture of a town's business life: banks, supermarkets, shopping centers and other commercial enterprises. Check for local and intercity bus service and taxi companies. Look under the listing for "airlines" or "airports" to see if there is a local airport and which airlines service it. See how many hospitals there are. A telephone book also gives an up-to-date listing for the chamber of commerce office and the senior citizens' center.

Continuing Education

I just can't pass up the opportunity to climb on the soapbox and push an idea I'm enthusiastic about, something that grows more popular as time goes by: continuing education for seniors. Throughout the country, community colleges, adult education centers and universities are adding classes and programs expressly tailored to older adults' needs. More than two-thirds of U.S. colleges and universities offer reduced rates or even free tuition to older citizens. You won't feel like the proverbial sore thumb in a setting where you have company your own age.

But continuing education for retirees is more than a pleasant learning experience; the classroom is a tool for retirement adjustment. Signing up for a class in Chinese cooking, fly-tying or rock polishing puts you in social contact with others from the community. An adult classroom is a great place to make friends with lively, stimulating people who share your interests, folks whose horizons are broader than Monday Night Football or tomorrow's Family Feud show. Taking classes is a quick, sure-fire way of becoming part of your new community.

Many schools will allow you to audit the more serious courses, that is, take the class but not have to worry about quizzes, tests, finals or term papers. You get the intellectual benefit and fun out of a course without the tension of having to do the homework or participate in class discussions.

If you have a trade or special skills of some sort, an even faster way of getting known is to offer to teach a class. Community colleges and adult education programs are often strapped for cash to hire full-time teachers and therefore welcome the opportunity to add classes with part-time or volunteer teachers. If your skills are needed, schools often don't require a teaching degree, just experience and the ability to communicate it to others.

Once, when my wife and I moved to a small Oregon city, I taught a couple of community college classes in freelance writing. Not for the money—which was almost nothing—but for the opportunity of meeting townspeople with a common interest in writing. The class was a resounding success, for we made half a dozen friends and received an invitation to join a local writer's group. Our entrance into the town's social life was immediate and satisfying.

But even if you have no intention of taking classes, a community college or university can be important to your lifestyle. Most schools provide the community at large with a wide selection of social and cultural activities, benefits which wouldn't exist without the school's presence. You don't have to be a registered student to attend advertised lectures and speeches (often free) given by famous scientists, politicians, visiting artists and other well-known personalities. Concerts, ranging from Beethoven to boogie-woogie, are presented by guest artists as well as the university's music department. Stage plays, Broadway musicals and Shakespeare are produced by the drama department, with season tickets often less than a single performance at a New York theater. Some schools make special provisions to allow seniors to use their recreational facilities. And art exhibits, panel discussions and a well-stocked library are often available to the public.

What to Look For

To sum it all up, the following is a list of requirements my wife and I personally consider essential for a successful retirement relocation. Your needs may be different; feel free to add or subtract from the list, and then use the list to measure communities against your standards.

1. Safety. Can you walk through your neighborhood without fearful glances over your shoulder? Can you leave your home for a few weeks without dreading a break-in? Most retirees feel that safety is the most important condition of all in selecting a new home.

2. Climate. Will temperatures and weather patterns match your lifestyle? Will you be tempted to go outdoors and exercise year-round, or will harsh winters and suffocating summers confine you to an easy chair in front of the television set?

3. Housing. Is quality housing available at prices you're willing and able to pay? Is the area visually pleasing, free of pollution and traffic snarls? Will you feel proud to live in the neighborhood?

4. Nourishment for Your Interests. Does your retirement choice offer facilities for your favorite pastimes, cultural events and hobbies, be it hunting, fishing, adult education, art centers, or whatever?

5. Social Compatibility. Will you find common interests with your neighbors? Will you fit in and make friends easily? Will there be folks from your own cultural, social and political dimensions?

6. Affordability. Are goods and services reasonable? Can you afford to hire help from time to time when you need to? Will your income be high enough to be significantly affected by state income taxes? Will taxes on your pension make a big difference?

7. Medical Care. Are local physicians accepting new patients? Does the area have an adequate hospital? (You needn't live next door to the Mayo Clinic; you can always go there if your hospital can't handle your problem.) Do you have a medical problem that requires a specialist?

8. Distance from Family and Friends. Are you going to be too far away from those you care for, or in a location where nobody wants to visit? If you would rather they wouldn't visit, you may do better even farther away.

9. Transportation. Does your new location enjoy intercity bus transportation? Many small towns have none, which makes you totally dependent on an automobile or taxis. How far is the nearest airport with major airline connections? Can friends and family visit without driving?

10. Senior Services. Senior centers should be more than merely places for free meals and gossip; there should be dynamic programs for travel, volunteer work and education. What about continuing education programs at the local college?

ARIZONA

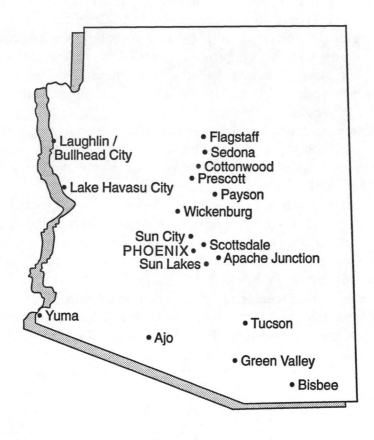

- Laughlin /
  Bullhead City
- Lake Havasu City

- Flagstaff
- Sedona
- Cottonwood
- Prescott
  - Payson
- Wickenburg

Sun City •
PHOENIX • • Scottsdale
Sun Lakes • • Apache Junction

- Yuma

- Ajo

- Tucson

- Green Valley

- Bisbee

A rizona is the third most popular state in the nation for those seeking new horizons for their retirement (Florida is first, and California is second). It may be of interest to note that of all the states that send retirees to Arizona, California sends the most. You'll also find many moving to Arizona from Florida, many of whom are on their second move; they tried Florida retirement first.

So many retirees are choosing Arizona retirement that 20 percent of the state's residents are over the age of 55. That's one out of every five—most of them voters—so you can be sure senior citizen issues garner a lot of attention, from the local city council to the governor's office. So, what's the big attraction for Arizona retirement? The answer is twofold: Arizona's weather and Arizona's gorgeous scenery. Low property taxes and plenty of cultural and recreational opportunities add frosting to the cake.

Arizona is also a great state for playing tourist whenever the mood strikes. There's no need to sit at home, not when Arizona has more national parks and national monuments than any other state for your visiting pleasure. You can also visit the state's innumerable golf and tennis resorts, Indian villages, natural scenic splendors, dude ranches, and desert and mountain playgrounds.

The nice thing about Arizona weather is that retirees have a wide range of climates from which to choose. That's one of the benefits of being retired: you no longer have to put up with the weather in your home town; you now have a choice in the matter. That old saying, "some like it hot, some like it cold," applies to Arizona weather. You can choose either one.

Hot weather fans (I happen to be one of them) can't do better than southern Arizona. If ever there were places that deserved the description of year-round summer, it would be Phoenix, Tucson or Yuma. It's true that during July and August, many more afternoons top 100 degrees than are under, but it's also true that December and January afternoons are always balmy, often 70 degrees and above. No matter how hot it gets in the daytime, Arizona's extremely dry air allows the heat to radiate rapidly so that the nights are usually cool. The air conditioning shuts down at night. With more than 300 days of sunshine each year and almost no rain, you have loads of opportunities to get outdoors. And just think about it: no snow shovels, no tire chains, no rubber boots or windshield scrapers!

Since most everywhere you go will be air conditioned, from the shopping mall to the racetrack grandstand, there's no need to suffer during the hottest part of the day. Most people hit golf balls or play tennis early in the morning and take their deserved naps in the afternoon. It's never too hot (or too cold) to get out in the early evening for a brisk walk.

Another reason many people choose to retire in Arizona's hot and dry areas is for health concerns. The arid climate alleviates symptoms of certain chronic diseases such as arthritis and asthma. Some find they're able to cut down on medication, others eliminate taking drugs entirely.

Other people prefer cooler weather (as does my wife). They dislike air conditioning and don't mind a little snow. Many find continual summer boring; they adore the invigorating changes in seasons. The place for them is the Arizona mountains, any of a dozen cool locations where air conditioning is optional or even absurd. When Flagstaff thermometers climb out of the 70s in the summertime, it's considered warm; on rare occasions when it tops 90, it's a heat wave. In Phoenix or Yuma, on the other hand, a 90-degree August day would indicate a cold front passing through. This book lists a number of Arizona mountain communities that provide four-season climates—without excessive snow—and pleasant summers. Some locations described here happen to be among our favorites, places we might consider for retirement ourselves, were we not already committed to where we live now.

Arizona receives very little rain, because the high Pacific Coast mountains block moisture-laden clouds from the ocean. This is particularly true in the southern reaches of the state. Most rain clouds that reach the dryer sections of Arizona are blown up from the Gulf

---

Arizona
"The Grand Canyon State"
48th state to enter the Union
February 14, 1912

State Capital: Phoenix
Population (1990): 3,677,985; rank, 24th
Population Density: 32.4 per sq. mile; urban: 83.8%, rural: 16.2%
Geography: 6th state in size, with 114,000 square miles, including 492 square miles of water surface and 24% in forested land. Highest elevation: Humphreys Peak, 12,633 feet; lowest elevation: Colorado River at southwest corner of state, 100 feet. Average elevation: 4,100 feet.
State Flower: Saguaro Cactus
State Bird: Cactus Wren
State Tree: Palo Verde
State Song: Arizona March Song

of Mexico in the summer months, and not very often at that. The mountain and northern parts of the state receive considerably more rain and snow, but compared to Eastern states, or even with California, even the wettest parts of Arizona seem arid.

Despite scanty rainfall, the state has a fascinating variety of plant and animal life. Characteristic plants in the desert regions are cactus, mesquite, yucca, agave, creosote bush, and sagebrush. More than a hundred varieties of cactus are found in Arizona, ranging from the little prickly pears to the giant saguaro, which sometimes towers 50 feet above the desert floor. Numerous plants remain dormant during the long, dry spells—only to burst forth in blossom at the first hardy rain shower.

Coyotes, mountain lions, antelope, deer and wildcats range mountain and desert alike. The desert is the home base of creatures such as rattlesnakes, scorpions and the venomous gila monsters, whose bite is fatal to small animals, but who are so shy and sluggish that it's extremely rare to hear of one biting a human. Higher altitudes are often covered with forests of pine, juniper and ponderosa, great habitat for deer, raccoons and other denizens of the woods. The best part about both desert and mountain landscapes is they're accessible to everyone. About 45 percent of Arizona's land is owned by the federal government. It isn't fenced; there aren't any keep-out signs. If you feel like strolling through government-owned deserts or forests, you can darn well do it.

Much of the state's wealth lies in its mineral deposits. Rich copper veins make Arizona one of the great copper-producing areas of the world. Arizona also ranks among the leading states in the production of gold, lead and silver. (Most of the uranium mined in the United States comes from the Colorado Plateau region.) Unless the government changes its laws, you are permitted to prospect on federal land and stake a claim if you hit it rich. The chances of your doing that are extremely small; you probably wouldn't recognize a valuable mineral if you stubbed your toe on it, and also, most land has been prospected many times before. But there's always that chance. I personally know amateurs who've made discoveries and who did right well.

Arizona's West Coast

After the wild Colorado River exits the Grand Canyon, it heads south toward Mexico and the Sea of Cortez. Along the way, it is captured by a series of dams that provide peaceful lakes to contrast nicely with the wild desert hills and canyons that enclose the river. Over the years, the river's rush to the sea has carved fantastic sculptures from sandstone, making this one of the more scenic stretches of river-highway in the West. Sand brought from the West's hinterlands, carried by rapid currents and deposited by lazy eddies over eons, has left sandy beaches all along the length of the river. Arizonans like to refer to this ancient length of sandy riverbank as "Arizona's West Coast."

Along this stretch of waterway—from the Arizona town of Parker on the south to the Nevada town of Laughlin on the north—growing numbers of retirees and snowbirds settle in every winter. The numbers increase every year, with more and more buying homes and staying year-round. Nestled between the rugged Mohave and Chemehuevi Mountains, with wide open desert vistas, the shimmering waters of Lake Havasu reflect the nearby peaks. The lake's 45 miles of fishing, boating and water recreation bring vacationers back over and over. Naturally their thoughts turn to this desert lake when time comes for retirement.

For years commerce along the river consisted of basic services opening seasonally to supply fishermen with bread, bait and beer, but that was about all there was. But once development took off, there was no stopping it. Places like Bullhead City and Lake Havasu have grown from small clusters of trailers and fishing shacks—with catfish and mallards as the major attractions—into virtual cities with all the facilities needed for comfortable retirement. This is one of the fastest-growing areas of its kind in the country.

History

The first Arizona settlers were Native Americans who built some sophisticated, multi-story buildings that awe present-day tourists to no end. The settlement at Oraibi dates from A.D. 1200, making it one of the oldest Native American communities in what is now the continental United States. The first Europeans didn't show up until 1528 when Cabeza de Vaca, shipwrecked off the Gulf of Mexico coast, meandered through Arizona on his way back to Mexico. His stories about golden cities sparked the interest of the Conquistadores, so they mounted an expedition into Arizona in 1539.

The Spanish wasted no time in settling Arizona, doing some farming and lots of mining. They discovered silver in Arizona and New Mexico and several valuable copper deposits which are still mined to this day. In 1821, when Mexico won her independence from Spain, Arizona became part of New Mexico Territory and permitted American traders to enter the region. When war with the United States broke out in 1846, the Mormon Battalion captured Tucson, and the territory became part of the United States.

Until the late 1800s, when Arizona's mining and agriculture became significant to its new owners, immigrants were mainly interested in finding ways to cross Arizona and get to California without losing their scalps to Apache war parties. The returning 49ers, now armed with a knowledge of mining, began locating valuable gold and silver deposits and rediscovering mines worked by the Spanish two centuries earlier. Tales of the wealth to be found were told by wagon drivers who had crossed the region, bringing in many of the first settlers. The wagon and stagecoach routes used by the Arizona pioneers later became the network over which the modern state highway system was developed.

ARIZONA TAXES
Ariz. Dept. of Revenue, 1600 W. Monroe, Phoenix, AZ 85007; 602-255-3381

Income Tax	Single	Married Filing Jointly	
Taxable Income	Rate	Taxable Income	Rate
$0 - $10,000	3.25%	$0 - $20,000	3.25%
$10,001 - $25,000	4.00%	$20,001 - $50,000	4.00%
$25,001 - $50,000	5.05%	$50,001 - $100,000	5.05%
$50,001 - $150,000	6.40%	$100,001 - $300,000	6.40%
$150,001 and over	6.90%	$300,001 and over	6.90%

General Exemptions $2,100 single, $4,200 married filing jointly; $1,500 blindness, $2,300 each dependent; additional $2,100 for 65 or older.
Public/Private Pension Exclusion $2,500 / None.
Social Security/Railroad Retirement Benefits Full exemption.
Standard Deduction $3,500 single, $7,000 married filing jointly.
Medical and Dental Expense Deduction Limited to amount in excess of 2% of adjusted gross income; fully deductible in 1996.
Federal Income Tax Deduction None.
Other Credit for property taxes or rent for low-income people over age 65.

Sales Taxes
State 4.7–5.5%, generally 5.0%; **County** up to 10% of state; **City** 0.5–3.2%
Combined Rate in Selected Towns Phoenix: approx. 6.7%; Tucson: 7.0%
General Coverage Food and prescription drugs exempt.

Property Taxes
Local property taxes may not increase by more than 2% annually. Real property taxes may not exceed 1% of market value. Intangible personal property is also subject to state taxation.
Tax Relief for Homeowners age 65 or older or disabled; income ceiling $3,750 single, $5,500 married (excluding Social Security); max. benefit $502.
Homestead Credit 35% of school tax; $500 max. reduction; no income limit.
Veterans & Spouses Up to $2,340 assessed value ($54,600 market value); income ceiling $8,000 ($12,000 if children under 18 living at home).

Estate/Inheritance Taxes
Arizona imposes only a pick-up estate tax, which is a portion of the federal estate tax and does not increase the total tax owed; no inheritance tax.

Licenses
Driver's License Required within 10 days of establishing residence. Written and vision tests required. Fee: $7, good for four years.
Automobile License Tags issued by other states are valid until expired, but if you buy property or work, you must obtain Arizona plates within 10 days. Registration: $12 plus $4 per $100 of value; min. $23.50, max. $1,200.

Phoenix

*We moved here from Michigan the last day of August. Every day
for the next three weeks, the temperature was over 100 degrees!
But the warm, balmy winter made it all worthwhile.*

—Sherry Trask

Let's start our investigation of Arizona with the location the
largest number of retirees choose for their new retirement homes:
the area around Phoenix.

Located in the appropriately named Valley of the Sun, Phoenix
is Arizona's largest city as well as the state's capital. Phoenix
sprawls over miles of desert landscape, encompassing a wide variety of neighborhoods, catering to all budgets and lifestyles. The
metropolitan area is even larger than statistics would suggest,
because more than 20 other cities begin where Phoenix ends. The
sum total is a bewildering number of possible retirement choices.

Retirees who relocate in the Valley of the Sun usually do so
because of the more than 300 days of sunshine they can count on
each year. Rarely will they get rained out at one of the area's more
than 130 golf courses. All types of outdoor recreation are available
year round in the Phoenix area. You'll find tennis courts in almost
every neighborhood, miles of hiking trails and access to some of
the country's best spectator sporting events. It never gets too warm
for outdoor fun, because you can always get out in the morning or
evening and stay indoors, in air-conditioned comfort, during the
afternoon.

Phoenix is named after the legendary bird which rises from the
ashes of its destruction, and appropriately so, because early settlers
in the 1860s founded the city on the ruins of an ancient Indian city.
The newcomers restored the sophisticated irrigation systems left by
the mysterious Hohokam Indians who abandoned them four centuries earlier, and a new civilization arose to replace the vanished
one. Within the city limits you can visit an archaeological dig at
Pueblo Grande, the site of a Hohokam Indian village which was
deserted about 1450. A few miles southeast are the ruins of Casa
Grande, a four-story housing complex built of layers of caliche
mud. This too, was abandoned in the mid-1400s for reasons that
remain baffling to this day.

Some say the image of a bird rising from the ashes of a fire is
also an appropriate description of Phoenix in the summertime. In
July and August, temperatures match those of the glowing ashes of

a medium-size bonfire. Don't you wonder how people survived there before the days of air conditioning? It's easy to say that folks get used to heat, and they do to a certain extent in a dry climate, but when the thermometer hits 115, as it often does here, that's more than just heat. Best stay inside and keep the air conditioner going. But with relative humidity in July and August at only 20 percent, and with air-conditioned homes, automobiles and shopping centers, there's no need to be uncomfortable in Phoenix.

Recreation and Culture   A large benefit of living in or near a major metropolitan area is the wide variety of cultural, recreational and social opportunities at your beck and call. Professional sports fans are in heaven here, with the NFL Cardinals playing big-league football at Sun Devil Stadium, the Phoenix Roadrunners of the International Hockey League duking it out at the Memorial Coliseum and the Phoenix Suns playing NBA basketball at America West Arena. Soon to come will be a big-league baseball team in a brand-new stadium in downtown Phoenix. Spring baseball training camps host the Oakland Athletics, the Chicago Cubs, the Milwaukee Brewers, the California Angels and the San Francisco Giants. Local fans get a chance to enjoy exhibition games well in advance of the regular season.

The Phoenix area is also known for racing events. You'll find horse racing, automobile racing, greyhound racing (dogs, not buses) and drag races sponsored by the National Hot Rod Association.

Making a Choice   Because of Phoenix's size—it goes on and on forever—it's difficult to generalize or choose only a few neighborhoods that invite retirement living. Because retirement is such a big deal here, you not only have hundreds of neighborhoods in which to retire, but small towns in all directions, any of which may suit your particular lifestyle. It's up to you to investigate.

Every imaginable lifestyle is available to retirees here. Some folks prefer elegant "gated" communities, where every facet of your social and recreational needs is met by professional social directors. Usually these developments restrict residents to 50 years or older and provide snazzy recreation centers and country club facilities. Other retirees prefer open, multi-generational neighborhoods where you make your own friends and choose your own recreational activities. Satisfactory retirement neighborhoods come in all flavors and price ranges, from expensive to moderate to downright cheap. Mobile home living is popular here, and again, you can find everything from luxurious, golf-course developments with country clubhouses, to incredibly cheap parks where you can purchase an older, eight-foot wide unit for under $2,000. You may not love the neighborhood, however.

Therefore, if Phoenix weather and amenities are what you're looking for, you'll have to do a lot of investigating on your own. It would take an entire book to evaluate every neighborhood. Rent a car, if you didn't bring one with you, and spend a few days looking around. You have lots of choices.

To give you some clues, we're going to present a couple of traditional, well-organized, seniors-only retirement communities in the Phoenix area: Sun City and Sun Lakes. Next we'll discuss two open, multi-generational communities: Scottsdale on the high end of the scale and Apache Junction on the economical end. But when you visit, by all means, do not confine your investigation to these communities. Take your time and make sure you're making the correct decision.

PHOENIX AREA	Jan.	Apr.	July	Oct.	Rain	Snow
Daily Highs	67	84	105	88	7	–
Daily Lows	38	52	78	57	in.	

Two Sun Cities

When we retired, we thought we'd have lots of time on our hands.
But we keep so busy with hobbies, volunteering and socializing
that we have to schedule time to go on vacations.

—Lloyd and Caroline Landress

In 1960, on New Year's Day, a new concept in retirement made a dramatic appearance in the Arizona desert. The Del Webb Corporation unveiled its first retirement-oriented model homes in a newly created community called Sun City. One of the first retirement developments to feature a large-scale, self-contained city restricted to mature residents, Sun City promised "an active way of life" for retirees. Before a single home was put on the market, a shopping center, golf course and recreational facilities were in place. The shopping center provided space for a supermarket, variety store, laundromat, barber shop, drug store and a service station. These facilities were essential, for at that time Sun City sat way out in the desert, a long way from the city. (Today, it's been swallowed up by Phoenix's expanding metro area.)

Del Webb officials expected as many as 10,000 curious visitors that first day. To their surprise, 100,000 showed up. Immediately, 237 homes were snapped up by the public, and by the end of the year sales reached 1,250. Prices were as low as $8,000, but it was not just price alone that sold the buyers. They bought the concept of Sun City's invigorating lifestyle, with year-round golfing, shuffleboard, dance clubs, socializing and volunteerism. By the time all 8,900 acres had been developed and sold, Sun City's population reached 46,000.

Sun City's seven recreation centers and 11 golf courses are owned and operated by residents who pay $100 per person yearly membership. A few other amenities at Sun City are a 40-acre recreation center, the 7,169-seat Sundome Center, a library, seven medical complexes, restaurants, banks and many other business conveniences.

Developers around the nation monitored Sun City's rapid growth and began jumping on the bandwagon. Today, you'll find 2,400 of these adult retirement communities around the nation. More Sun City developments in the Southwest are under way in Tucson, Las Vegas and Georgetown, Texas. This concept of over-50, organized communities changed the way many people view retirement.

Riding on the wave of success, Del Webb Corporation purchased another 7,100 acres another few miles west of Sun City, and began all over with Sun City West. The development currently has 25,000 of the projected 31,000 residents in their homes, enjoying the benefits of four multi-million dollar recreation centers, eight 18-hole golf courses, a 203-bed hospital and a performing arts center.

Not everyone will enjoy the homogeneity of planned retirement; some folks prefer a multi-generational neighborhood. But obviously, many others like the idea of having neighbors and friends of their own age, who share the same values and world views. An added benefit is not having hordes of teenagers roaming the streets on skateboards, motorcycles or hotrods. (Relatives under age 19 are only permitted to visit here. We're told this has cut teenage vandalism and crime to almost nothing.) Without a population of children, property tax dollars instead go toward community upkeep and improvements, rather than to support schools.

This pre-arranged lifestyle particularly suits those moving from another area, who have no acquaintances here, and who don't want to invest a lot of time trying to make friends and developing recreational interests. It's all right here in one package.

Real Estate One reason homes in the original Sun City sold so quickly is they were priced right. Starting at $8,000, the more expensive ones topped out at about $15,000. Even though dollars were worth more in those days, these prices were attractive and the quality clearly satisfactory. As development continued, a need for more features and more square footage pushed prices a bit higher. Then when the supply of homes was gone, and development started at Sun City West, buyers moved in that direction.

This made homes in the original Sun City a great buy, especially for those with low budgets. Perfectly nice two-bedroom homes on no-maintenance lots sell for as little as $40,000. Townhouses go for even less. In fact, 90 percent of the old Sun City homes are priced in the $45,000-$130,000 range. Buy one and you are part of the community with access to all facilities.

Sun City West offers a higher-quality home, and prices follow the quality, as you might expect. Low-end, two-bedroom townhouses start at about $90,000, with luxurious four-bedroom homes going for well over $250,000.

After just one tour through the model homes, one feels tempted to buy immediately. The architecture is bold and imaginative (to match the payments); the furniture is top quality and luxurious. A word of caution: it's terribly easy to stand in the middle of one of these well-lighted and professionally furnished places and imagine how happy you might feel living there. Try to picture how the place will look furnished with your pink sofa (the one with the stained cushions), that comfortable but threadbare recliner and that wooden floor lamp that was a wedding present from your sister-in-law. If the place still feels like your dream home, then buy it.

Recreation and Culture In addition to the marvelous activities always going on next door in Phoenix, Sun Cities residents participate in more than 250 community, service and social organizations. The Sundome Center for the Performing Arts is the country's largest single-level theater and presents some spectacular entertainment ranging from country music giant Kenny Rogers, velvet-voiced Mel Torme to concerts by a 95-instrument symphony orchestra.

Arizona State University offers non-credit enrichment courses in Sun City or credit courses at ASU West. Rio Salado Community College offers special interest classes at various convenient locations.

When Grandkids Visit Take 'em to see one of the big league sports teams. Just about any time of the year, you'll find football, basketball, or hockey games going on. Several major league baseball teams hold spring training here, with numerous regularly scheduled exhibition games for the public. Indianapolis race cars thrill crowds here, as well as stock car racing and even dragboat racing!

Important Addresses and Connections
Chamber of Commerce: 12211 W. Bell Rd. #204, Sun City, AZ 85372
Daily Newspapers: *Daily News-Sun*, 10102 Santa Fe Dr., Sun City, AZ 85372; *Arizona Republic*, P.O Box 2243, Phoenix, AZ 85004
Real Estate Agent: Camelview Realty, 4512 N. 40th St., Phoenix, AZ 85018
Airport: Phoenix Sky Harbor, a half hour away
Bus/Train: Greyhound and Amtrak serve the vicinity

Sun Lakes

We used to live in the San Francisco Bay area, and even though the weather there is mild, it was too foggy and cool for us. My husband is a retired golf pro, and he loves the fact that he can play every day, and he doesn't have to bundle up.

—Rita Lundahl

South of Phoenix is another example of a planned retirement development, but with a more expensive, luxurious tone. In several respects, this is the Scottsdale of seniors-only communities. It comes as no accident that Sun Lakes bears more than a passing resemblance to its counterpart west of Phoenix. Why? Because this miniature Sun City was started by Ed Robson, who got his start in construction working for Del Webb. He found a location about 23 miles south of downtown Phoenix and started off with mobile homes in 1972. Soon he realized that he could construct a quality, luxury home for little more than the cost of a double-wide mobile, so he switched to luxury homes. The result is today's community of 12,000 residents, divided into four country-club neighborhoods, each with its own golf course and clubhouse. Although golf is Sun Lake's central theme, there are a multitude of opportunities for other activities such as tennis, swimming, fitness and arts and crafts. Nine conveniently located tennis courts make this sport the second-most-popular outdoor recreation.

Sun Lakes is far out in the country, with a quiet atmosphere similar to that which must have characterized Sun City when it began years ago. However, the way Phoenix is growing, it's just a matter of time until the megalopolis swallows Sun Lakes as well. This is a place for those who want country club living and who will make use of the facilities, for you are also purchasing quality surroundings. An impressive number of shopping facilities make it unnecessary to travel to Phoenix, not even for major purchases. But when you want to go to the big city, Interstate 10 access is just two miles away. The fact that Phoenix is nearby and an easy drive over the interstate is one of the features about Sun Lakes many retirees admire. "It's a straight shot up the interstate to the airport," said one gentleman, "so it's no problem when our children visit."

Recreation and Culture For continuing education, two community colleges are within commuting range, with Chandler Community College just a hop, skip and a jump away. Arizona State University is also conveniently reached by freeways.

Of course, golf is why many retire in Sun Lakes, and that's why they buy homesites on the golf course. For these people, there is no other sport but golf. However, one of the nice things about being so close to Phoenix is that you can participate in any or all events available to Phoenix residents.

Living Costs and Real Estate The cost of living is about the same in Sun Lakes as in Phoenix, however housing here will be considerably higher. The homes here emphasize luxury and quality, and the result is higher home prices. In many ways, Sun Lakes resembles the much larger Sun City complexes north of Phoenix, but prices start at $129,000 and go up to as much as $300,000. This is compared to Sun City West's average new-home price of about $92,000. Resales of conventional homes are also high, ranging from $80,000 to $350,000, and mobile home resales start at about $50,000.

Crime and Safety The crime rate here is said to be exceptionally low, and several residents maintain that this is one of the safest places they've ever lived. For those who want to be extra safe, two of the four Sun Lakes neighborhoods are "gated." Only those with legitimate business are allowed in.

When Grandkids Visit If you're ready to retire, you are old enough to have clear memories of World War II—maybe old enough to have fought in it—so take the grandkids to the Champlin Fighter Museum and the Confederate Air Force. The Champlin Museum features only fighter planes from both World Wars; the Confederate Air Force specializes in keeping WWII planes in flying order, with bombers being the specialty. The kids can climb up into a genuine B-17, past machine guns and ammunition belts and into the bomb bay.

Important Addresses and Connections

Chamber of Commerce/Senior Center: Sun Lakes Homeowners Association, inside each development

Weekly Newspaper: *Sun Lakes Splash*, 9532 E. Riggs Rd., Sun Lakes, AZ 85248

Real Estate Agent: Val Amica, Sun Lakes Realty, 9666 E. Riggs Rd., Sun Lakes, AZ 85248

Airport: 20 minutes to Phoenix Sky Harbor Airport

Bus: no local bus; private shuttle company to Phoenix airport

Scottsdale

The taxes on our home here in Scottsdale are a quarter of what we used to pay in New Jersey. Yet our home is twice as nice.
— Mr. and Mrs. Bill Adair

In Arizona, the word "Scottsdale" is a synonym for high-class, luxurious and expensive. This gilt-edged city of 135,000 on Phoenix's eastern limits (and its neighbor, Paradise Valley) is to Arizona as Palm Springs or Beverly Hills is to California. As such, it's become a retirement haven for those who don't mind paying more in return for sophistication, Saks Fifth Avenue–style shopping and gourmet restaurants galore. Obviously a lot of well-heeled retirees fall into this category because 40 percent of Scottsdale's population is over 50 years of age. Billing itself as "Arizona's Playground," the city is also proud of its vast recreational opportunities.

The accent on retirement here is away from Sun City–style, closed, seniors-only communities. Instead, Scottsdale retirees choose neighborhoods where they blend with residents of mixed ages, similar to the settings they left in their home towns. This gives Scottsdale a different look, a distinct residential countenance that avoids mile after mile of similar dwellings. Most homes are custom built or constructed in small enough numbers to look stylistically different from one another.

Scottsdale has some of the most elegant and opulent shopping districts and residential neighborhoods we've encountered anywhere in the country. Majestically landscaped boulevards are lined with so many fabulous, prestige-name stores that your credit card vibrates as you drive past. Sumptuous residential neighborhoods display homes so opulent and palatial that you'll hate yourself for not being able to afford one. Scottsdale may have a poor neighborhood, but we've never stumbled across it. Well, we did find one ghetto area where people drive Buicks instead of BMWs.

An additional boost to Scottsdale's reputation as a place to retire comes from the FBI's crime report, which ranks the city in the upper 25 percent for personal safety. This is the best score of any of the Arizona towns reviewed in this book.

Lest you write off Scottsdale as a place for only the ultra-rich and snobbish, let's take a look at some surprising statistics. First, Scottsdale's cost of living is only slightly above Phoenix's and not far above national averages. While real estate prices are higher than most other Phoenix locations, median sales prices in Scottsdale are still below Sedona and Prescott markets and, in fact, are below many of the more mundane Southwestern locations covered in this book. This lower median sales price doesn't mean that homes in Scottsdale are cheaper than in Prescott, it just means Scottsdale has a much larger inventory of homes in less-expensive ranges. When many more homes in the $100,000-$130,000 range sell than in the over $500,000 class, the median sales price drops.

However, for the ultimate in scenic values for the price, don't fail to investigate north Phoenix's Cave Creek and Carefree developments on Scottsdale's northern border. If you can afford homes in the $200,000 and up range, the quality of these desert neighborhoods is unmatched. Towering mountains with rugged peaks overshadow granite boulders, enormous saguaro cacti and classic Sonora Desert vegetation that surround Southwestern-style homes on large lots. Carefree and Rio Verde homes tend to be the more expensive, but our favorite locale is the slightly less costly Cave Creek area. There you might find a lovely home on a one-acre desert landscaped lot for under $200,000. One acre is a small lot here, and $300,000 is a more common asking price, however. Farther north, in the Tonto Hills, luxury homes are perched high enough to view Phoenix in the distance and also enjoy 10-degree cooler weather.

The West's Most Western Town In addition to its spiffy, upscale reputation, Scottsdale cultivates yet another image by calling itself "The West's Most Western Town." This concept manifests itself in the original town center which used to be the elegant shopping district before the name-brand stores moved to more opulent quarters on Scottsdale or Camelback roads. Today, this older area affects Western storefronts that house yuppie bars and restaurants or sell expensive Western-style clothing and souvenirs. Every January the city celebrates this heritage with 30 days of parades, street dances and the inevitable hokey shoot-outs on Main Street by actors. Local residents seem to take this Old West theme to heart; you'll see more ex-New Yorkers wearing wide Stetsons, snakeskin boots and expensive Western shirts than any place this side of Las Vegas.

But Scottsdale isn't all glitz and rodeos. It's one of the Southwest's leading art centers with 120 galleries displaying works of local and international artists. Once the shoot-out on Main Street ends, the Scottsdale Celebration of Fine Arts takes over until April with exhibits of oil, watercolor and pastel paintings, sculpture, jewelry and ceramics, all by local artisans.

Real Estate Scottsdale spreads out over 185 square miles, with hundreds of distinct neighborhoods. It's impossible to characterize all of them. Suffice to say that just about anywhere you might wish to live here will be in quality surroundings although some areas will be more spiffy than others. Deliberately or accidentally, Scottsdale has managed to keep neighborhoods tasteful, with Southwestern or Mediterranean architecture, and for the most part has avoided the tract-home look that plagues many fast-growing communities.

We were surprised to find a few homes offered in acceptable neighborhoods for around $100,000. Average three-bedroom homes in average neighborhoods were offered at $110,000 to $150,000. The average sales price is about $129,000, which shows there is a large market of lower price homes. Older condos and townhouses can be found for $60,000 and up.

Medical Care With such a large percentage of the population of Scottsdale near or over retirement age, health care servers have responded by providing some of the best facilities in the region. In addition to three excellent hospitals, this is home of the new $50-million Mayo Clinic. Numerous other medical establishments are scattered all over the Phoenix area. Scottsdale has over 600 doctors, about 150 dentists and more than 20 nursing homes.

Recreation If the Phoenix area sounds like a golfer's paradise, with 130 golf courses around the area, consider that 20 of these golf courses are in Scottsdale, and several new layouts are under construction. Fourteen of these golf courses are public, including the Tournament Players Club of Scottsdale (permanent home of the PGA Phoenix Open and the Senior PGA Golf Tournament). Nineteen driving ranges are waiting to help keep your swing in shape. Tennis buffs will find 50 public courts at numerous city parks, with lessons given at Indian School and Scottsdale Ranch Parks.

When you live in Scottsdale, you'll want to take full advantage of the mountain views and pristine environment by getting outdoors as much as possible. Scottsdale maintains a green belt with nearly 40 miles of city-maintained, multi-use paths. Residents regularly use them for biking, jogging, hiking and strolling. There are also 200 miles of unpaved recreational trails for hiking and horseback riding.

The city's park system offers a variety of facilities that appeal to folks of retirement age, such as full-size swimming pools, exercise rooms and dance studios. Daily admission to swimming pools is $1 for adults. Programs include swimming lessons, diving and synchronized swimming teams.

Culture and Education Scottsdale and surrounding communities offer many adult lifelong learning programs, with interesting classes in just about anything you might imagine. The Scottsdale Community College offers an Elderhostel Program as well as a great continuing education program. Those over 62 get a 50 percent discount for certain courses.

Senior citizens are invited to join a program called Older Adult Service and Information System (OASIS) in which adult volunteers are trained to enhance reading, writing and communication skills of grade school students.

With the University of Arizona located next door in Tempe, Scottsdale is exposed to the cultural influences of a large school. The city has its own symphony orchestra, which performs at the Scottsdale Center for the Arts, in addition to the center's theater productions, concerts and other cultural offerings.

When Grandkids Visit Try a picnic at the McCormick Railroad Park on East Indian Bend Road. In addition to a one-mile ride on a train, you'll enjoy seeing old railroad cars, a turn-of-the century locomotive and two restored train depots. When the kids get tired of trains they can ride an old-fashion merry-go-round.

Important Addresses and Connections

Chamber of Commerce: 7343 Scottsdale Mall, Scottsdale, AZ 85251
Senior Services: Scottsdale Senior Center, 10440 E. Via Linda, Scottsdale, AZ 85258
Daily Newspaper: *Scottsdale Progress Tribune*, 7525 E. Camelback, Scottsdale, AZ 85251
Real Estate Agent: Distinguished Properties, 6500 Scottsdale Rd., Scottsdale, AZ 85253
Airport: Phoenix Sky Harbor International is practically next door
Bus/Train: Scottsdale is served by its own city buses and Phoenix bus service, as well as Greyhound and Amtrak; complimentary Dial-a-Ride is available for the elderly or disabled

Apache Junction

What do I like about Apache Junction? Well, it's hot, it's desert, and it's sunny all the time. I can see the mountains every day. So, what's not to like?
— Mary Jacobson

Not far from Scottsdale, our lower-cost example of Phoenix area retirement is Apache Junction. It doesn't have the charisma or charm of Scottsdale (few places do), but it also doesn't have the price tag. One of Phoenix's many commuter bedroom communities, Apache Junction is fast acquiring a dual personality in its role as a popular retirement destination for both permanent and temporary residents. Retirees from the Midwest and East are ending their retirement search when they discover Apache Junction's laid-back attitude and the area's year-round summer. Over the last ten years, the permanent population has doubled, almost to 20,000. Most of this increase can be attributed to retirees.

Only a half-hour drive via the fast-moving Superstition Freeway from downtown Phoenix and Sky Harbor Airport, the town can almost claim rural status due to its position on the border between city and desert. In the distance, the Superstition Mountains rise above the desert floor, presenting a mysterious fortress-like appearance. Once the stronghold of fierce Apache warriors, these mountains also are the source of the most famous "lost gold mine" of all times. The Lost Dutchman's Mine has drawn adventurers for a century of searching and exploring the canyons and cliffs of the Superstitions hoping to find the treasure. According to legend, at least eight men have died mysteriously in their quest for the Lost Dutchman. But don't let this discourage you, by all means, have a look. (By the way, the mine was lost, not the Dutchman.) Every February, the Lost Dutchman Days festival is celebrated with concerts, a rodeo, a parade and a carnival.

Apache Junction sits on the western end of the famous Apache Trail, which is also known by the mundane name of Highway 88. This 78-mile stretch of winding, scenic road follows the ancient trail used by Apaches to traverse the canyons of the Salt River to present-day Roosevelt Lake. This road is a slow but interesting route to the lake. About 25 miles of the road is gravel, with occasional steep dropoffs at the road's edge; it can be impassable in wet weather.

Snowbird Heaven The town of Apache Junction has long been a favorite with RV enthusiasts and snowbirds who travel to Arizona each winter. They enjoy it here because the town welcomes them so warmly and because the city of Phoenix is easy to visit. More than 40 mobile home and RV parks accommodate some of these visitors. Their number is said to approach 35,000 for the season (hopefully not all at the same time)! The main complaint we hear from full-time residents is that many businesses cater to snowbirds and close their doors for the summer season. Fortunately, other communities and Phoenix itself have any type of business connections you might need without regard to season.

Regular retirees, looking for a place to live all year, are also moving here, finding that year-round residence is easier than traveling back and forth with each change of seasons. In addition to a warm welcome, retirees find some of the best real estate buys in the state here. A variety of lifestyles are available in Apache Junction: homes on rural acreage, quiet single family neighborhoods, mobile homes, and over-55-only retirement complexes. The city ranks in the top 25 percent of safe places as reported by FBI statistics.

Real Estate Most homes in Apache Junction range from $60,000 to $90,000, with excellent value for the dollar. Mobile homes are plentiful and reasonably priced. The higher the elevation in the foothills, the more expensive the property. Homes with acreage, nice views and stables for horses routinely top $200,000, still bargain priced when compared to similar properties around Scottsdale. The more spiffy places are found at or near the "fence line"—that is, as close to the national forest as possible, for you can't build on that land. Local people claim that just this small difference in elevation causes an amazing drop in temperature. It's still hot in the middle of a July day, but not as hot as the valley floor.

Medical Care Valley Lutheran Hospital is just six miles west of Apache Junction, and numerous other hospitals are available in the Tempe, Mesa and Phoenix metropolitan areas. Scottsdale's Mayo Clinic is less than 20 miles away.

Recreation and Culture In addition to the multitude of golf courses available in the Phoenix area, seven more golf courses are within a short drive of Apache Junction. Since I'm not a golfer, I must admit something puzzles me—that is, some of the courses listed specifically mention "grass" as part of their description. Maybe I'm wrong, but this leads me to believe that some Arizona courses are made of sand?

Fishing enthusiasts can travel to several lakes within a 16- to 30-mile range of Apache Junction, and the Tonto National Forest lies due north, with trout streams, game-filled woods and endless hiking trails and campgrounds.

For hardy adventurers with tough bottoms, Central Arizona College offers a five-day horseback trek into the Superstition Wilderness. The school also is host to Elderhostel programs for people over 55, with courses in liberal arts and sciences.

When Grandkids Visit Take 'em to the Goldfield Ghost Town. It's only about three and a half miles out of town and entertains the kiddies with fake gun battles and tours through an old mine. At one time the town boasted three saloons. Today there's still one saloon open, a place where you can duck inside to down a stiff one while the kiddies watch fake gunmen shoot it out in the street with those gawdawful loud blank cartridges. You might want to have more than one drink at this point.

Important Addresses and Connections

Chamber of Commerce: 1001 N. Idaho Rd., Apache Junction, AZ 85217
Senior Center: 1177 N. Idaho Rd., Apache Junction, AZ 85217
Daily Newspaper: *Apache Junction Daily Bulletin*, 860 S. Saguaro Dr., Apache Junction, AZ 85220
Real Estate Agent: Century 21 Mtn. View, 1000 W. Apache Trail #107, Apache Junction, AZ 85220
Airport: Phoenix airport is about 20 minutes away
Bus: Greyhound connects with Phoenix

Flagstaff

We tried Florida retirement first, then came here for a visit. Of course, we stayed. We can't get over how beautiful the mountains look or how lovely the trees are with snow on them in the winter.
—Evelyn and George Fraley

This northern Arizona city sits near the base of the San Francisco Peaks, which rise to 12,670 feet in the distance. The mountains provide a breathtaking backdrop for Flagstaff and its 50,000 inhabitants. This is an excellent example of Arizona's diversity in climate and outdoor activities. Only two and a half hours north of Phoenix—"where summer stays all year round"—Flagstaff is proud of its four distinct seasons. One of these seasons is definitely winter. The 7,000-foot altitude here guarantees full mountain winters, with copious snow—as much as 20 inches in some months and more than 90 inches for the year. To some folks snow is an attraction, for others a pain in the neck. This is one Arizona location where you may want to keep your snow shovel handy.

Summers are delightful, with temperatures seldom topping 80 degrees (while Phoenix cooks at over 100 degrees). Summer evenings are always cool—air conditioning is not needed here—and you'll sleep under blankets every night. Profusions of spring wildflowers make hiking trails delightful, and fall is punctuated by aspens displaying brilliant yellows to complement the reds and purples of deciduous trees and the deep green of the evergreens.

Flagstaff is small enough to avoid being a metropolis, yet large enough to supply all the shopping, restaurants, churches and service organizations you'd ever need. A large mall provides 65 indoor shops with chain department stores such as Sears and J.C. Penney. The city received its name from a large flagstaff which was erected for a Fourth of July celebration back in the 1870s, and the downtown shopping area capitalizes on this with an old-town motif. Quaint shops, galleries and bistros are the order of the day here.

Recreation and Culture   Outdoor sportsmen will find fishing and hunting opportunities without equal. Fishing in nearby streams and several recreational lakes yields great catches. For hunters the area is excellent, with annual hunts for deer and elk. Just 80 miles north is Lake Powell, with an incredible amount of shoreline. Flagstaff has numerous golf courses and dozens of tennis courts for spring, summer and fall recreation. Horse racing is popular in the summer and dog sled races in the winter. A 15,000-seat indoor multi-purpose dome hosts Division I Big Sky varsity football games as well as other sporting events. Skiing is 15 miles away at the Snow Bowl on San Francisco Peaks. Cross-country skiing is also available closer to town.

Northern Arizona University, a well-regarded institution, hosts numerous fine art presentations. From theatrical productions to museums, the university makes Flagstaff one of the cultural centers of the Southwest. Coconino Community College, just a few years old, enhances continuing education in Flagstaff. Joining the schools in filling a culture and arts schedule is the summertime Festival of Arts, which includes concerts, theatre, films and other visual arts. The Festival in the Pines is a place to buy superb arts and crafts. The Flagstaff Symphony hosts several fine performances from October through April. And Flagstaff's Winter Festival stages events from competitive skiing and skating to dog sled races.

Real Estate   A wide variety of homes are available here in both rentals and sales. Although housing costs are almost 20 percent above national averages, all price ranges, tastes and budgets are accommodated, from log cabins in the pines to luxury homes on the golf course. Utility costs are low, which brings the overall cost of living down to about 7 percent above average. Some of the less expensive areas are the Grandview and Bow and Arrows subdivisions, where homes sell in the mid $70,000 to $100,000 range.

You'll also find expensive locations such as Lakeside Acres, where homes range from $220,000 to over $1,000,000.

Medical Care Because of its position as the largest town in the area, Flagstaff has developed a strong base of medical facilities and health professionals. A new 126-bed hospital offers most medical specialties, everything from neurosurgery to plastic surgery. A new cancer center is equipped with the latest technology. Two air shuttles and a fleet of ground ambulances bring emergency cases to the hospital within a 130-mile radius of Flagstaff.

When Grandkids Visit A trip to the Grand Canyon might be in order. It can be almost a two-hour drive, but several tour companies will take you by bus if you prefer not to drive—they include visits to early day and contemporary Native American cultural sites. In town, Coconino Center for the Arts offers ever-changing exhibits, including the Festival of Native American Arts. A third possibility, for summer, is the ski-lift at Snow Bowl. It features a 6,450-foot-long chairlift which climbs to a panoramic vista at 11,500 feet. They say you can see the Grand Canyon from the top.

Important Addresses and Connections
Chamber of Commerce: 101 West Route 66, Flagstaff, AZ 86001
Senior Center: 101 W. Santa Fe Ave., Flagstaff, AZ 86001
Daily Newspaper: *Arizona Daily Sun*, P.O. Box 1849, Flagstaff, AZ 86002
Real Estate Agent: Shattuck Realty, 804 Beaver St., Flagstaff, AZ 86001
Airport: Pulliam Airport, with daily commuter flights to Phoenix
Bus: both a city bus and Greyhound serve the area

FLAGSTAFF	Jan.	Apr.	July	Oct.	Rain	Snow
Daily Highs	42	57	82	64	21	97
Daily Lows	15	26	51	31	in.	in.

Prescott

First we tried retirement near Phoenix. When we found out that we couldn't take the heat and traffic, we started looking around. Fortunately we found Prescott before we had to look too far.
　　　　　　　　　　　　　　　　　　　—Eric and Esther Jensen

The picturesque city of Prescott, often compared with Sedona as a premier Arizona retirement location, consistently receives recommendations from retirement writers as a great place to retire. In fact, Peter Dickinson, the dean of retirement authors, selected Prescott as his retirement home. That should tell us something. Indeed, Prescott does compare well with Sedona, yielding all the desired features for gracious retirement plus a gorgeous mountain setting. Although Prescott doesn't exactly match Sedona's scenic wonderland (few cities in the world can), it stands head and shoulders above most other Southwestern mountain locations. A majestic mountain backdrop of pine forests overshadows the city, and tastefully designed homes nestle among tall ponderosas and steeply rolling foothills.

Prescott differs in one major aspect: Sedona is new, with modern construction and homesites architecturally designed for today's living, while Prescott is mature, one of Arizona's oldest communities. Residents are proud of Prescott's small-town America image, with conservative architecture, Victorian homes and over 400 buildings listed on the National Register of Historic Places. The town was founded in 1863 after gold was discovered in the headwaters of the Hassayampa River. The following year it was already large enough to be named the Arizona Territory capital.

Self-proclaimed "Everybody's Home Town," Prescott does indeed have a home town feeling even though its business district indicates a small city rather than a small town. With 32,000 city population and 75,000 in the total shopping area, it's anything but smallish. Prescott's downtown area centers around an old-fashioned square, complete with a traditional courthouse and the mandatory bronze statues. The park-like setting seems to invite residents to gather during numerous community celebrations and ceremonies. It's a place where you can park your car and walk to shopping and restaurants, instead of driving to each destination. (Folks don't worry too much about crime here, since Prescott ranks in the upper 30 percent of the FBI's crime safety charts.) One side of the square faces a heritage of the early mining-town days, "Whiskey Row," once a block-long string of saloons, gambling palaces and places of lesser fame, today a charming collection of antique shops, fine restaurants and boutiques. The chamber of commerce is also located on the square, and is unusually helpful to potential retirees.

Prescott is surrounded by jagged peaks, often snow-covered, and a forest of Ponderosa pines (reputedly the largest tract in the world) overlooks the city. Prescott's movie-set panorama not only rivals Sedona's, but residents claim the weather is better here and that the four seasons are more sharply delineated. The elevation averages about 5,400 feet, which means cooler summers than in most of Arizona, with daily highs rarely climbing out of the 80s, and then dropping to the 60s every evening. On the other hand, winters are colder, too, with several good snowfalls every year. Winter lows are in the 20s at night, but almost always warming into the 50s by noon.

Our last visit to Prescott was in January, two days after a three-inch snow. The sky was brilliant, most of the snow gone after two 60-degree afternoons, although it still looked pretty on the ground and clinging to the needles of the gracious Ponderosa pines.

Recreation and Culture Yavapai College, a two-year institution, offers a non-credit "retirement college" with 900 students over the age of 62. Other cultural activities include musical performances by the Phoenix Symphony, community theater and several museums. Prescott's activity calendar has something going on every month of the year, items such as art shows, horse racing, parades, music festivals and even a Cowboy Poetry gathering.

Actually, it seems like something is happening every *week*, with horse racing throughout the summer, a Frontier Days celebration, art shows, a bluegrass festival and the year topped off with the famous Christmas tree-lighting ceremony and parade. The city's holiday lighting has earned it the title of the "Christmas City."

As you might expect, the rugged mountains, soaring pines and sparkling lakes inspire local artists. Their work can be enjoyed at galleries at Yavapai College, Mountain Artists Guild, Southwest Artist Association and Prescott Fine Arts. The latter group also presents a full season of theater, ranging from musicals to drama, comedy to melodrama.

If you enjoy golf, Antelope Hills is a municipal facility featuring two 18-hole courses. Prescott Country Club also has an 18-hole course 13 miles east of town, open to the public and PGA approved. Prescott also has public tennis courts, racquetball, and both indoor and outdoor Olympic-size pools. Three golf courses and five tennis facilities are part of the recreational scheme, along with hiking, camping, fishing and horse trails. Trail maps are available at the Forest Service office and from the chamber of commerce. Should you be unable to control the urge, 7,600-foot Granite Mountain offers exciting rock-climbing opportunities. Local lakes are stocked with trout, bluegill, bass and catfish. There's even a gambling casino on the Yavapai Indian reservation.

Medical Care Health care is above average here, with nearly 100 physicians and surgeons serving the community, and private doctors are accepting new patients. The Yavapai Regional Medical Center, a 129-bed hospital, and a large Veterans Affairs Medical Center are both conveniently located.

Living Costs and Real Estate We found housing prices somewhat higher than we expected. They are a bit lower than rival Sedona, but not by much. Surprisingly both communities have higher average housing prices than even legendary Scottsdale. There appears to be an abundance of rentals, however, for those who want to try the area for a few months before making any decisions. I predict that with Prescott's growing popularity, housing prices will probably continue to creep up. Occasionally an acceptable place can be found for as low as $65,000, but mostly homes sell above $100,000, and those places with views overlooking the valley can easily cost $200,000 and above.

In the older parts of the city, there are several neighborhoods of Victorians and areas of modest, smaller homes. Most of Prescott has been built on rolling, uneven terrain, not suitable for mass-produced tract homes, so most building tends to be custom, designed to fit on the individual lot.

The median price of a condo is $90,000, with more modest ones priced several thousand less. Rentals in Prescott range from $450 for a one-bedroom apartment to anywhere from $600 to $1,200 for a three-bedroom house.

Prescott Valley For those seeking less costly housing, yet close to Prescott, the place to look is in nearby Prescott Valley. This is a quickly growing community, in the process of developing its own reputation as a retirement destination.

With fewer steep hills, Prescott Valley permits cluster construction, which keep prices down and quality high. The valley is literally sprouting with new, more affordable homes. New homes here start in the $80,000 range, and offer more square footage, larger lots and more amenities than similar prices will buy in Prescott. Of course, you sacrifice view for more housing for the dollar. But, the city of Prescott is only 20 minutes away and large-scale shopping even closer.

When Grandkids Visit They'll enjoy Prescott Animal Park, six miles north in Heritage Park, where you'll see exotic animals in their natural settings. Or try any number of museums, not the least of which is the Sharlot Hall museum, filled with Arizona pioneer memorabilia as well as prehistoric Native American artifacts. The three-acre grounds feature pioneer buildings, an old-time locomotive and demonstrations of early-day Arizona handicrafts and ways of life.

Important Addresses and Connections

Chamber of Commerce: P.O. Box 1147, Prescott, AZ 86302
Daily Newspaper: *Prescott Courier*, P.O. Box 312, Prescott, AZ 86302; twice-weekly: *Prescott Sun*, 238 N. Marina, Prescott AZ 86301
Senior Center: Lloyd Roe Center, 335 E. Aubrey, Prescott, AZ 86301
Real Estate Agent: Coldwell Banker High Country Realty, Connie Sue Class, 116 N. Marina St., Prescott, AZ 86301
Airport: Prescott Municipal, with commuter service to Phoenix
Bus: Greyhound provides service to Cottonwood and Phoenix, and the Prescott Transit Authority serves the local area

PRESCOTT	Jan.	Apr.	July	Oct.	Rain	Snow
Daily Highs	50	67	89	72	18	20
Daily Lows	20	33	56	36	in.	in.

Cottonwood

When I retired, we looked for someplace with a slow pace, clean air and water, with interesting scenery. We found Cottonwood, and we looked no further. —a chamber of commerce volunteer

Midway between Prescott and Sedona is a strategically located retirement possibility in the picturesque Verde Valley. News about Cottonwood and nearby Clarkdale seems to be spreading by word of mouth, for the area receives scant coverage in retirement publications. But the word is apparently getting around because 26 percent of the Verde Valley's population is over 65.

Although Cottonwood's scenic values pale when compared to nearby Sedona or Prescott, most Verde Valley homes enjoy mountain vistas in almost any direction. The rolling hills around

Cottonwood itself aren't wooded, as they are in Prescott or Sedona, yet the valley is completely surrounded by the Prescott National Forest. Cottonwood is the largest community here, the commercial and shopping center for the entire valley.

Cottonwood and Verde Villages, right on Cottonwood's city limits, have a combined population of about 16,000. Clarkdale has around 8,500 inhabitants. This population supports adequate shopping, and because it's only 17 miles from the Interstate 17, transportation is better than many areas of middle Arizona. A local bus service, called CATS (Cottonwood Area Transit System), operates six days a week and picks up door to door in response to phone calls. Greyhound buses stop at Camp Verde, 14 miles away, and daily shuttles take you to the Phoenix airport.

The Verde Valley sits at a much lower altitude than either Prescott or Sedona—at an elevation of 3,300 feet—so Cottonwood receives much less snow. Nevertheless, the Verde Valley's air is just as crystal clear and crisp. Its location puts it close to many natural wonders: desert trails, mountain forests, rivers and lakes. And a big attraction is that property prices are far less than in the large, congested areas in and around Phoenix.

Recreation and Culture   Over 150 miles of rivers and streams wind through the Verde Valley, so opportunities for fishing, hunting, canoeing or river rafting are essentially unlimited. Golf and tennis facilities are abundant in nearby Sedona. And Yavapai College has a branch, Verde Valley Campus in Clarkdale, which offers small classes for continuing education.

Medical Care   Cottonwood's 104-bed Marcus J. Lawrence Hospital is known as one of the finest diagnostic and treatment centers in Northern Arizona. It has a large medical staff, an excellent emergency department and is equipped with the latest modern technology. The facility serves a wide area here and is the nearest emergency clinic for the Sedona area. Presently, there are 40 physicians on the medical staff.

Real Estate   Homes here are bargain priced when compared with Cottonwood's expensive neighbors, Sedona and Prescott. Since most growth here has occurred in the past 10 years, the majority of homes are fairly new. Prices range from mobile homes on individual lots and fixer-uppers in the $40,000 range to elegant hillside homes at $150,000.

When Grandkids Visit Don't miss a trip to Jerome, a ghost town in between Cottonwood and Sedona. Nicknamed "The City in the Sky," Jerome deserves the description, for it clings to the brink of an incredibly steep mountainside and extends downward a breathtaking 1,500 feet! Streets wind and switchback from brink to the valley below in an almost gravity-defying manner. Substantial brick buildings, homes and businesses—mostly abandoned today—are reminders of Jerome's colorful past. At its peak in 1929, when 15,000 lived in this roaring, violent town, it had the reputation of being "the most wicked city in America." Today the town is making a comeback: up to 400 residents from its low point of 100 in 1955.

Important Addresses and Connections

Chamber of Commerce: 1010 S. Main St., Cottonwood, AZ 86326
Senior Services: Verde Valley Senior Citizens' Ctr., 102 E. Pima St., Cottonwood, AZ 86326
Weekly Newspaper: *Verde Independent-Bugle*, 116 S. Main, Cottonwood, AZ 86326
Real Estate Agents: Sexton Realty, 565 S. Main St., Cottonwood, AZ 86326
Airports: nearest is Phoenix Sky Harbor
Bus: shuttles take you to Phoenix, plus there's local bus service and door-to-door on call

COTTONWOOD	Jan.	Apr.	July	Oct.	Rain	Snow
Daily Highs	58	77	95	82	13	5
Daily Lows	28	42	66	64	in.	in.

Payson

And the sun was setting in a blaze of gold. From the Rim I took a last lingering look and did not marvel that I loved this wonderland of Arizona.
—Zane Grey, famous Payson retiree (from *Tales of Lonely Trails*)

Located in the center of the world's largest stand of virgin Ponderosa pines, nestled in a breathtaking valley just below Arizona's majestic 7,000-foot Mogollon Rim, the town of Payson is another favorite candidate for mid-Arizona retirement. And, it's an easy two-hour drive north of Phoenix. Payson sits at about the same altitude as Prescott, at 5,200 feet, offers the same four-season climate as Prescott and similar spectacular scenery, but it doesn't share Prescott's or Sedona's high housing costs. In fact, local boosters like to refer to Payson as "the poor man's Sedona." Prices are surprisingly affordable, with many modest cabins and small houses scattered through the wooded hills.

Payson was never a well-kept secret with Phoenix residents. This little mountain town, with cool breezes, pine trees and gorgeous scenery, has been a favorite summer getaway for decades. With July and August temperatures 15 to 20 degrees below those in Phoenix, you can understand Payson's popularity! When the Phoenix pavement bakes in 110-degree August days, Payson residents play golf in 89-degree sunshine. In the evening they'll be wearing sweaters, for temperatures always drop below 60 degrees.

Yet Payson's altitude isn't so high that winters aren't mild enough for hiking, fishing or horseback riding, with occasional snows for cross-country ski treks. During the three coldest months, temperatures always approach 60 degrees by afternoon.

Payson started out with a split personality. On the one hand were summer residents who delighted in their part-time homes tucked away among the pines. They loved to design their places as Swiss chalets, complete with frilly curlicues along the roof lines, Swiss-style shutters and other artsy-craftsy touches. On the other hand were local folks, those who lived here all year, who preferred to define their image as rugged outdoorsmen, proud of rodeos and their Old West heritage. The result is a sometimes humorous mixture of architecture styles. Western log cabins, with wagon wheel and longhorn motifs, sit cheek-to-jowl by alpine cottages with pink-and-green wooden scallops around the windows and split front doors painted with bouquets of flowers. Oddly enough, because the neighborhoods are so woodsy and loaded with trees, the homes exude charm instead of clashing. Even Swiss-style mobile homes don't look out of place in such a lovely setting.

Zane Grey, the famous Western author, was one of Payson's earliest boosters. He wrote several books while living in his dream cabin in Payson and intended to make his permanent home here. Mr. Grey wrote in 1920 (in *Under the Tonto Rim*), "I love the great pine and spruce forests, with their spicy tang and dreamy pace, murmuring streams and wild creatures."

Unfortunately, Grey became furious when local officials refused to allow him to hunt bears out of season. So despite the murmuring streams, wild creatures and dreamy pace, Zane Grey left Payson in a huff, never to return. For years, his cabin was a tourist attraction, but it tragically burned to the ground in 1990, presumably torched by a gang of bears.

Retirees here have plenty of folks their own age to play with. Almost 60 percent of the population is over 55 years of age. The chamber of commerce utilizes retirees, with 29 volunteers working in the chamber office. "We couldn't operate without 'em," said the local chamber manager.

The retired community is quite active here, with many projects going on at one time to keep everyone who wants to work busy. One popular community project is operating a Humane Society. Volunteers work very hard trying to find a home for every stray dog or cat that comes into the shelter. They dread having to put animals to sleep. They dread it so much, in fact, that they simply don't do it. The result is that the Humane Society shelter grows larger and larger every year as new strays take up residence in the Payson retirement home for animals. Should you move to Payson, don't be surprised if the first group to call on you is not Welcome Wagon, but rather representatives from the Humane Society, begging you to take in a pet or two.

Recreation and Culture With mild year-round weather, Payson is the place for outdoor sports. The spectacular Mogollon Rim is just a few miles to the north of town, where hunting, fishing, hiking and sightseeing are legend. And Roosevelt Lake is only 30 miles from Payson, a very popular place for boating and fishing and famous for championship bass tournaments.

Payson claims to be the site of the world's oldest continuous rodeo. The event has grown from a local contest between cowhands to a world-class event attended by top rodeo hands from all over the country. The community celebrates with a rodeo dance, parade and a fiesta.

Adding to the Western-outdoor theme is the State Championship Loggers Sawdust Festival, with power-saw bucking, log tossing and ax throwing. On the gentler side of the entertainment scene are two popular musical events: the Country Musical Festival and the Old Time Fiddlers Contest. The Tonto Community Concert Association presents an impressive schedule with classical music, folk musicians and dance companies. The Rim Civic Orchestra, an all-volunteer group of musicians, presents two concerts a year, as well as performing at various civic functions. Programs consist of everything from Bach to ragtime.

For indoor sports, a nearby gambling casino, operated by the local Native American tribe, brings revenues to the community as well as affording entertainment at the casino's 476 slot machines. The casino is a welcome source of employment for Payson residents, providing some part-time work for retirees.

Eastern Arizona College has offered classes here since 1976, and is in the process of establishing a permanent campus. Senior citizens can enjoy continuing education experiences in a small school setting.

Living Costs and Real Estate
Although there are a couple of upscale neighborhoods where homes are quite substantial and expensive for the area, most neighborhoods are relaxed, with inexpensive housing. Mobile homes are interspersed with conventional housing, particularly in the less-expensive areas, but with lots of trees and natural landscaping, they blend in just fine.

Price-conscious buyers will find Payson a true retirement bargain. They might well find less-expensive housing elsewhere, but not with the gorgeous setting. Mobile homes on large wooded lots can be bought for as little as $45,000, and conventional homes start in the $70,000 range, and average from $65,000 to $90,000. In upscale areas in town, homes can top $500,000, but the value for the dollar is incredible. Rentals are said to be rather tight except for the off season.

Medical Care
Because of the older population, the local non-profit hospital is in the process of enlarging and becoming a cancer treatment center for northern Arizona. Facilities are excellent; the Payson Regional Medical Center is the only round-the-clock hospital for nearly 25,000 full- and part-time residents of the Rim Country area, including the Tonto Apache Reservation. Another feature of the health care situation here is that Payson is less than a two-hour drive to the Mayo Clinic in Scottsdale, as well as to numerous excellent medical facilities in the Phoenix area.

When Grandkids Visit
Be sure and visit the Payson Zoo. It started out with a dozen studio animals for movies and TV commercials. But they started taking in cast-off zoo animals, retired circus beasts and injured local wildlife. Randy, the zoo's manager, just couldn't turn any animal away. Today the zoo is home to 60 animal

refugees and is still growing. A local society takes collections for their support. Randy says that when animals come into his life before he has accommodations ready for them, he takes them into his one-bedroom trailer. At one time he was living with three baboons, a deer and a bobcat. The zoo features a genuine lion and at least one tiger.

Important Addresses and Connections

Chamber of Commerce: 100 W. Main St., Payson, AZ 85547
Senior Center: located on Main Street
Weekly Newspaper: *Payson Roundup/Mogollon Advisor*, 708 N. Beeline Hwy., Payson, AZ 85541
Real Estate Agent: Rim Valley Real Estate, 511 S. Beeline, Payson, AZ 85547
Airport: shuttle service is available to Phoenix Sky Harbor
Bus: bus service connects the area with Phoenix, 94 miles to the south

PAYSON	Jan.	Apr.	July	Oct.		Rain	Snow
Daily Highs	53	70	93	76		21	25
Daily Lows	24	35	59	40		in.	in.

Sedona

Every morning when we wake up we look outside, drink in the view, feel joyful and congratulate ourselves for being able to live in Sedona.
—Linda Parker

Most popular retirement locations offer much the same kinds of services, housing, shopping and other amenities necessary for everyday living. The major differences are price variations, transportation, recreational and cultural opportunities. Some have prettier scenery than other places, sometimes the weather is better. Occasionally you'll find a retirement town that stands out in one respect or another. Rarely will you run across a town which stands out to the extreme. Sedona is one of these places. Sedona's incomparable scenic wonders rank it among a half-dozen retirement destinations that soar high above the ordinary. Your first view of Sedona is guaranteed to take your breath away, and you'll never get over that initial shock.

The best way of experiencing Sedona's impact is by driving from Flagstaff over the slow, 27-mile Oak Creek Canyon road. This is often described as one of the most scenic highways in North America. The pavement winds and twists through thick pine forests and gnarled oaks, with distant glimpses of deep gorges and arroyos embellished with enormous natural stone sculptures. Fantastic shapes of spires, chimneys and buttes never fail to bring sighs of amazement.

When you reach Sedona, the canyon broadens and drops into a wide amphitheater overshadowed by enormous red, pink and orange rock formations. Brilliantly hued cliffs and rugged spires of florid sandstone ascend majestically above the town. The rich greens of Arizona cypress, junipers and Piñon pines contrast dramatically with the red background framed by the deep blue Arizona sky—a sight not easily forgotten.

On our first visit to Sedona several years ago, we had a curious feeling of déjà vu. The place seemed strangely familiar, as if we'd visited here often. This odd feeling kept nagging until it suddenly hit us! Western movies! We'd seen this exact scenery in innumerable Cowboy-and-Indian movies. Countless bands of Apache warriors attacked wagon trains as they lumbered past these red rock formations. Cavalry troops galloped along the trails, and stagecoaches surrendered so many strongboxes full of treasure that we half expected to see a posse arrive at any moment.

Hollywood discovered Sedona and Oak Creek Canyon in the 1920s, beginning a relationship continuing to this day. With all this astounding scenery, it is quite understandable. Actually, Zane Grey first portrayed Sedona artistically; he fell in love with the place, describing it in his popular novel, "Call of the Canyon." When Hollywood was ready to film the story, Grey insisted that it be shot on the Sedona location. Since that time hundreds of films and TV commercials have capitalized on the dramatic rock formations as background settings. A local group, called the Sedona Film Commission, is engaged in promoting the area for more films.

Hollywood artists and technicians came so often that many decided to relocate; some still call Sedona home. This "Red Rock Country" has long attracted artists of all dimensions, who draw inspiration from the country's fantastic vistas. New Age settlers and spiritual seekers also find Sedona a desirable location, for healing and emotional rejuvenation. In the mid-1970s they proclaimed their discovery of four electromagnetic energy sources in the area called vortexes. Today a community of alternative healing practitioners provides a varied schedule of workshops and events here.

The number of retirees who select Sedona as their home base is truly impressive. The head of the senior citizens center estimates that around 40 percent of the population are retired. "This makes for an interesting mix of retired folks, artists, New Age devotees and business people," he said.

The town has around 16,000 residents, although the business district and facilities make the town seem much larger. Tourism is big here, and tourist money supports an unusually wide range of restaurants (35 of 'em). Since growth has been recent, most construction is new and well maintained. People understand the beauty and practicality of natural landscaping to blend their homes into Sedona's beauty. A bonus is that desert landscaping doesn't includes lawns that continually need mowing.

Sedona's altitude is 4,300 feet—that's 3,200 feet higher than Phoenix, only two hours away by car, and 2,700 feet lower than Flagstaff, which is less than an hour away. (Some guidebooks list Sedona as being at a 4,400-foot altitude. Since the town slopes downward, it all depends on where you measure.) This altitude means warmer winters than Flagstaff and cooler summers than Phoenix.

Lest I make Sedona sound like paradise on earth and start a stampede, let's take a look at two downsides frequently mentioned by residents. First of all, this is an expensive place for property. Secondly, traffic is unusually heavy on Sedona's few main thoroughfares. Traffic is aggravated by the continual flow of tourists gawking at the scenery, grabbing parking spaces and generally getting in everybody's hair. On the other hand, Sedona's quality of life and stunning landscape greatly lessen the impact of these inconveniences.

Recreation and Culture Sedona surely is a place to cultivate latent talents or to appreciate the artistic talents of others. Sedona has between 200 and 300 resident artists, which accounts for the 35 art galleries and exceptionally active community art center. Two theater groups present year-round dramas, plus several ad hoc performances by a senior citizen center group. Another theater group presents outdoor performances on summer evenings.

A local arts and cultural commission tries to focus the efforts of all talented people in the community into interesting, year-round projects. The Theater and Music wing of the Artists and Craftsmen Guild presents programs ranging from jazz to the classics, and the arts center holds monthly art exhibitions to augment the many art galleries in town. Other highlights of the seasons are the two-day Hopi Artists Gathering, a sculpture show, the Native American Arts and Crafts Fair and the Sedona Chamber Music Festival. Each fall, internationally renowned musicians gather to present a full day of musical celebration called "Jazz on the Rocks."

Sedona golfers have their choice between two nine-hole and two 18-hole golf courses. The unique settings provide golfing enthusiasts with breathtaking views at every turn. Courses stay open for year-round golf. The area also supports five tennis club resorts. Camping, fishing and hiking are exceptionally popular and accessible because 77 percent of the countryside is government forest service land—open to everyone. The wilderness begins at the edge of town. Hiking and horseback riding trails abound, with or without tour guides.

Living Costs and Real Estate Sedona has grown rapidly in recent years, with affluent retirees and successful artists a large segment of new residents. As a result, property prices have kept pace with growth. This is not a place to look for bargain-basement real estate; views like this do not come dirt cheap. Some are expensive showplaces, constructed to take full advantage of the natural beauty of the panorama, but you'll also find less costly homes that do quite the same. Manufactured homes start at $45,000 and go up to $130,000; conventional homes on quarter-acre lots start at $150,000. For a nice view, add $30,000. One prestigious development asks $315,000 for its entry-level homes, $900,000 for its top-of-the-line places, with building lots starting at $160,000. Expect to pay from $800 to $1,200 a month rent for a house and $600 and up for an apartment. The development of Oak Creek, on Sedona's edge, often has available rentals, but overall, rentals in the area may be difficult to find.

Medical Care A new medical facility is under construction, but until it's completed, the nearest ones are in nearby Cottonwood and another in Flagstaff, 27 miles to the north (on the slow winding road). But the area does have paramedics, ambulances, an out-patient health care center, and a medical evacuation helicopter. Also, an adequate number of doctors, dentists and optometrists take care of residents.

When Grandkids Visit Take 'em to Red Rock State Park. The park offers three main trails designed to suit whatever energy level you care to expend. The Smoke Trail follows Oak Creek through lush wooded areas, always with spectacular views of the red rock formations along an easy half-mile hike. You might want to bring a fishing rod and try to hook a trout. Overnight camping isn't permitted here, and you must pack out what you bring in.

Important Addresses and Connections

Chamber of Commerce: P.O. Box 478, Sedona, AZ 86336
Senior Services: 331 Forest Rd., Sedona, AZ 86336
Twice-Weekly newspaper: *Red Rock News*, 296 Van Deren St., Sedona, AZ 86336
Real Estate Agent: Sedona Realty, 3950 W. Highway 89, Sedona, AZ 86339
Airport: commuter flights to Phoenix
Bus: van shuttle to Phoenix airport

SEDONA	Jan.	Apr.	July	Oct.	Rain	Snow
Daily Highs	55	72	95	78	17	9
Daily Lows	30	42	65	49	in.	in.

Bisbee

Even though more and more tourists are visiting Bisbee, it doesn't tarnish the charm. And Bisbee's charm is why I love it here.
—Judy Perry, local artist

Tucked away in a steep canyon in the rugged Mule Mountains of southern Arizona—the domain of the great Apache warriors Geronimo and Cochise—the town once called "Queen of the Copper Camps" is making a dramatic comeback. When I first wrote about Bisbee, it had just suffered a jolting financial disaster. Some homes were selling, completely furnished, for as little as $500. If nobody had the $500, houses were sometimes abandoned without even bothering to lock the doors. By the time we visited, things had taken a turn for the better, with retirees coming in to buy the cheap real estate and rebuild the town. Since then Bisbee has dramatically changed direction, from a semi-abandoned mining town to its newer role as an enchanting retirement "discovery."

Once a wild, wide-open city of 25,000 miners, merchants and adventurers intent upon making their fortunes, Bisbee's pace today is slow and quiet. Since the town is off the standard tourist track, not that many visitors disturb the ghosts of yesteryear. A stroll through Bisbee's narrow streets is like stepping into the past Daytime sounds are muted; after midnight the streets are all but deserted. Although ghosts of the past can almost be seen, Bisbee is far from being a ghost town. Residents express great satisfaction with Bisbee's balance between quiet leisure and fulfilling activities.

More than just a source of bargain housing, Bisbee's colorful history matches its picturesque desert-mountain setting, only a few miles from the Mexican border. Its narrow, winding streets epitomize a classic style of mining towns of the late 19th century; it's a place frozen in time. The town's architectural style is appropriate, a mixture of authentic Victorian and Western mining camp, with brick and clapboard construction dating from the 1890s and even earlier. Because of steep hills and ornate Victorian construction, people often describe the town as having a certain San Francisco atmosphere—without the cable cars, of course.

What happened to Bisbee? Disaster struck quite suddenly, back in 1975, when Phelps-Dodge, the mining company that sustained Bisbee's economy, ceased operations. Panic and despair struck the canyon's households. Families began leaving in droves. If Bisbee hadn't been the county seat, disaster would have been total.

This collapse happened near the end of the "flower child" movement of the '60s and '70s. Word circulated through the underground that Bisbee was a great place to "be." Young adventurers, intellectuals, artists and a few loafers floated into town on a wave of fading idealism. Some bought furnished homes for almost nothing; others squatted in vacant houses.

When retirees heard about these bargains, they created a new wave of immigration to Bisbee. Gradually, members of the Love Generation decided that making money was really "where it's at," so they sold their homes to retirees for profits and moved on to join the Yuppie Generation. One needs big bucks to buy the obligatory BMW; that kind of money isn't easily earned in Bisbee.

Fortunately, many of the new wave didn't want to leave; they had fallen in love with Bisbee. These "kids" are now in their 40s and 50s, with graying hair, moving inevitably toward senior citizen status. Fortunately for Bisbee, those who stayed were loaded with talent: artists, writers and intellectuals. Enough creative people stayed to give Bisbee the reputation and flavor of an artists' colony.

Today's population has stabilized at just over 8,000. You'll no longer find boarded-up storefronts downtown, either. They are all occupied and bustling with profitable businesses. Numerous shops and boutiques dispense antiques, gifts, crafts, jewelry and tourist goods, and art galleries display the works of local artists.

This colorful downtown section, known as "Old Bisbee," happens to be one of Bisbee's major tourist attractions. In its heyday 47 saloons watered the thirsty center of town, affectionately known as "Brewery Gulch." Historians consider Bisbee to have been the "liveliest spot between El Paso and San Francisco." The fame of Brewery Gulch's dance hall girls lives on today with stories of Crazy Horse Lill, Kate Elder (Doc Holliday's mistress) and Black "Jack" a woman who dressed as a man and robbed stages. A few saloons remain, enough for atmosphere, but most have been converted into art galleries or studios.

Revisiting today, we find even more retirees have selected Bisbee for permanent homes. An increase in retiree population and income always creates a healthy snowball effect on commerce, services and organizations serving the community. Prosperity has gradually returned to Bisbee. Naturally, this wave of bargain-hunting home buyers pushed selling prices up. But since prices started at an incredibly low level, real estate is still an excellent buy. Turn-of-the-century homes and well-preserved Victorians are available in town, as well as more conventional housing in the outlying districts of Warren and San Jose.

Bisbee's climate is excellent, with enough altitude (5,300 feet) to keep the summers pleasant, plus low humidity to make the winters brisk, but not bitter. During our January visit the thermometer dropped into the 40s by midnight, yet we walked around town in light sweaters, feeling perfectly comfortable. Many summer residents come here from Phoenix and Tucson, fleeing the baking, 100-plus-degree, July-August season. One reason for the cooler summer temperatures is that the steep canyon walls cast early shadows across the town to block the afternoon heat of the desert sun. A sign painted prominently on one of the downtown buildings proclaims that Bisbee has the "best climate in the world."

Shopping is adequate, with additional heavy shopping in Douglas, 23 miles to the east. Douglas is on the Mexican border, across from Agua Prieta, where some folks like to shop for Mexican bargains. Just a few miles south is the border town of Naco, also a place to browse for south-of-the-border items.

Recreation and Culture Bisbee has one nine-hole golf course at Turquoise Valley Golf & RV Park; this course is one of the oldest in the Southwest!

Bird watchers enjoy the San Pedro Riparian National Conservation Area, 15 miles from Bisbee, and Ramsey Canyon, some 25 miles distant. Not limited to birds, visitors are treated to sightings of all sorts of wildlife: javelina, mule deer, coyotes and, of course, the ubiquitous desert jack rabbit.

The cultural ambience here centers around the creative colony of artists and craftspeople. Various galleries feature works by Southwest and local artists, poetry readings, dinner theater, and Old West melodramas. The Bisbee Arts Coalition (BAC) is a community-based volunteer organization dedicated to promoting art, humanities and cultural activities. Cochise College, based in Douglas, has a branch in Bisbee. The school provides many personal growth opportunities in continuing education and lifelong learning.

Real Estate Be aware that the days of bargain homes are long gone. Of course, fixer-uppers can occasionally be found, and satisfactory housing can still be located for under $50,000. Mid-range housing runs between $60,000 and $90,000. At one time, the really old, historic places were bargains, and retirees had fun remodeling to bring them up to acceptable standards. For many people, renovating and rejuvenating an old house is enjoyable, a chance to allow artistic and creative abilities to run rampant. However, prices for old homes have skyrocketed in the past few years. You'll pay much more per square foot for an old Victorian than for a brand new place. And, there are few new homes because there's very little building underway. There's no room and no infrastructure. For this reason, rentals are difficult to find. Places that used to be for rent are now owner occupied.

Medical Care Medical facilities are noteworthy for a small town: a 49-bed hospital with eight full-time doctors and an ambulance service. Other medical professionals include five dentists, two optometrists, a chiropractor, and an osteopath.

When Grandkids Visit A trip to the Copper Queen Mine is in order. The mine is right in the center of town. A mining ore car takes you underground for a one-hour tour of the copper mine. Visitors, wearing helmets and headlamps, can see how miners worked this famous ore deposit.

Important Addresses and Connections

Chamber of Commerce: 7 Naco Road, P.O. Box BA, Bisbee, AZ 85603
Senior Center: 300 Collins Road, Bisbee, AZ 85603
Daily Newspaper: *Bisbee Daily Review*, 12 Main St., Bisbee, AZ 85603
Real Estate Agent: Mule Mountain Realty, 602 Hwy 92, Bisbee, AZ 85603
Airport: commuter airlines fly out of Bisbee-Douglas International Airport, 17 miles away
Bus: there's a local bus operated by Catholic Community Services and shuttle service to Tucson Airport

BISBEE	Jan.	Apr.	July	Oct.	Rain	Snow
Daily Highs	57	74	89	77	16	4
Daily Lows	33	47	65	51	in.	in.

Ajo

We moved from California five years ago, and it's been amazing how new folks moving into Ajo have changed the looks of the town, by planting trees, landscaping and sprucing up their properties.
— John and Irene Martin

One of my favorite retirement success stories took place in a little mining town in the Arizona desert. The setting was Ajo, a small mining town about 120 miles west of Tucson and 110 miles south of Phoenix. The town of Ajo's economic mainstay was a huge open-pit copper mine which provided employment and good wages for working families. This was a thriving community with more than 10,000 inhabitants. Suddenly, without previous warning, Ajo's backbone shattered when the mining company made an out-of-the-blue corporate decision. The word went out: shut down the Ajo copper workings! Disaster struck.

Caught without regular paychecks, working families wasted little time in packing their belongings and skinning out for greener pastures. Almost overnight, Ajo dwindled to a skeleton of its former self, down to 2,800 residents, and dropping toward ghost status. Many homes in Ajo belonging to the mining company—used as employee housing—were dumped on the real estate market, offered for as low as $13,000. Privately owned properties were sacrificed at give-away prices. One real estate broker explained, "At one time we had 600 houses listed for sale and nobody interested in buying."

Those residents who remained in Ajo were determined to make a go of it. They embarked on a campaign to encourage retirees to join them and save Ajo from becoming an abandoned wreckage. One of my earlier books—*Retirement Choices*—highlighted Ajo, described the situation, and urged retirees to take a look as a possible place for inexpensive desert retirement. The word soon got out, and buyers eager for affordable retirement property visited, liked what they saw, and began snapping up bargains.

Once low-cost company housing was disposed of, the real estate market stabilized. But prices leveled out at what most folks would still consider rock bottom. As of summer of 1995, the listing price of homes on the Ajo market ranged from $25,000 to $149,500. Many homes were offered around $45,000. This would be for a substantial, three-bedroom place on a nice-size lot.

Because retirees purchased the vast majority of these homes, Ajo embarked on a new career: from mining center to retirement center. The reverse shift in population created a satisfying snowball effect on the economy. Retirees moving into Ajo put pressure on the community for more goods and services, thus creating jobs and bringing working families back into Ajo to fill these jobs. Today's population approaches 5,000, far more than half of them retirees.

Another shift in Ajo's place in the universe took place when several thousand retired snowbirds started flocking into town to enjoy a few weeks or months of warm desert winter, something they wouldn't have done back when Ajo was an industrial mining town. The extra money they spend here further enhances the economy. Thus creating even more jobs for working families. "One nice thing about Ajo," said a one retired couple, "is that we have a mixture of young and old. We have about 600 children in our school, and many young adults to balance out the social scene."

Originally, Ajo was located a short distance from its present site, but in 1916 a rich ore deposit was discovered underneath the town, so the corporation decided to move the company town to its current location. Now, the term "company town" often creates negative pictures, visions of smokestacks, clapboard row houses and company stores. This isn't always the case, and certainly these images are incorrect in Ajo. Because the town needed to be moved, a decision was made to rebuild with refinement and style.

The mining superintendent in charge at that time hired an architect to design a "garden city." The result is an unusually tasteful palm-lined plaza, an oasis that looks more as if it belongs to a desert spa than an Arizona mining camp. The Ajo Community Health Center replaced the company hospital and does a creditable job of taking care of local residents, with two doctors on staff and one doctor on call. Further legacies of the company town are facilities originally built for corporate executives, but now available for public use. One example is the country club with its golf course and other amenities. It's now operated as a non-profit organization for the benefit of Ajo residents.

The plaza is quite comfortable, a place where local retirees congregate to exchange greetings and comment on the earth-shaking events that rarely happen here. Crime? Hardly. I can't imagine a place with more personal safety than Ajo.

Residents keep in touch with the world via cable TV (with about ten channels), a weekly newspaper and daily delivery of the Phoenix and Tucson papers. An interesting transportation development is La Tortuga Transit, a rural bus project that connects the town with Tucson and points in between. Whenever enough local people get the urge, they arrange for La Tortuga Transit to run them up to Laughlin, Nevada, to challenge the gambling casinos there.

The weather is typical of the Arizona desert. Even though the altitude is 1,750 feet, it still gets hot in the summer. The local chamber of commerce describes Ajo as "the place where summer spends the winter" or "the town where warm winters and friendly smiles await you." The chamber of commerce also claims that Ajo is noted for having the best climate in the country, with warm winters and continuous sunshine that other parts of Arizona cannot equal. Notice that the emphasis is on the winter climate. Since I've never been here in the summer, I can only go by statistics, but these clearly suggest that it gets hot there.

Recreation and Culture

The country club's nine-hole golf course is supplemented by lighted tennis courts, a swimming pool, bowling alley, rifle range, equestrian center and numerous parks and picnic grounds. Although the golf course is nine holes, it's rated by the Arizona Golf Association as 18 holes (rating 68.1, slope 111). The club has a lounge and restaurant.

Medical Care   The Ajo Community Health Center is open daily from 8 to 5, with a doctor on call around the clock. This is an outpatient clinic providing primary care, laboratory, X-ray and pharmacy services. On-call emergency care is also available, with plane or helicopter ambulance transportation to Phoenix and Tucson. Two doctors and two dentists maintain practices in Ajo.

When Grandkids Visit   Take 'em to the Organ Pipe Cactus National Monument, just south of town, where they can see enormous stands of organ pipe cactus, virtually the only place where they can be found in the United States. Spectacular saguaro cactus with soaring, uplifted arms and other desert vegetation also decorate this unspoiled desert land. Your grandkids might also enjoy a visit to Puerto Peñasco, Mexico, a couple of hours drive down to the Sea of Cortez, on Cholla Bay. The town of Puerto Peñasco isn't too spectacular, but it is Mexico, a foreign country, and the natives love to see gringos enjoying themselves and spending money. Beaches here are uncrowded and seem to go on forever, with great swimming and fishing fun for all.

Important Addresses and Connections

Chamber of Commerce: 321 Taladro, Ajo, AZ 85321
Senior Center: Senior Citizens Center, 1215 Center St., Ajo, AZ 85321
Weekly Newspaper: *Ajo Copper News*, 33 Plaza, Ajo, AZ 85321
Real Estate Agent: Copper Crown Realty, 41 Plaza, Ajo, AZ 85321
Airport: Tucson is nearest connection
Bus: service to Tucson three times a week

AJO	Jan.	Apr.	July	Oct.	Rain	Snow
Daily Highs	64	82	103	88	6	2
Daily Lows	50	56	78	61	in.	in.

Tucson

We moved here from Illinois and were delighted to find so many other folks from Illinois have moved here. Not surprised, just delighted. We've formed an informal club of ex-Illinois residents.
—Mr. and Mrs. C.V. King

Tucson sits in a high desert valley with the majestic Catalina Mountains in the north, the Santa Rita mountains on the south and the Rincon mountains to the east. Dry, crisp air and Sonora Desert landscaping qualify Tucson as one of the nation's better winter destinations. The valley's elevation of 2,300 feet guarantees an agreeable year-round climate, with summer temperatures about five degrees cooler than Phoenix. In fact, an inch or two of snow usually touches down in the winter. Summers are still hot, just not quite as hot as Phoenix.

Many neighborhoods are as Southwestern chic as you'll find anywhere in the state. This is particularly true on the northern environs, where the land rises into gentle hills with a Palm Springs or Scottsdale look. The city's Mexican and Pueblo heritage is evident in home styles; low, adobe homes with red-tiled roofs are interspersed with modern ranch-style architecture and Spanish-colonial styles. These influences go further than home styles; Spanish is widely spoken—for many a first language—and a plethora of restaurants specialize in cuisine from nearby Mexico.

Its 420,000 inhabitants qualify Tucson as a moderately large city, and it is still growing. The fastest-increasing age group here is the over-60 crowd, which used to account for 20 percent of the population but is now over 30 percent. Since it's the over-60 group who are most likely to vote, it's no surprise that senior citizens get fair treatment in this city. The well-appointed Tucson Senior Citizens Center clearly shows the attention that city politicians show retired people.

Retirees will find living costs in Tucson pretty much average, with a slightly below-average housing market. Warm and pleasant winters don't demand much in the way of heating costs, but this is offset by obligatory air conditioning in the summer. Crime levels are admittedly higher that many Southwestern cities, but police point out that high numbers of offenses in certain areas raise the averages for the entire city. As is generally the case, the better the neighborhood, the lower the crime rates.

Tucson has its share of organized retirement and over-55 residential developments. With beautifully designed homes, extensive sports centers, shopping and medical facilities, these complexes are small cities in themselves. One adult community, Saddle Brooke, calls itself the "youngest adult community" because it sets its lower age limit at 45 years of age instead of the usual 55. Housing prices in these adult communities range from $70,000 to $170,000. Typically, these retirement retreats feature 18-hole golf courses, shuffleboard, tennis courts, jogging tracks, clubhouses complete with cardrooms, dance floors, exercise rooms and, of course, the obligatory swimming pools.

Twelve miles northwest of Tucson's downtown, one of the newer Sun Cities is under way. Currently about 3,600 residents live in this upscale development, with a projected 5,000 inhabitants when finished. This 1,000-acre active adult community is even closer to the Catalina Mountains—you feel as if you can reach out and touch them—and is surrounded by natural desert vegetation and a golf course with impressive views of the nearby mountains. This is one of the highest-quality Sun City settings, and homes are priced accordingly.

Many smaller, apartment-type retirement quarters are available in and around Tucson. They range from places where renters must be "active" to those offering "senior care" concepts, a euphemism for "nursing home." You'll also find the growing concept of "life care" centers, in which apartments are provided for those who are still active, then rooms with housekeeping care, and eventually nursing care for those who need it.

The Armory Park Senior Citizens Recreation Center (in downtown Tucson) is a model of its kind. Senior citizens take an energetic part in running the center and have no trouble getting all the volunteer help they need. At any one time several hundred volunteers are on call as they try to use everyone's special skills. For example: retired accountants and tax practitioners give free income tax assistance. Others teach handicrafts such as jewelry making, crocheting and painting. A senior citizens housing authority high rise is across the street from the center and another is planned, making it convenient for everyone to participate.

Recreation and Culture
The University of Arizona, located in Tucson, greatly enriches the community's educational, cultural and recreational life. Classes, lectures, plays and concerts are an

ongoing boon to retirees. Probably due to the university's influence, Tucson is the only city in the state with its own opera company, and it also has a light opera company that stages Broadway musicals. The Tucson Symphony Orchestra, Ballet Arizona and the Arizona Theatre Company add to the cultural offerings.

For outdoor activities, there are 35 golf courses in Tucson's immediate vicinity, some played in deep canyons, others in open desert. City and county parks have numerous handball and racquetball courts, swimming pools and many organized recreational programs. There are more than 300 tennis courts in the Tucson area, many of them lighted for night play. It may come as a surprise that winter skiing is available just 30 miles away at Mount Lemmon Ski Valley, the southernmost place to ski in the nation.

The Colorado Rockies major league baseball team holds spring training here, with the attendant exhibition games, and there's also a triple-A Pacific Coast League team that plays through the season. For other organized sports, fans drive two hours to Phoenix. A greyhound track operates year-round.

Real Estate   Living costs here are about the same as most Arizona cities, about average nationally, but the wide range of real estate prices makes Tucson practical for almost any budget. Buyers have a wide selection of neighborhoods ranging from inexpensive to out-of-touch with reality. The average home sells for around $100,000 or less. Condos start in the $65,000 range and continue on up from there.

Tucson is also a popular place for mobile home living. The newspaper's classified section usually has listings from mobile home parks who are advertising spaces for rent, something rare in many metropolitan areas. A space in one of Tucson's adult mobile home parks can be found for as low as $125 a month. The nicer ones charge more, with $200 considered a fairly high rent. Compare this with $350 to $400 in some cities, and you'll understand what a bargain mobile-home living is in Tucson.

With so many parks to choose from, you would be well advised to do some shopping. Some parks are primarily for working people, and their interests and social lives are intertwined with friends who live somewhere else. These parks will seem cold—not that people are unfriendly, but they prefer their lives to be more private. Other parks have mostly retired folks, where you'll find plenty of activities and neighborly retirees. Visiting a park residents' meeting or attending one of the bingo sessions can tell you worlds about who your new neighbors might be.

Medical Care Arizona's only state medical school is located here with a teaching hospital at the University Medical Center. Fifteen hospitals in the area offer excellent medical care, with about 3,000 beds in all.

When Grandkids Visit It's absolutely obligatory to visit Old Tucson Studios, about a dozen miles west of the city. It'll look familiar to you and the kids, since more than 300 films and TV thrillers have been made here. You'll see where John Wayne held off the Indians and where countless bad guys bit the dust in the middle of Main Street. Stunt men dressed as outlaws and lawmen demonstrate how movie shootouts are done, and a museum shows other cinema effects. You might want to bring earplugs for the shooting sprees.

Important Addresses and Connections
Chamber of Commerce: 130 Scott Ave., Tucson, AZ 85701
Senior Services: 900 Randolph Way, Tucson, AZ 85700
Daily Newspaper: *Tucson Daily Star and Tucson Citizen*, 450 S. Park. Ave, Tucson, AZ 85714
Real Estate Agent: Tucson Assoc. of Realtors, 1622 Swan Rd., Tucson, AZ 85712
Airport: Tucson International
Bus/Train: there's Greyhound and city bus service, as well as Amtrak

TUCSON	Jan.	Apr.	July	Oct.	Rain	Snow
Daily Highs	65	81	98	82	12	2
Daily Lows	38	50	71	56	in.	in.

Green Valley

When I was a school teacher, I used to spend my summer vacations visiting friends here in Green Valley. When I retired, I just knew I had to move here.
—Jennie Rygiel

Most exceptionally successful retirement communities became popular by accident, either as a byproduct of tourism or because of unusually pretty surroundings, and are almost always situated near a good-sized shopping area or city. Green Valley is an exception to the general rule, for it stands complete as an age-restricted retirement center and was planned to be that way.

Originally an unlikely development dream on a high rise of desert land 25 miles south of Tucson on Interstate 19, Green Valley turned out to be not so unlikely after all. Today more than 20,000 people, the overwhelming majority of whom are retired, call Green Valley their home. One source reports that the average age here is in the upper 60s, and residents come from all over the world. Although some inexpensive property can be found here, most of the area is more upscale than you might expect. The average household income here is surprisingly high for a retirement community: over $44,000. Thirty-one percent of Green Valley households have incomes over $50,000.

Green Valley is unincorporated, and folks seem to prefer it that way. Less taxes, fewer bureaucrats, more time for golf. The town sits at an altitude of 2,900 feet at the foot of the Santa Rita Mountains (an Apache hangout in the olden days) and is 40 miles north of Nogales and Old Mexico. It's about eight miles long and two miles wide, divided by the interstate. One advantage Green Valley has over nearby Tucson or Phoenix is its higher elevation. Residents say summer temperatures are consistently five degrees cooler than Tucson and ten degrees cooler than Phoenix. On the hottest July and August days, low humidity permits night temperatures to drop 30 to 40 degrees. An escape from summer's hottest days can be found 20 miles away in the 9,000-foot elevation of the Santa Rita Mountains. Temperatures in the pine-shaded Madera Canyon, with an elevation of 4,000 feet, average 20 degrees cooler than Green Valley. But Green Valley winter daytime temperatures are similar to Tucson or Phoenix, averaging from the mid-60s to the low 70s.

A study of the local telephone directory clearly demonstrates the "melting pot" character of Green Valley. In addition to phone numbers and addresses, the local directory lists the residents' former home towns as well as their occupations before retirement. The directory lists retirees from all 50 of the United States and 10 Canadian provinces who have selected Green Valley for their new homes. Residents from many other countries also make Green Valley their home. Your neighbors could come from Australia, Costa Rica, England, France, Ireland, Germany, Sweden or any of 26 other foreign countries from six continents. Among the United

States, California and Illinois each account for 14 columns of names in the phone directory, with Michigan filling 11 columns and Minnesota and Wisconsin seven columns each. Green Valley residents take advantage of this diversity by forming clubs based on their place of origin. You'll find clubs from the Dakotas, Michigan and Tennessee—most states are covered. A large number of retirees are Canadians, some spending only the winters here. There's even a British Women's Teapot Club.

Complete facilities include several large shopping centers, and the rec center for Green Valley is quite comprehensive, with facilities for arts and crafts, sewing, lapidary work and photography. A swimming pool, jacuzzi, sauna and exercise room complete the recreational picture.

Not all of Green Valley is restricted to over-50 folks, so there are youngsters around to keep the makeup of the community from being one-dimensional. Instead of an R.S.V.P. program, seniors are served by a volunteer organization called Friends In Deed, which fills much the same function.

Recreation and Culture
Golf is Green Valley's traditional outdoor sport, after all, it started as a development around a golf course. There are six local courses, three 18-hole courses open to the public and three private courses. They range from traditional wide layouts to tournament-quality designs. Tennis is also popular here with 13 courts, eight of them lighted for night play in specially designed facilities at recreational centers run by Green Valley Recreation. For less strenuous exercise, Green Valley offers shuffleboard and swimming at 25 pool facilities, some of which require membership. There's also a bowling alley.

Surprisingly, fishing is possible even in the middle of the desert. Three fish-filled lakes are within one hour's drive from Green Valley. Less than 20 minutes from the community is one of the nation's best-known birdwatching sites at Madera Canyon.

Many seniors take advantage of the non-credit courses at Pima Community College, with interesting classes including art, dance, history, language arts and literature. For art classes in painting, woodworking and ceramics, many depend on Green Valley Recreation. Also of interest are classes in jewelry-making, quilting and ballroom dancing. Just a short drive away is Tucson, a city that has been called "a cultural oasis in the desert." Green Valley folks regularly travel there to hear the Tucson Symphony, the Tucson Pops Orchestra or the Arizona Light Opera Company.

Real Estate Living costs here are about the same as most Arizona towns, about average nationally, but the wide range of real estate prices makes it possible for any budget to make a selection. According to the chamber of commerce, sale prices of homes in the past few months were from $24,000 to $300,000. Rentals for unfurnished apartments start at $325 monthly, with an annual lease, and $900 and up for furnished units on a seasonal contract. Two full-service retirement apartment complexes are available.

The low end of the housing market consists of the original townhomes which were built by the first developer. They were intended for folks to live in while their golf-course homes were built. They are perfectly livable and attractive, if somewhat small. The one-bedroom townhomes can usually be purchased for as little as $30,000 to $42,000. A two-bedroom unit sells for $35,000 to $48,000. Larger, conventional housing in excellent neighborhoods starts at $85,000. The interesting thing about Green Valley neighborhoods is that they are all nice looking, well-kept and delightfully landscaped with low-maintenance desert plants, cactus and ornamental rock. Lawnmower salesmen would starve here.

Medical Care Green Valley has two highly rated nursing homes and a 24-hour emergency clinic, plus two private clinics and a 60-bed health care center. Four ambulances with trained emergency medical technicians are standing by, and Tucson hospitals are 20 miles away by Interstate 19.

When Grandkids Visit Check out the San Xavier Del Bac Mission on Tohono O'Odham Indian Reservation. Of all the missions founded by Jesuit Father Kino, this is the only one still in active use. Today it's operated by the Franciscans. Another possibility is the Titan Missile Museum, once a launching site for Intercontinental Ballistic Missiles (ICBMs), now an interesting museum with tours deep into the workings.

Important Addresses and Connections

Chamber of Commerce: P.O. Box 566, Green Valley, AZ 85622
Senior Services: Green Valley Rec., P.O. Box 586, Green Valley, AZ 85622
Twice-Weekly Newspaper: *Green Valley News*, P.O. Box 567, Green Valley, AZ 85622

Real Estate Agents: Barbara Hinton, Real Estate Connection, 101-58 S. La
   Canada, Green Valley, AZ 85614; Dick Smith, Century 21 (has rentals),
   191 W. Esperanza Blvd., Green Valley, AZ 85614
Airports: Tucson International, 23 miles north, with shuttle service
Bus: Citizen's Auto State provides service to Tucson

GREEN VALLEY	Jan.	Apr.	July	Oct.	Rain	Snow
Daily Highs	65	82	98	82	12	2
Daily Lows	38	50	71	56	in.	in.

Wickenburg

*When we found out that we could play golf every day in the win-
ter in Wickenburg, we bought a condo and moved from
Washington.*
                                                        —Charles Jamison

Wickenburg has a population of 6,000 and is the shopping center for 20,000 in the area. An impressive 30 percent of the town's
population are retired. About an hour's drive northwest from
Phoenix, the town of Wickenburg is attracting retirees who don't
want to accept the neatly arranged, orderly and secure life of Sun
City or the bustle of traffic-bound Phoenix. A measure of big-city
life has found Wickenburg, however, with the installation of a traffic light a couple of years ago.

In small-town Wickenburg, they savor the tang of the Old West.
The town has been famous for years for its guest ranches (they
used to call 'em dude ranches), which go way beyond being simply places to herd cattle. They come complete with amenities such
as swimming pools, tennis courts, and sometimes a golf course.
Although guest ranches are still popular with tourists, the retirement emphasis is on small-acreage places where you can keep riding horses and live year-round.

This area is highly mineralized and was the site of a considerable gold rush back in the late 1800s. Several rich mines encircled
the town, with millions of dollars worth of the glittering mineral
taken from the ground. Although most of the richest locations have
been worked out over the years, enough remains to keep the local
people busy prospecting and panning for the gold that the old-
timers may have missed. Not only gold: other valuable minerals

such as silver, copper, turquoise, mercury, nickel and tungsten crop up within a 25-mile radius of Wickenburg. Don't expect to become rich panning for gold, however, because yesteryear's miners were pretty busy. The town celebrates its Wild West past every February with Gold Rush Days, a weekend of rodeos, gold panning and dressing up in period costumes.

It does get hot in the summertime, with July and August posting highs of 100 degrees and above. But like most Arizona desert country, low humidity takes much of the sting from the high temperatures. Winter nights can be cold, with frost common, but day temperatures are quite pleasant, with shirt-sleeve weather being the noonday norm.

Medical Care Because of the large number of seniors, health care is adequate with a 34-bed hospital and many doctors in private practice. Fifty minutes of driving takes you to excellent Sun City hospitals, which specialize in problems of the elderly.

Living Costs and Real Estate The cost of living here is about on a par with Phoenix, which is slightly above the national average. However, land here is abundant and fairly inexpensive, so building lots are typically sold by the acre, and you get more land for your money that you could expect in Phoenix. You may keep horses in your yard if you care to; the local horse population is considerable. You can saddle up and go for a ride through open desert and brush country in almost any direction you care to ride. Since almost all of the surrounding land is owned by the federal Bureau of Land Management (BLM), nobody can interfere with your rides. You don't know how to ride horseback? No problem, local saddle clubs with friendly members will help you get started. The clubs organize numerous social activities centered around horseback riding, from afternoon rides for beginners to the grueling Desert Caballeros Ride for seasoned horsemen, who come from all over the country to participate.

Wickenburg has several mobile home parks, with many living units used only part of the year, their owners choosing to live elsewhere during the hot summer months. At one time it was possible to buy a lot and install a mobile home, but nowadays this is frowned upon by the city council.

Recreation and Culture Wickenburg simply isn't large enough to provide a wide variety of cultural offerings. Several art galleries display works of local artists. The local Community Center hosts Sunday afternoon concerts by a civic group called Friends of Music. For theater, symphony concerts and other major cultural events, it's necessary to travel an hour away to Phoenix.

To play golf in Wickenburg, you need to belong to a club. The Wickenburg Country Club is the least expensive, with monthly memberships of less than $100. The high-price spread is Los Caballeros Golf Club. However, avid golfers claim it's worth the more costly fees, because Los Caballeros is supposed to be one of the top ten courses in the state.

When Grandkids Visit Check out the Desert Cabelleros Western Museum in downtown Wickenburg. You'll find a collection of minerals, fossils and artifacts from ancient Native American tribes who used to inhabit the region. Or you might want to picnic south of town where the normally dry Hassayampa River surfaces to form an unusual oasis of green willows and cottonwoods.

Important Addresses and Connections

Chamber of Commerce: P.O. Box Drawer CC, Wickenburg, AZ 85358
Senior Services: Wickenburg Community Action Program, 256 N. Washington St., Wickenburg, AZ 85390
Weekly Newspaper: *The Sun*, 179 N. Washington, Wickenburg, AZ 85390
Real Estate: Coldwell Banker, 300 N. Tegner St., Wickenburg, AZ 85390
Airport: Phoenix Airport
Bus: there's Greyhound, but no local bus service

WICKENBURG	Jan.	Apr.	July	Oct.	Rain	Snow
Daily Highs	67	79	103	82	11	2
Daily Lows	30	48	70	52	in.	in.

Lake Havasu City

Retirees in Lake Havasu City have two ways to go. They can either shut themselves up in their homes and become hermits or get down to the chamber of commerce and find out about all the clubs, groups and social activities. If you were an Elk or Kiwanis back home, no reason you can't be the same in Havasu.

—Bob Ramsdell

Before it became Lake Havasu City, the shore here was just plain Lake Havasu, another place snowbirds kept secret, a quiet, inexpensive location to escape the rigors of winter. Snowbirds would enjoy the winter, acquire a deep tan, and then pack up their RVs and head north for the spring. Of course, those who visited always returned the following year to enjoy the quiet lake, good fishing and a delightful summer-like winter.

The catalyst for change was Robert P. McCulloch, who flew over the lake one day in search of a good place to test his outboard motors. He spotted an abandoned Army Air Corps landing strip, which is now the airport of Lake Havasu City. He started to dream, and plan.

In August 1963, McCulloch purchased 16,630 acres of virgin territory on the Arizona side of the lake and began designing a city. At first the idea of relocating a manufacturing enterprise in an isolated desert hamlet seemed outlandish at the time. But it worked out just as McCulloch dreamed, and brought prosperity and growth. Gradually the economy bootstrapped itself, and outsiders started buying lots and building winter homes.

McCulloch's next wild idea occurred when he discovered that the famous London Bridge was for sale. Stone by stone the 170-year-old Tudor bridge was dismantled in London, shipped through the Panama Canal to Long Beach and trucked to its new location on the shore of Lake Havasu. A problem developed when it turned out the bridge was too short to span the engorged Colorado River at this point. It turned out not to be a problem when a part of the river was simply diverted under the bridge. The promotional effort paid off, for today the bridge is a sure-fire tourist attraction and a plus for the economy of the region.

From its original, unpretentious beginnings, Lake Havasu City has boomed to over 36,000 full-time residents. Homes and condos, trailers and mobile homes, businesses and services of all descriptions appeared as if by magic. An estimated 6,000 to 8,000 additional winter residents swell the population and add to the general prosperity.

Of all the Southwestern retirement destinations we've investigated in the past several years, we have to admit that Lake Havasu City is one of the most surprising. Every time we come here we're amazed at the amount of innovative construction, new businesses, nice restaurants, and the increased number of full-time retirees who choose to live on the treeless banks of a desert lake. The surprising

thing is the touch of quality in all of this. The city has grown gracefully, not just a quick-and-easy expansion and taste take the hind-
most. Havasu City combines all the convenience of a much larger
population center with quality surroundings worthy of a high-class
spa or resort. Adding touches of class are the spectacular scenic
sculptures—cliffs, canyons and ragged peaks—which never fail to
draw gasps of astonishment from our lips when we pass through
Havasu.

True, in July and August, you'll bake. But not much more than
in Phoenix. And like Phoenix, winter's balminess and gentle
warmth makes you forget the rotisserie of summer. For some reason, Lake Havasu City is a bit warmer in the winter than rival
Bullhead City, a bit north. January averages five degrees warmer,
with 67-degree high temperatures, yet summer highs are about the
same, only a little over 108 degrees. Yes, that's 108 degrees—but air
conditioning quickly drops the thermometer down to 72 degrees,
so, as they say, "don't sweat it."

Lake Havasu City, as a retirement choice, is different from many
popular locations. The economy doesn't count on retirees for sus-
tenance. On the contrary, the region's booming economy attracts
so many working families, many with children, that retirees are a
true minority. There's no question about Lake Havasu's having a
multi-generation, home-town feeling. As the chamber of commerce
director pointed out, "Lake Havasu City isn't just another walled-in
senior community. It's multi-generational, vibrant, yet easy paced
at the same time."

Medical Care Because of the high number of retirees, the
Lake Havasu area enjoys a more complete health care system than
ordinarily found in communities of similar size. A 99-bed acute-care
hospital, staffed with 35 physicians, and a 120-bed nursing center
serve the community. The hospital is in the process of expanding
by 50 percent, by the way. For unusual medical problems, a state-
certified life support/air evac is available around the clock.

Recreation and Culture Some fishing enthusiasts insist
on living as close to the source of prey as possible, so mobile home
parks right on the river become their choice, and RV parks dot the
riverbanks, each with its own boat-loading ramp and nearby bait
shop. By the way, boating and fishing aren't the only sports
enjoyed here. Four golf courses courses, five tennis facilities and at
least one bowling alley will keep you active.

Those who like slot machines and roulette wheels will feel at home here. It isn't necessary to drive to Las Vegas; gambling palaces on the Nevada side of the lake draw throngs of senior citizens who can't wait to contribute their money. Five times daily, ferry boats obligingly shuttle rich passengers to the casinos on the Chemehuevi Indian Reservation on the California side, and then fetch poorer but wiser passengers back to the Colorado side. Free buses will carry you to the Nevada gambling town of Laughlin, where casinos will also cheerfully accept your money

Attending to higher cultural needs than blackjack and poker are the Lake Havasu Art Guild, the Drury Lane Theater Company, the Havasu Light Opera Company and a community choir and orchestra. For those interested in continuing education, Mohave Community College offers unique and challenging course options. A gem and mineral society provides outlets for rockhounds and collectors.

Year-round events crowd the calendar here. Golf and tennis tournaments, art festivals and a Dixieland jazz festival are among the many happenings throughout the area. A "Snowbird Jamboree" takes place in the winter, as you might imagine, while a Hava Salsa Challenge and the Blue Water Invitational Regatta break the routine in the summer. October is time for the yearly celebration to commemorate the opening of London Bridge.

Senior Services A bustling senior center provides a dial-a-ride service in addition to the customary bridge games, arts and crafts, health maintenance and nutrition programs. The Lake Havasu Senior Center holds line dancing classes three times a week, has a wheelchair lift van and home delivers meals. The community college offers fee discounts to senior citizens, and some activities are coordinated with Arizona State University, including drama performances, concerts and lectures.

Living Costs and Real Estate The cost of living here barely tops the national average. High utilities and medical care costs are offset by low home prices. Despite all this growth, housing costs are generally lower than in other metropolitan areas of Arizona and markedly lower than comparable housing in southern California. According to the Lake Havasu Board of Realtors, single-family detached homes range in price from $45,000 to $400,000 (for golf course sites), with an average selling price of $65,000. Townhouses and condominiums are available from $35,000.

Apartments and home rentals are plentiful and available from $275 to $700 per month. Residential lots average around $9,000.

Crime and Safety According to the FBI's statistics, the Lake Havasu area is one of the safest in the country, ranking in the top 20 percent of low-crime areas. The police department's 56 law officers are supplemented by a 37-member Citizens Volunteer Program who donate thousands of hours each year to maintaining the area's reputation for safety.

When Grandkids Visit They'll be interested in the London Bridge, a roller rink, and all of the great things to do at the Aquatic Center. Boating, water skiing and jet skiing are popular with the younger set, as well as swimming and cane-pole fishing for catfish from the banks of the Colorado River lake. Several boat tours entertain and inform as they cruise the waters. For that special treat, you and your grandkids might like to try parasailing, soaring 300 feet above the waters of the lake below, like eagles on high and... on second thought, maybe you wouldn't like that.

Important Addresses and Connections

Chamber of Commerce: 1930 Mesquite Av., Lake Havasu City, AZ 86403
Senior Center: 2223 Swanson Ave., Lake Havasu City, AZ 86403
Daily Newspapers: *Lake Havasu City Herald*, 2225 W. Acoma Blvd., Lake Havasu City, AZ 86403; *Today's Daily News*, 1890 W. Acoma Blvd., Lake Havasu City, AZ 86403
Airports: Lake Havasu City Airport, with several commuter connections to LA and Phoenix
Bus/Train: none

LAKE HAVASU CITY	Jan.	Apr.	July	Oct.		Rain	Snow
Daily Highs	67	87	109	91		4	–
Daily Lows	37	54	79	58		in.	

Bullhead City/Laughlin

I don't know why any sensible person would retire here, unless they liked fishing, hiking, and other outdoor sports, or unless they were looking for an inexpensive place to live. Of course, 67 percent of the population here are retirees.
—Thurston Daniels

About 55 miles north of Lake Havasu City, Bullhead City is an alternative for those who enjoy low desert retirement. Unlike Lake Havasu City, which was planned, Bullhead seems to have taken the path of least resistance and simply followed the road and the Colorado River. Above the town, where the highway to Kingman crosses the river, is Davis Dam. This forms the lower end of Lake Mohave and the lower extremity of Lake Mead National Recreational Area.

Sitting across the river from each other, Bullhead City and Laughlin are an odd-couple combination of residential and high-life gambling personalities. Both places are booming to the point that it's difficult to guess how many people are living there. Bullhead City's population keeps growing, with about 27,000 at last count. New businesses open monthly to keep up with demand, ensuring adequate shopping for the area.

Laughlin is the southernmost point in Nevada where you can gamble, and an enormous percentage of the patrons are retirees. They come with canes, wheelchairs and even walkers, all determined to make a killing. I'm not exaggerating; when we last visited Laughlin, I made a survey by counting the number of obviously under-age-60 slot-machine players in each row of 20 machines. The average was one under-60 youngster for each row of 20. The casinos long ago discovered that putting slot machines and senior citizens together can be a lucrative proposition.

Until the casinos began riding high, Bullhead City was a sleepy fishing village, not much more than a scattering of winter retirement places and fishing marinas. But with Laughlin constantly needing more employees for motels and casinos, Bullhead City's growth kept pace as workers and retirees increased their numbers. Today the casinos employ thousands; many retirees enjoy full-time or part-time jobs doing everything from cleanup to dealing blackjack.

Rapid ferry boats shuttle tourists and casino employees over the river, and more retirees are choosing to live on the Nevada side of the river. An added benefit of being a Nevada resident is no state income taxes on all of those gambling winnings. If you don't win, you can join Gambler's Anonymous at the Bullhead City Senior Center. Don't be surprised to see me there.

Recreation and Culture The most popular recreation here involves exercising slot machine handles or throwing a pair of

plastic cubes across a green felt table and shouting, "Come on, baby!" This is immediately followed by the words, "Oh, no!" When you grow tired of these recreational opportunities or run out of money (quite likely), you'll find plenty of conventional activities to amuse you. Six golf courses, three 18-hole and three 9-hole layouts, can be found within a short drive of town.

The Bullhead chamber of commerce is continually trying to think up activities to keep residents and tourists on the Arizona side of the river. As a result, their activity calendar is generally full, with something going on every week. Everything from chili cookoffs to jazz dance combos. At the time of our last visit the chamber was promoting a Harley Davidson rally; 30,000 bikers were expected. It seemed like a good idea, but all 30,000 immediately checked into the casinos on a round-the-clock basis, leathers, helmets and all. Another cultural event which was scheduled for May 13 was the "Country Fair & Burro Barbecue." Not being overly fond of burro steaks, we passed on that one.

Real Estate Property costs vary widely in Bullhead City, as does the range of quality. At the low end of the scale are single-wide mobile homes with prices to match the caliber, and at the top of the line are elegant riverfront homes for half a million or more. Houses on the Nevada side of the river tend to be newer, more expensive and located in better looking neighborhoods. Older homes in acceptable neighborhoods on the Arizona side seem to sell between $65,000 and $95,000.

Medical Care A new extended-care facility for senior citizens operates in conjunction with Bullhead Community Hospital and is located across the street from the hospital.

When Grandkids Visit They'll probably want to see another of those reconstructed ghost towns with gunfights and Western street drama. Oatman is the place here, about 14 miles from Bullhead City, and it's surprisingly original, so much so that several Western movies have been filmed here. An added feature are the wild burros that roam Oatman's streets and sidewalks. These are descendants of animals who escaped captivity to avoid working in the mines years ago (can't blame 'em). The lazy burros hang around town mooching snacks from tourists—burro pellets are sold everywhere—and head for the hills when day is done.

Important Addresses and Connections

Chamber of Commerce: 1251 Highway 95, Bullhead City, AZ 86429

Senior Services: Mohave Senior Programs, 1885 Trane Rd., Bullhead City, AZ 86429

Daily Newspaper: *Mohave Valley Daily News,* 2435 Miracle Mile, Bullhead City, AZ 86439

Real Estate Agent: Bullhead City Real Estate, Inc., 1951 S. Hwy. 95, Bullhead City, AZ 86442

Airport: Laughlin-Bullhead Airport, with commuter connections

Bus: Greyhound, shuttle to Las Vegas McCarren Airport

BULLHEAD CITY	Jan.	Apr.	July	Oct.	Rain	Snow
Daily Highs	62	84	108	90	4	–
Daily Lows	42	56	79	62	in.	

Yuma

We love Yuma as our winter home. When it looks like rain in Oregon, we start packing and we know we're going to have great summer weather while our Oregon neighbors are getting wet.

—Bob and Rose Gleason

Yuma, the last of the Colorado River towns, anchors Arizona's southwest corner, where the mighty Colorado crosses into Mexico on its way to the Sea of Cortez. At this point, the river loses some of its majesty. Much of its flow has been siphoned off along the way to irrigate truck farms, supply drinking water to dozens of communities and make ice cubes for casinos. A sleepy little desert town just a few years ago, Yuma's growth can be described as explosive. Since 1980, its population has increased by 30% to 57,000.

Only the center part, or "old town," shows evidence of its age and historic past. Everything else looks brand new. Originally described as "the great crossing place of a very wide and treacherous river," this was a trading center for early day adventurers and settlers.

In those days, Yuma's most noted landmark was its infamous Territorial Prison, a place as grim and dreaded as modern-day Barstow, California. (Well, almost as grim.) Of the prisoners who attempted escape, 26 were successful, and eight died from gunshot wounds. Fortunately, escaping from Barstow is much easier; you simply tromp on the accelerator pedal and away you go. Actually, prison life wasn't all that bad; because of the massive adobe walls, the cells were one of the cooler places in a Yuma summer. In 1907, the prison was closed, becoming a high school for a while, then free lodging for hobos during the depression and finally a museum.

Because of its low desert altitude (only 138 feet), summers here are exceptionally hot. Throughout the year, residents expect just a little more than three inches of rain. Think about that for a moment; three inches of rain is what most Eastern cities receive in one moderate rainstorm. Make no mistake, this is desert!

Yuma's winter population triples, as snowbirds from all over the country descend upon the area, bringing motorhomes, trailers and campers. But like the Rio Grande Valley area, Yuma convinces many snowbirds to nest for year-round retirement.

Living Costs and Real Estate   Yuma has the lowest cost of living of any Arizona retirement site discussed in this book. Real estate is also the lowest in the state. Median home prices are 18 percent below average, balanced by utility costs 18 percent above average. In 1994, there were in excess of 700 dwellings on the market with prices starting at $35,000, with the median price $69,000. Obviously, it's a buyer's market here.

Many retirees take advantage of nearby Mexico for inexpensive prescription drugs, dental care and experimental medications not yet approved in the U.S. (although most have been in Europe). A Marine Corps base is located within the city limits, sharing its runways with private and commercial aircraft. Residents are treated to an interesting display of Marine fighter jets and airliners alternating on take off. This base provides PX, commissary and medical care for military retirees.

Recreation and Culture   For gaming activity, Yuma Greyhound Park presents live dog racing and pari-mutuel betting on horses as well as greyhounds. Then there's the Cocopah Gaming Center, a tribal casino south of Yuma on Highway 95, for those who love to fight the slot machines. Because of the large influx of seniors in the winter, these facilities do quite well.

Outdoor sports quite naturally tend toward the warm weather variety. Several golf courses offer desert play which best be completed early in the morning on most summer days. The other major outdoor interest here is fishing in the Colorado River. Great bass fishing is enjoyed here, with catches of bluegill, crappie, and king-size catfish to fill your boat.

Even though Yuma can hardly qualify as a "college town," several institutions of higher learning are situated here. Arizona Western, a two-year state college, offers continuing education programs. A branch of Northern Arizona University is also located in Yuma, about as far south as a northern branch can be. Two private colleges complete the roster.

Medical Care One major hospital and various care centers attend to the medical needs of Yuma retirees. A major home care service is available. Because of the large number of seniors here, medical care is said to be excellent.

When Grandkids Visit The Colorado River can be a central attraction for kids. A recently developed historical park on the river, Yuma Crossing, shows how Yuma was in the days of the Wild West, before the railroad arrived. Along with the usual staged gunfights, the children will enjoy the overall Western theme. Another special treat might be to fish from the banks of the Colorado River, one of the few places in the world where you can be in the middle of the desert and pull in a catfish.

Important Addresses and Connections

Chamber of Commerce: 377 S. Main St., Yuma, AZ 85364
Daily Newspaper: *Yuma Daily Sun,* 2055 Arozoa Ave., Yuma, AZ 85364
Senior Center: Yuma Adult Center, 160 First St., Yuma, AZ 85364
Real Estate Agent: Century 21 Group, 1595 S. First Ave., Yuma, AZ 85364
Airport: Yuma International Airport
Bus: both a city bus and Greyhound serve the area

YUMA	Jan.	Apr.	July	Oct.	Rain	Snow
Daily Highs	69	85	107	91	3	–
Daily Lows	43	56	80	62	in.	

COLORADO

- Fort Collins
- Steamboat Springs

- Boulder

- DENVER

- Grand Junction

- Colorado Springs

- Durango

When you think of mountain scenery, the state of Colorado has to figure big. With some of the most gorgeous mountains on the continent—several passes climb over 10,000 feet—the highways that cross them are so high that some folks have trouble breathing. When they do catch their breath, the mountain scenery immediately takes it away again.

These magnificent mountains are Colorado's greatest natural resource. Much more than a tourist attraction, they are rich in minerals and teem with wildlife—deer, antelope, elk, black bear, and bighorn sheep. About one third of the state is forested with ponderosa and lodgepole pine, spruce, Douglas fir and aspen. The forests are rich in fur animals, such as muskrat, raccoon, beaver and fox, and game birds such as pheasant, quail and grouse, which are all protected by carefully regulated hunting laws. Mountain streams are the hideouts of rainbow and german trout, and lakes hold trophy bass and schools of perch.

Even though Colorado is famous for its Rocky Mountain scenery, with forested slopes and snowcapped peaks, much of the state is in high desert with equally interesting landscapes. The eastern portion of the state, from Denver to the Kansas state line, is pure great plains, sparsely populated and not the type of landscape one normally thinks of when talking about retirement.

On the western side of the Rockies the Colorado Plateau spreads out into a vast, arid tableland with plateaus that rise 4,000 to 8,000 feet above sea level. In places, the region is wildly eroded into a jumble of flat-topped mesas and steep-walled canyons. Deep canyons along the Gunnison and Yampa Rivers are some of the most spectacular in the world. These great differences in elevation cause Colorado's climate to vary widely from one part of the state to another, thus giving newcomers a wide choice of surroundings. Most areas have certain weather characteristics in common: lots of sunshine, low humidity and not an over-abundance of rainfall.

Colorado has a lot to offer the retiree: legendary mining towns, ultra-modern cities, farmlands and forests, mountain peaks and desert dunes. Full-time retirees like the reasonable housing, low property taxes and mild winters in most parts of Colorado. Some folks choose to retire in Colorado on a seasonal basis. Many part-time retirees love the state for its wonderfully refreshing summers, maintaining homes in high-altitude, picture-postcard locales; then they return to their Phoenix or Yuma homes before snow begins to cover the ground. Others come here for the opposite reason, to enjoy superb skiing and Colorado winter sports.

Yet the state is more than an outdoor paradise. Modern cities and progressive towns are scattered all over Colorado, places that provide all the amenities of civilized, cultured retirement. University towns, residential communities and tourist attractions offer delightful lifestyles for retirees, and all are close to Colorado's outdoor wonderlands.

A word about high-altitude living: those with health problems might want to consult their doctors before considering a move into high elevations. At high altitudes, oxygen is less dense, and humidity is 50 to 80 percent lower than at sea level. You need to breath more deeply to draw enough oxygen into your lungs. Sudden changes in environment from low to high altitudes can produce symptoms of nausea, rapid heartbeat, fatigue and other problems—for some people, not all. Usually, your body adjusts to lower oxygen supplies and dryness in the

> **Colorado**
> "Centennial State"
> The 38th state to enter the Union, Aug. 1, 1876
>
> **State Capital:** Denver
>
> **Population (1990):** 3,307,912; rank, 26th
>
> **Population Density:** 31.9 per sq. mile; urban: 80.6%, rural: 19.4%
>
> **Geography:** 8th state in size, with 104,091 square miles, including 496 square miles of water surface and 33% in forested land. Highest elevation: Mt. Elbert, 14,433 feet; lowest elevation: Arkansas River, near Kansas, 3,350 feet. Average elevation: 6,800 feet.
>
> **State Flower:** Rocky Mountain Columbine
>
> **State Bird:** Lark Bunting
>
> **State Tree:** Blue Spruce
>
> **State Song:** Where the Columbines

air after 48 to 72 hours. Many people, like the author, experience no altitude symptoms other than initial drowsiness at altitudes over 11,000 feet. That's no problem; I simply take an extra nap every day until my body adjusts. When my body adjusts, I still take an extra nap. I'm retired—I nap when I want to.

History

Early native peoples known as Basket Makers or Cliff Dwellers—probably related to the Anasazi of Arizona—established a sophisticated civilization that flourished in what is now Colorado from about AD 100 to 1300. Possibly a great drought, lasting from 1276 to 1299 may have forced them to abandon their dwellings high in the canyon walls. It's all very mysterious; another possible scenario is that they were chased away by invading tribes coming down from Alaska. Their multi-storied apartment buildings are well-preserved in Mesa Verde National Park and in the Yucca House and Hovenweep National Monuments.

By the 1700s, when Spanish and French explorers visited the area, the civilized tribes had long been replaced by nomadic, sometimes fierce, plains tribes—the Cheyenne, Arapaho, Comanche, and Kiowa. The Ute tribes mostly controlled the mountain regions where many retirees are now settling.

In 1803 the United States acquired the eastern part of Colorado from France as part of the Louisiana Purchase. The rest belonged to Spain and became part of Mexico when Spain relinquished claim to her western posessions. Then, in 1848 Mexico decided (at gunpoint) that it might not be a bad idea to hand over the rest of Colorado to the United States via the Treaty of Guadalupe-Hidalgo.

Early adventurers who explored the Colorado territory bore famous names like Kit Carson, John C. Fremont and Zebulon Pike. These "mountain men"—fur traders and hunters—established early settlements and forts as they followed the existing Indian trails that usually paralleled the courses of the rivers. Today, Colorado's major highways and interstate pavement cover these same trails.

The big development boom began in 1859; the gold and silver strikes opened the floodgates. Colorado became the destination of thousands of fortune seekers and immigrants. "Pikes Peak or Bust" became a national slogan. The final connection was forged in 1870 when a railroad linked Denver with the Union Pacific. Modern development was underway and hasn't slacked off a bit since.

COLORADO TAXES

Colorado Dept. of Revenue, 1375 Sherman, Rm. 186, Denver, CO 80261
303-620-4123

Income Tax
Flat rate of 5% of Federal taxable income
Personal Exemptions or Credit Not applicable.
Public/Private Pension Exclusion $20,000 for persons age 55 and older.
Social Security/Railroad Retirement Benefits Exempt.
Benefits Exemption To extent excluded from federal taxable income; any taxable portion included in federal AGI also subject to further $20,000 exclusion.
Standard Deduction None.
Medical and Dental Expense Deduction To extent excluded from federal taxable income.
Federal Income Tax Deduction None.

Sales Taxes
State 3.0%; **County** 0.25%–4.0%; **City** 1.0%–5.0%
Combined Rate in Selected Towns Denver: 7.3%; Colorado Springs: 6.4%
General Coverage Food and prescription drugs are exempt.

Property Taxes
All real and personal property subject to state and local tax.
Tax Relief for Homeowners and renters 65 or older, or disabled, or surviving spouse 58 or older; income ceiling $7,500 single; $11,200 married; maximum benefit: $500.
Deferral Program Homeowners 65 or older are eligible for a homestead deferral of real property taxes. Local option deferral for non-gaming property homeowners if tax is 130% or greater than prior year's tax owed. Maximum benefit is equity in the property.
Other At local option, homeowners 60 or older may work at minimum wage for local taxing entity in lieu of tax bill owed.

Estate Tax/Inheritance Taxes
Colorado does not impose an estate tax nor an inheritance tax. It imposes only a pick-up tax, which is a portion of the federal estate tax and does not increase the total tax owed.

Licenses
Drivers License Colorado requires a driver's license with 30 days of establishing residence. A vision test is required upon surrender of old driver's license. Fee: $15 for five years.
Automobile License Taxed according to weight, with registration fee, $9-$16.10 plus $5.50 for title, and about 2 percent tax on value. A car with value of $12,000 would pay around $240 per year.

Boulder

There's something special about living in a university town. But Boulder is special among all university towns.

—Susan and Wayne Merwin

A growing retirement trend is toward college towns. Even if they haven't the slightest interest in continuing education, retirees often find that a university influences a community, serving as an exciting source of entertainment and cultural stimulation. Many of these social and cultural activities wouldn't exist without the school's presence. You don't have to be a registered student to attend lectures and speeches (often free) given by famous scientists, politicians, visiting artists and other well-known personalities. Concerts, ranging from Beethoven to boogie-woogie, are presented by guest artists as well as the university's music department. You can attend the school's stage plays, Broadway musicals and Shakespeare productions with season tickets that cost less than a single performance at a New York theater. Some schools allow senior citizens the use of recreational facilities and access to well-stocked libraries.

Therefore, without hesitation, I highly recommend Boulder as one of the better examples of university retirement locations. In addition to the University of Colorado at Boulder's intensely active college atmosphere, Boulder's immediate surroundings are as beautiful as you could imagine. It's about 27 miles northwest of Denver, with the Flatiron Mountains and snow-covered peaks looming in the background and Rocky Mountain National Park just minutes away. This wonderfully cosmopolitan city of 83,000 inhabitants is the home of the University of Colorado. The university, students and faculty impact the city's environment in many pleasant ways, carrying the institution's intellectual excitement into the community as a whole.

The school's influence is most obvious in the center of the city, as you stroll along the renovated downtown pedestrian mall known as Pearl Street. This vibrant historic preservation district is the focal point of the city, its traditional heart and soul. Mimes, jugglers and musicians mingle with the crowds, adding a touch of magic to the scene, something you'd expect to find in San Francisco or Paris, rather than Colorado. All generations mix here, as a place to meet for coffee, read a newspaper or magazine, or perhaps browse a book store or a boutique. Pearl Street offers a great selection of good restaurants, art galleries and specialty shops, of a variety and quality seldom seen in downtown areas of today's cities. Pearl Street is the site of continual activities, formal and ad hoc, the site of art festivals, practicing musicians, birthday celebrations, a place for people-watching and relaxing. In short, downtown Boulder is a user-friendly, enjoyable place to visit.

The University of Colorado encourages retirees to enroll in classes for credit or as auditors. But for those who don't feel up to total immersion in the university's curriculum, an extraordinary senior center operated by Boulder Housing and Human Services gives classes in everything from papermaking to computers. They even offer sailboat instruction on Boulder Reservoir and day trips to archaeological sites and theaters in Denver. Coupled with an active volunteer program, this is one of the better senior programs we've seen.

Boulder's winter looks bad statistically—that is, if you consider snow bad—because Boulder catches even more snow than Denver! December and February receive the heaviest blankets of the white stuff, but like Denver, daily temperatures climb high enough to get rid of it quickly. It doesn't hang around for long. Most days of the year can be spent walking, biking or with other outdoors activities. Summer makes amends by providing gloriously sunny and comfortable days.

Recreation and Culture   The Boulder area offers plenty of opportunity for outdoor recreation. You'll find three public (and one private) golf courses and 44 tennis courts. If you don't know how to play, Boulder Senior Services provides golf and tennis lessons. You can even take classes in canoeing. Lessons aren't necessary to utilize the 150 miles of hiking trails in Boulder's immediate vicinity. Ski buffs will be happy to learn there are ten ski areas within 110 miles. Indoor sports fans will be happy to discover that there are 37 gambling casinos within 46 miles of Boulder.

When football or basketball season rolls around, Boulder, like any college town, comes alive with enthusiasm. Even non–sports fans are drawn into the gaiety when pep rallies and celebrations charge the air with excitement. The best part is, tickets to college sporting events are usually very affordable, sometimes free.

Among the outstanding cultural events generated by the university is its Shakespeare festival, one of the top three in the country. There's also a nationally praised Bach Festival and the Colorado

Dance Festival. Every summer the Chautauqua Auditorium sponsors a very popular film series as well as dance, music and dramatic presentations. The list of festivals, musical productions, expositions and dramas are far too long to be presented here. It seems there's not a day in the year without two or more choices of interesting activities going on.

Living Costs and Real Estate The cost of living here is about 13 percent above national averages, mostly because of the high cost of housing, which is 49 percent above average. The last two years have seen a spectacular rise in selling prices of homes, with about a 25-percent increase since 1992. The average sales price of three-bedroom homes in early 1995 was an astounding $273,000. Town homes and condos had an average sales price of $123,000.

Note that these are average sales prices; this doesn't mean that what most of us would consider an average house sells for $273,000. As mentioned in the introductory chapter, the problem with averaging prices is that when an extraordinary number of expensive luxury homes sell, this raises the average sales price of ordinary homes. When five homes sell for $120,000, and two homes sell for $520,000 each, the average sales price is $273,000. This is the case in Boulder; a home selling for $273,000 isn't what most folks would consider an "average" home, even though the price is average. Homes selling for over $500,000 are common there, as are homes selling for under $120,000.

Rentals are correspondingly high, with two-bedroom apartments renting from $650 to $1,300. Partly this is due to student pressures on the rental market and partly because of a slowdown in the building of new units.

Medical Care The largest health care center is Boulder Community Hospital, with a full staff of physicians and 265 beds. With Denver just a half-hour drive away, the total hospital and doctor situation is excellent for retirement. The County Health Department operates a Wellness Program for people 55 and older, conducted at the Boulder Senior Services facilities. Registered nurses perform screening tests on blood sugar, cholesterol and blood pressure.

When Grandkids Visit One option is to visit the Fiske Planetarium on the University of Colorado campus. You'll enjoy an armchair travel trip around the galaxy on the Star Show. The Friday evening show is followed by free stargazing through telescopes at the university's observatory. A self-guided tour of the Colorado Scale Model Solar Systems gives the grandkids (and yourself) a sense of where planets are in relation to one another.

Important Addresses and Connections

Chamber of Commerce: 2440 Pearl Street, Boulder, CO 80302
Senior Services: 909 Arapahoe Ave., Boulder, CO 80302
Daily Newspapers: *Daily Camera*, 1048 Pearl Street, Boulder, CO 80302;
   Colorado Daily, 839 Pearl Street, Boulder, CO 80302
Real Estate Agent: Century 21, 1120 Main, Boulder, CO 80302
Airport: 50 minutes from the new Denver International Airport
Bus: City bus with discounts for senior citizens and intercity connections
   to Denver

BOULDER	Jan.	Apr.	July	Oct.	Rain	Snow
Daily Highs	41	66	88	70	17	90
Daily Lows	17	45	57	40	in.	in.

Colorado Springs

Could one live in constant view of these grand mountains without being elevated by them into a lofty plane of thought and purpose?
—Gen. William Jackson Palmer, founder, Colorado Springs, 1870

Pikes Peak dominates the view from every part of Colorado Springs, towering 14,110 feet high, presenting an ever-changing picture depending on the angle of the sun, the clouds, and the amount of snow. The altitude of the city is a bit higher than Denver, at 6,035 feet. It would seem only natural that Colorado Springs should receive more snow than Denver, but oddly enough, it receives about 30 percent less snow.

Although today's Colorado Springs is booming, with high-tech industries bringing in more residents daily, the town doesn't look like a boom town. As it grew over the years, the city matured gracefully. The result is that you'll find a variety of housing and neighborhoods, ranging from older stately homes to modern planned communities and custom homes built in outlying wooded areas. Today's population of 315,000 makes Colorado Springs a good-sized city, yet it's an easy place to drive in, with wide roads and boulevards accommodating traffic and seldom bogging down with gridlock as so often happens in some cities this size.

The central section of town is vintage Colorado, with comfortable and affordable residential environs. As you move outward, neighborhoods become newer and more expensive. Most neighborhoods are safe too, for Colorado Springs ranks 83rd in personal safety out of the 213 cities surveyed, placing in the top 40 percent. Tri-Lakes area, a few minutes' drive north of Colorado Springs, boasts several newer, upscale communities: the towns of Monument, Palmer Lake and the luxury developments of Woodmoor and Gleneagle.

The military plays an important role in Colorado Springs' economy. The North American Air Defense Command (NORAD) is headquartered in nearby Cheyenne Mountain. The Fort Carson Army Base, Peterson Air Force Base and the U.S. Space Command are all located in or around Colorado Springs. As if this weren't enough, the Air Force Academy is located on the northern side of the city. Many military families choose to retire here because of their experience with the town while stationed at one of the military installations.

The Air Force Academy joins an amazing number of institutions of higher education in Colorado Springs. Besides Colorado State University, there are branch campuses here of four or five other universities, two junior colleges and several private colleges. This spacious academic environment can't help but have a beneficial impact on the community. Colorado State University, for example, presents plays, lectures, concerts, and book signings to the public, sometimes free, sometimes for a modest admission charge. However, on the down side, with off-duty military personnel and students competing for part-time work, the job market will probably be tight.

Recreation and Culture

Most retirees who decide to move to Colorado Springs will have some golf clubs tucked away in the moving van. Area courses are famous far and wide. This is where the annual World Senior Tournament is held, as well as the Ladies' and Mens' Invitationals and the Ladies' U.S. Open. Golfers may select from seven public and 11 private courses.

Because of the great skiing available, some sports fanatics golf in the morning and ski that afternoon. Colorado is famous for hunting, fishing and river rafting, as well, and Colorado Springs is in the middle of it all.

For continuing education, Pikes Peak Community College offers a program of unlimited courses for $11 for those over 60 years of age. The University of Colorado gives senior citizens 50 percent off tuition for those auditing classes.

Near the Colorado College campus is the Fine Arts Center, with a 450-seat theater hosting performing arts series, classic film festivals and lectures. This is where the American College Players put on Broadway plays and musicals during the summer, while the Civic Music Theater performs all year round. The Fine Arts Center also houses the Taylor Collection of Native American and Hispanic art and an art school. Also, during July and August, the Colorado Opera Festival is held at Pikes Peak Center, and the Broadmoor International Center presents theatrical events and concerts.

Living Costs and Real Estate The cost of living is just slightly below national averages, but is nevertheless 15 points below Denver. This is due in part to exceptionally low utility costs, some 20 percent below average. This becomes important when heating a home during the long winter season.

Housing is also lower than in Denver, although not remarkably inexpensive. Prices vary widely, with the less-expensive places in the center of town, where you can often find something in the $60,000 bracket. On the northern side of the city prices tend to be higher; the selling price of an average single-family home there is around $85,000, and in some upscale areas, prices begin at $128,000. There's at least one gated community with prices starting in the mid-$90,000 range.

Apartments are currently experiencing a low vacancy rate. This is the result of population growth and a slow rate of new apartment construction. Waiting lists are sometimes necessary, but it may be worth it. Two-bedroom rentals in full-service facilities, including clubhouse and fitness centers, start around $550 and one-bedroom places for $400. Since heating costs are usually included in the rent, apartment living can be economical.

Medical Care Colorado Springs is a healthy place to be sick because of abundant medical facilities here. Memorial Hospital has a burn unit and specializes in intensive coronary care and cancer treatment. Other medical facilities are Penrose Community hospital, St. Francis Hospital and Cedar Springs Hospital, with a total of 1,000 beds. Colorado Springs is the home of the oldest Visiting Nurses Association in the state. Of interest to veterans are the military hospitals at the Air Force Academy and the Army hospital at Fort Carson.

When Grandkids Visit An hour or two could be well spent at the Garden of the Gods. Hike the trails through this 940-acre park where fantastic natural sculptures have been eroded from red sandstone bluffs. Among other items there is a balancing rock and one formation that resembles "kissing camels." For real camels, there's the Cheyenne Mountain Zoo, on the other side of town, with over 500 animals on display.

Important Addresses and Connections

Chamber of Commerce: P.O. Drawer B, Colorado Springs, CO 80901
Senior Services: 1514 N. Hancock Ave., Colorado Springs, CO 80903
Daily Newspaper: *Gazette Telegraph*, 30 S. Prospect St., Colorado Springs, CO 80903
Real Estate Agent: Sue Gindhardt, Century 21, 481 Hwy 105, Monument, CO 80132
Airport: Colorado Springs Airport provides major airline service
Bus: there's a good local system and an intercity bus, TNM&O, that connects with Greyhound

COLORADO SPR.	Jan.	Apr.	July	Oct.	Rain	Snow
Daily Highs	41	60	85	65	15	43
Daily Lows	16	33	54	37	in.	in.

Denver

I love the seasons here, and I especially love to watch the snow falling and making things beautiful. Since I live in a condo, I don't have to get out to shovel it, so I can love snow from my balcony window. It usually melts the next day, just in time for shopping.
—Dorothy Trask

Back in 1858, a few flakes of gold were discovered in the waters of Cherry Creek, where it emptied into the South Platte River. This unleashed the famous "Pikes Peak or Bust" gold rush that almost overnight boosted the little mining camp into the city of Denver. More gold and silver were discovered in nearby mountains, and Denver became the natural place to spend mining profits. So, from the beginning, Denver became Colorado's showplace of culture, a place for elegant mansions and glittering entertainment. With the finest restaurants, stores and theaters between San Francisco and St. Louis, it is not surprising that it acquired the title "Queen City of the Plains."

The largest city within a radius of 600 miles (an area almost the size of Europe), Denver has a population of 468,000 and a metropolitan population of close to 2 million. As the center of commerce for this large area, Denver maintains its "Queen City" title with its large infrastructure of culture, arts and commerce, much larger than most towns of this size. Its restaurants, theaters and department stores are geared for customers coming from the entire area.

This is a clean city, with pleasant, tree-shaded residential areas and loads of inexpensive apartment buildings. Most homes are built of brick, especially older ones. According to a common story, an early-day mayor owned a brick factory, so he passed laws that all homes must be constructed of brick. Maybe it's not true, but the brick construction does add a special touch to Denver's architectural flavor.

Many economical neighborhoods offer bargain housing, but there are some districts that might cause retirees to feel uncomfortable. These neighborhoods are the ones that push Denver down on the personal safety charts. Much crime in these areas is gang-related, and rarely involves seniors, but why bother? Understand, crime rates here aren't horrible—ranking 126th out of 213 places—but I'd recommend looking over a neighborhood closely before making any decisions. Good places to look for safe housing possibilities are the outlying areas such as Aurora or Littleton. From there, it's a quick shot downtown for shopping, theater or cultural events.

Denver is also called the "Mile-High City," and indeed you will be precisely one mile high if you stand on the west steps of the State Capitol building. Actually, compared with other Southwest locations discussed in this book, Denver's mile-high status is no big deal, being almost 2,000 feet lower than places like Santa Fe or Flagstaff. Of course, the altitude affects the weather, and Denver's weather is interesting from the perspective of a retiree. At first glance it would seem to be a horrible place to winter, what with a yearly snowfall of 60 inches! Seems like every winter, TV newscasts feature Denver's airport buried under banks of drifting snow. But that's only part of the story. Yes, it can snow a foot or more overnight, but within a couple of days, if not the next day, it's all gone, and you'll be basking in 65-degree sunshine! The sun shines on Denver about 300 days a year, bringing more hours of sunshine than places like Miami or San Diego. Even the coldest months average 47 degrees every afternoon. Snow doesn't have a chance to stick around. Furthermore, the dryness of the air fools you into thinking it is far warmer than it really is.

Recreation and Culture Denver golf courses are open for play all year, and there have been as many as 30 playing days in January. The city operates seven golf courses and often sponsors tournaments between courses. Ten more golf courses, eight of them open to the public, are scattered around the metropolitan area. Both horse and greyhound racing tracks operate part of the year, with the doggies running from June 16 through February 10.

If you like to visit museums and art galleries, you'll have a ball here. Denver boasts six art museums, 16 historical museums, four natural history museums and 29 art galleries. That's in addition to many outdoor parks and displays that are essentially open-air museums. The city of Denver also maintains a sort of museum with a herd of 40 buffalo in a natural setting 20 miles west of the city. These are the direct descendants of the last wild herd left in America.

Theatergoers have a wide choice, with four dinner theaters and several other conventional houses. The Denver Center for the Performing Arts hosts professional touring, cabaret and resident theater presentations. Denver has its own opera, with in-the-round and proscenium-staged productions featuring international artists.

About 30 casinos are within an easy drive of Denver, notably in Central City, Blackhawk, Cripple Creek and Georgetown. The casinos provide buses which will take you to the gambling joints and refund your bus fare. Sounds generous, but not to worry, they'll get it all back before you leave.

Living Costs and Real Estate A few years ago, Denver was the most depressed big-city market we found anywhere in the country. The reasons were twofold: first, the oil shale boom had inflated new construction, and second, the savings-and-loan industry (industry or racket?) had been disbursing construction loans and financing homes, apartments, office buildings, for anyone who asked. Then, when the petroleum companies suddenly pulled out of the shale exploration business and fired most of their employees, the boom turned into a disheartening bust.

However, the market made a remarkable turnaround. Today homes sell for 14.8 percent over national averages. This is responsible for an overall cost-of-living at 6.5 percent over national average. Utility costs are lower, which helps keep down living costs. Home and condo prices and rents vary widely, depending upon what part of the city or suburb you choose.

Medical Care Saint Joseph Hospital offers a service called Med Search, a free physician-referral service. This helps newcomers find a conveniently located specialist or general practitioner to meet their needs.

When Grandkids Visit The Denver Zoo might be just the place to take the little ones. The city is building a new $10 million home for its gorilla collection there. The zoo's exhibit is nicely laid out, with spacious, natural habitats for the animals (at $10 million it oughtta be spacious). The newest exhibit is a rainforest display called Tropical Discovery, which is drawing thousands of people interested in tropical habitats.

Important Addresses and Connections

Chamber of Commerce: 1445 Market St., Denver, CO 80202
Senior Services: 135 California St. #300, Denver, CO 80202
Daily Newspaper: *Rocky Mountain News*, 400 W. Colfax, Denver, CO, 80204; *Denver Post*, 1560 Broadway, Denver, CO 80202
Airport: shuttle buses to Denver International Airport, 30 minutes away
Bus: there is a city bus as well as Greyhound service

DENVER	Jan.	Apr.	July	Oct.		Rain	Snow
Daily Highs	43	61	88	67		15	60
Daily Lows	16	34	59	37		in.	in.

Durango

The difference between Durango and tourist places like Telluride or Aspen is that we have a real town, with permanent people, employed in all kinds of trades and professions, yet we enjoy the ambience and excitement of a resort town.
—Don Ricedorff

Tucked away in a horseshoe of the San Juan Mountains in the southwestern corner of the state, Durango has been the gateway to southwestern Colorado's natural riches for more than 100 years. Indians and fur traders, miners and prospectors, ranchers and railroad engineers alike passed through Durango on the way to seek their fortunes. Many found that Durango itself was the treasure they sought. Two million acres of national forest surrounds the city and provides countless places for outdoor recreation, with hunting, fishing and hiking opportunities galore.

Although the town is relatively young—established little more than a century ago—the Four Corners Region where it's located boasts evidence of ancient glories. Two thousand years ago, this was home to a mysterious aboriginal culture known as the Anasazi (the Ancient Ones). For some unknown reason the Anasazi abandoned their sophisticated, several-storied apartment buildings and left the area to the next wave of inhabitants, the Ute tribes, who arrived a couple of centuries later. They were there to welcome the Spanish, who explored the region in the 1500s.

The town of Durango got its start in 1880, as a depot and roundhouse location for the railroad, and grew rapidly into a town of 2,000 residents just a year later. Before long the fledgling town boasted 20 saloons and 134 businesses. Today the population is 15,000 and still growing. Retirees make up a good percentage of the inhabitants; almost 30 percent are 62 or older. The business community and residents recognize the treasure of those original buildings constructed by Durango's pioneers which are still in use today. Parts of downtown have been named by the Colorado Historical Society as a national historic district, bestowing Durango with Victorian splendor and elegance.

Residents like the town because it's a pleasant and peaceful community with a below-average crime rate and above-average quality of living. A 6,500-foot elevation ensures a four-season climate with bountiful snowfall in the town, yet not so high an altitude that temperatures don't rise above freezing every winter day. With 85 percent solar exposure, snow removal is seldom a problem. You're also guaranteed cool summer evenings without the need of air conditioning.

Because Durango sits all by itself near the Four Corners area, by necessity it's become a self-contained little city. As Will Rogers one said, "Durango's out of the way and glad of it." All the shopping needs are met by commercial development in and around Durango. Turn-of-the-century hotels and commercial buildings abound in the business district, and an unusually high number of good restaurants serve a variety of cuisines. The year-round tourist business encourages upscale establishments, to the benefit of year-round residents.

Durango is also gaining recognition as an artist's colony. In addition to several well-known painters, half a dozen authors— novelists and non-fiction—make this their home, as well as a number of essayists, freelancers and poets. Three galleries here are nationally recognized for quality Native American arts, Navajo weavings, jewelry, paintings and sculpture.

Recreation and Culture
Skiing at Purgatory Ski Resort, 26 miles away, is reputed to be among the best in the country. Nine lifts and 250 inches of snow account for the resort's impressive increase in ski-hours. Although the resort has record snowfall, it also has record blue-sky days, which makes for great downhill fun. It's not too late to learn to ski, and Purgatory has a beginner's lift especially for those who are brave enough to give it a try.

Three 18-hole golf courses, 10 tennis courts and five walking trails in Durango encourage outdoor recreation. A growing sport, one which mature adults find enjoyable, is mountain biking. I'm assuming that the biking is down the mountain, not up, else it wouldn't be quite as fun.

The Animas River flows through town, offering excellent trout fishing, rafting, kayaking and other recreational activities. This is the third-most-rafted river in the state. You have your choice of a guided raft trip, or a do-it-yourself journey (or fiasco, depending on your experience in rafting). A guided fishing trip is an excellent way to learn fishing skills. Fishing at several stocked trout lakes in the area provides more restful adventure.

Hunting for big and small game is an attraction that draws tourists and brings local residents out during the seasons. Camping is also popular here, with over 900 campsites within a 40-mile radius.

Durango is also a progressive college town. Fort Lewis College, a four-year, fully accredited institution offers continuing education classes for local retirees. It also adds a vibrant dimension to the local lifestyle with cultural and artistic programs. A $5 million Community Concert Hall is planned for 1996. The theater's 600 seats will be arranged in a unique three-level arrangement with the closest seat only five feet from the stage and the farthest only 60 feet.

For those interested in archaeology, within an hour's drive of Durango are Mesa Verde Park, Crow Canyon Archaeological Center, Chimney Rock, the Anasazi Heritage Museum, and the Ute Mountain Ute Tribal Park.

Casino gambling, ever-increasing in the Southwest, is available near Durango. The Sky Ute Casino is 25 miles from town and the Ute Mountain Casino about 50 miles away. Slot machines, keno, bingo and poker games operate well into the wee hours of the morning to relieve you of your money.

Living Costs and Real Estate The cost of living here is slightly below national averages, and real estate prices possibly slightly higher than in some other Colorado locations. The reason for this is that there are fewer lower-end starter homes than elsewhere. Contractors prefer to build more upscale places, since they sell well. The average price for a three-bedroom home is $140,000, with starting prices around $80,000 and upper prices around $385,000. Condos start at $60,000 and reach $150,000 at the higher end of the scale. Homes with acreage and fantastic views start in the $150,000 range.

Medical Care Mercy Medical Center is the largest "rural" hospital in the state. It has 125 beds and is the regional referral center for specialized care throughout a six-county region. It has over 80 physicians on its medical staff. There's also skilled nursing care at Four Corners Health Care Center, with 156 beds and outpatient services for therapy.

When Grandkids Visit Try the Durango & Silverton narrow-gauge railroad, an authentic steam-powered train ride through the valleys and beside the peaks of the scenic San Juan Mountains. In continuous operation since 1882, this railroad line carried food and provisions to miners around the turn of the century and returned loaded with silver ore for the mills in Durango. If you can't get reservations on the train, only 36 miles from Durango are the most famous and best preserved cliff dwellings of the ancient Anasazi Indians at Mesa Verde National Park.

Important Addresses and Connections

Chamber of Commerce: 111 S. Camino Del Rio, Durango, CO 81302
Senior Services: 2424 Main Ave., Durango, CO 81301
Daily Newspaper: *Durango Herald*, 1275 Main Ave., Durango, CO 81301

Real Estate Agents: Coldwell Banker, 785 Main Ave., Durango, CO
  81301; The Wells Group, 901 Main Ave., Durango, CO 81301
Airport: La Plata Field, several commuter connections
Bus: "Durango Lift" takes you around town, and TNM&O bus service has
  connections with Greyhound

DURANGO	Jan.	Apr.	July	Oct.	Rain	Snow
Daily Highs	41	62	85	67	19	71
Daily Lows	10	29	49	31	in.	in.

Fort Collins

*We spent four out of our last five vacations in Colorado, so we
knew we wanted to retire there. After looking around, Fort Collins
is where we decided to settle.*
                                                    —Marie Edmond

This is another town that receives favorable reviews in national publications as a desirable place to live, work and retire. A scenic place with 90,000 residents and friendly neighborhoods, Fort Collins views the panorama of the nearby Rocky Mountains. The Cache la Poudre River runs along the upper edge of the city, a river famous for whitewater rafting, fishing and just plain scenic enjoyment. The upper stretches of the river are protected by the federal Wild and Scenic Rivers Act. This was the filming site for the first episode of the movie "Centennial." The river received its name back in 1836 when a party of French trappers cached an excess cargo of gunpowder on the river in preparation for a trip into the mountains. The French word for gunpowder is "poudre," thus the name "Cache la Poudre."

The city of Fort Collins seems to put special emphasis on services for seniors. There's an impressive list of activities continually in process, from senior employment and training to senior games and line dancing classes. Travel trips to Breckenridge Ski Area and to concerts in Boulder are other examples of city-sponsored activities, with door-to-door transportation provided at an additional fee of $2.00.

Recreation and Culture Skiing at world-class ski resorts is a matter of a few hours' drive from Fort Collins. The runs at Loveland Pass, an hour west of Denver, offer free skiing for those over 70. Don't laugh, one lady I interviewed in Colorado Springs moved here when she was 78 to take advantage of the great skiing.

River rafting on the wild and scenic Poudre River can be unlike anything you've ever tried. Although you might get doused with spray and rock and roll as you ride the waves, it's a sport that does not require strength or skill, at least not if you go rafting with a guide who will do all the work. If you prefer, you can go with a guide who has the passengers do the work. It's fairly safe, too, because you will be wearing helmets and life jackets.

Hunting and fishing are of course excellent anywhere in Colorado. The Poudre Canyon can be fished throughout its length. On the Poudre River, beginning nine miles northwest of Fort Collins, Colorado's famous "Trout Route" begins. Fishermen don't want to miss this. For those who like their outdoor recreation a bit less adventuresome, six public golf courses and plenty of tennis courts provide traditional exercise.

Fort Collins is home to Colorado State, second-largest university in Colorado, with more than 25,000 students, faculty and staff. Front Range Community College has an additional 3,500 students. The school gives 10-percent discounts off tuition for those over 60, 20 percent if you're over 70, and a full 30 percent for those students over 80 years of age. You can be sure that the student population makes a difference in the community. One way this manifests itself is in the quality and variety of inexpensive restaurants. When you put a large body of students and retirees into the restaurant-shopping area, you'll find better and more imaginative cooks.

Living Costs and Real Estate Like many Colorado retirement locations, Fort Collins is slightly above average in the overall cost of living. One item, however, is very favorable: utility rates. They run almost 25 percent below national averages. This is important in an area where winter heating bills will figure importantly into the family budget.

Although Fort Collins was established back in the mid-1800s, over 65 percent of its homes have been built since 1970. This points out the fast-growing nature of Fort Collins and also that it's a relatively modern-looking city. The average selling price for a single family home is about $120,000, with some in acceptable low-cost neighborhoods for around $60,000. Condos sell for about $60,000 to $85,000. The large college student population places pressures on rentals, so apartments aren't plentiful.

Medical Care Even though Denver is less than an hour away by Interstate 25, medical care here in Fort Collins is more than adequate. The Poudre Valley Hospital acts as the regional medical hub of northern Colorado. The facility boasts 235 beds with 11 surgical suites, and 12 intensive and coronary care unit beds. The hospital offers a Geriatric Assessment Program that gives medical, nutritional and daily living assistance for at-risk hospitalized senior citizens.

When Grandkids Visit An exciting white-water rafting trip down the Poudre River will get your blood racing as waves crash over the side of the raft and you paddle for dear life. If that sounds too daring, then think about going to City Park where you can rent a paddleboat on the lake. The grandkids can paddle. It isn't as exciting as a river trip, but who the heck needs racing blood, anyway? There's also a slow-moving miniature train to ride and tame geese to feed.

Important Addresses and Connections

Chamber of Commerce: 420 S. Howes St., Suite 101, Ft. Collins 80522
Senior Services: 1200 Raintree Dr., Ft. Collins, CO 80526
Daily Newspaper: *Fort Collins Coloradoan*, 1212 Riverside Ave., Fort Collins, CO 80524
Airport: commuter flights to Denver International
Bus: local bus service, Greyhound/Trailways, Senior Alternatives in Transportation (for in-town service), hourly bus/van service to Denver Airport

FORT COLLINS	Jan.	Apr.	July	Oct.		Rain	Snow
Daily Highs	43	61	88	67		15	60
Daily Lows	16	34	59	37		in.	in.

Grand Junction

I retired from making money, but not from work. I'm putting in more hours now on volunteer projects than I ever did when I worked for money. And I love it, because people here are so nice!
—Hazel Shoen

Grand Junction is another example of an economic disaster that turned out to be a bonanza for retirees, and how an influx of retirees helped turn the disaster into a success story. During the late

1970s, encouraged and subsidized by the government, oil companies began experimenting with the enormous oil shale deposits of Colorado and Wyoming. Thousands of workers flocked here to help develop this potentially valuable natural resource. Grand Junction participated in this welcome economic boom. New houses and apartments went up like mushrooms after a rainstorm.

Suddenly, the bubble collapsed. Slumping oil prices had made it too expensive to squeeze petroleum from the shale. One Sunday afternoon, Exxon announced that it was closing its $5 billion Colony Oil Shale Project. Grand Junction remembers this date as Black Sunday. Almost 8,000 workers lost their jobs. As quickly as they came, they began leaving. Knowing they hadn't even a prayer to make payments, many simply walked away from their homes. They couldn't even give the properties away because they owed more money on the mortgages than the market value. The few buyers who were in the market simply waited for foreclosure and then bought from the banks at bargain prices. As in Bisbee and Ajo, Arizona, the workers who lost their jobs suffered, both financially and from their shattered plans for the future.

The businesspeople who survived realized that the solution to the problem lay in attracting industry with a stable financial base, something not subject to boom or bust like petroleum. Economic incentives, such as free land for new and expanding industries, were offered. At the same time, they began concentrating on a special business, one that's clean, doesn't pollute the air, and brings in an obvious source of steady income: the retirement industry! Other nearby towns, such as Parachute, Palisade, Fruita and Clifton, joined in the movement to attract retirees.

Their efforts were successful. Gradually, the economy recovered, due in large measure to retiree money. Surplus homes were eventually purchased, and the population began rising once more.

Grand Junction would be a nice place to retire regardless of housing bargains. It's just a nice place to live. This is the largest city in western Colorado, located in a broad valley in high plateau country west of the Rocky Mountains. Its name came from its location near the junction of the Colorado and Gunnison rivers (the Colorado was originally called the Grand River). Grand Junction is the center of an urban area of some 105,000 people, although the town itself has a comfortable population of 39,000. Shopping malls, an active senior citizens center and excellent health care are among the attractions. A 4,500-foot altitude and low rainfall combine to ensure four pleasant seasons with an abundance of sunshine and mild winters. Golf and tennis are year-round sports adding to Grand Junction's desirability for retirement.

For some reason, the city ranks 149 out of 220 cities in personal safety. I find this puzzling, since everyone I've spoken with in Grand Junction swears that the town is safe. Sometimes these statistics can become out-of-balance because of the way crimes are reported and the type of offenses reported to the FBI. The local police chief points out that here all crimes are reported, which ups the rate.

Recreation and Culture
With mild weather, golf is a practical, almost year-round sport. Three 18-hole golf courses and one 9-hole layout afford plenty of opportunities to whack the balls. Two tennis clubs plus courts in public parks allow tennis players their exercise. River rafting and fishing on the Gunnison and Colorado Rivers are popular and convenient pastimes. Grand Junction is 45 minutes from Powderhorn Ski Resort on Grand Mesa and less than three hours from most major Colorado ski resorts. A series of trails for walking or biking follow the Colorado River for those who don't care to brave the ski slopes.

Mesa State College, a four-year institution, offers a variety of continuing education courses of interest to seniors. Grand Junction also has a Symphony Orchestra which presents concerts October through April.

Living Costs and Real Estate
After an initial bottoming out of the real estate market, it came back dramatically. In fact, both the cost of living and sales prices of homes are slightly above national averages today. According to a real estate broker, about 50 percent of today's buyers are retirees from out of state. Although the bargain-basement housing market is history, homes are still plentiful and some inexpensive places are always available. The average home sale is about $96,700, with 20 percent of those on the market advertised at $100,000 or under. Another 20 percent of the housing inventory on the market sells between $150,000 to $300,000. Rentals are rather scarce, since most buyers want to occupy rather than rent.

During the oil boom period, Exxon, one of the larger companies, was forced to enter the construction business to provide housing for its employees. The company developed a flat mountaintop, a place called Battlement Mesa, into a spiffy housing development.

The company constructed 684 residences, complete with a multi-million-dollar recreation center. When employees left, Battlement Mesa became an upscale retirement community.

Medical Care Grand Junction has four major hospitals: St. Mary's Hospital, 294 beds and in the process of enlarging; Community Hospital with 78 beds; Hilltop Rehab Center; and a Veterans Hospital. The veterans facility is the only one between Denver and Salt Lake City. Forty family practitioner physicians and 115 specialists serve the area.

When Grandkids Visit Because this was a heavy-duty dinosaur playground several million years ago, you might want to take the kids to Dinosaur Valley, a museum with dinosaur bones and fossils typical of that era. Seeing animated models of those prehistoric cuddly creatures ought to bring some slack-jawed attention from the grand-kiddies.

Important Addresses and Connections

Chamber of Commerce: 360 Grand Ave., Grand Junction, CO 81501
Senior Services: 550 Ouray Ave., Grants Pass, CO 81501
Daily Newspaper: *Daily Sentinel,* P.O. Box 668, Grand Junction, CO 81502
Real Estate Agents: Century 21, Love & Associates, Larry Goad, 1840 N 12th St., Grand Junction, CO 81501; Robert Bray Realtors, 1015 N. 7th St., Grand Junction, CO 81501
Airport: commuter airline connections to major regional hubs
Bus: no city bus service, but there's an on-demand shuttle for seniors, called Mesability Pickup, and regular Greyhound service

GRAND JUNCTION	Jan.	Apr.	July	Oct.	Rain	Snow
Daily Highs	36	65	94	69	8	25
Daily Lows	15	38	64	41	in.	in.

Steamboat Springs

There are so many genuine people who live here and work here and raise their families here. That's hard to find in a ski town.
—Barb Jennings

You say you love winter? You can't wait until ski lifts start running? Maybe Steamboat Springs is your town. Snuggled in a high valley at 6,700 feet, the town's alpine climate features low humidity, warm summer days and cool, crisp nights. It also features winter snow, from 170 to 450 inches! Most of that is on the slopes, thank goodness.

This is a charming, upscale place for those who enjoy delightful summers and abundant outdoor winter sports. While its winter "champagne powder" skiing brings winter sportsmen from all over the country, Steamboat Springs enjoys wonderful summer weather, just what you might expect from its Rocky Mountain setting. Even in July and August, temperatures rarely climb out of the 80-degree range, and every evening drops into the 50s.

The town's name came from a mineral spring that made a chugging noise that sounded like a steamboat to the early fur trappers who passed through the area. Over 150 mineral springs are found nearby, supplying medicinal waters for modern-day residents' hot tubs and baths at the public swimming pool.

Abundant wild game and rivers teeming with fish encouraged settlers, and the development of the town as a ski resort brought Steamboat Springs to its present population of about 7,000 inhabitants. Its early development is evident in the well-preserved Victorian homes and substantial brick business buildings which date from the late 1800s. Folks who've moved here recently say they appreciate the change from the hectic, crime-plagued lifestyle of big cities.

Although it sits on U.S. 40, a major east-west highway, Steamboat Springs is somewhat isolated, being 157 miles from the nearest big town, Denver. However, express shuttles to Denver airport, plus frequent shuttle flights from the local Yampa Valley Regional Airport, keep folks in touch with big-city civilization (for those who need that sort of thing).

Recreation and Culture Of course, the major recreational drawing card here is skiing. Steamboat Springs bills itself "Ski Town USA," and has produced more Olympic skiers than any other U.S. town. With 20 lifts, 108 trails and a 3,600-foot vertical rise to 10,500 feet, this area is recognized as one of the best in the country. The season lasts from Thanksgiving to Easter each year. Snowmobiling, sleigh rides and back-country skiing are also enjoyed.

Summer outdoor sports include one nine-hole and two 18-hole courses, including a Robert Trent Jones, Jr. championship course and two public tennis facilities. River rafting, hiking, camping and soaking in natural hot springs are other outdoor fun things to do here.

Colorado Mountain College/Alpine Campus, a two-year school, offers extensive continuing education classes. Steamboat Springs Arts Council coordinates a number of cultural groups including several dance groups, drama and music ensembles, the Ballet Northwest, Mountain Madrigal Singers and a writers' group.

Living Costs and Real Estate This is not a place to look for bargain real estate; it's an upscale area and property offerings show this. This higher-priced real estate pulls the overall cost of living up as well. Condos are big here, and practical, because they can be turned into rentals for any time you're someplace else. The average condo sold in 1994 for $110,334. The median sales price for a three-bedroom home was about $155,000. In the exclusive Mt. Werner area, the average selling price of a home was $380,026.

Medical Care Routt Memorial Hospital serves the community with 24-hour emergency care and 22 beds. The Northwest Colorado Visiting Nurse Association provides home health care, care for handicapped persons and the terminally ill, with a 15-person staff. There are a couple of small clinics, plus several doctors who are accepting new patients.

When Grandkids Visit Check out Fish Creek Falls, where water plunges 280 feet in a spectacular display. This is a place for picnicking and exploring hiking trails. Innertubing on the Yampa River might appeal more to the grandkids than to us mature folks.

Important Addresses and Connections

Chamber of Commerce: PO Box 774408, Steamboat Springs, CO 80477
Senior Services: 1255 Lincoln, Steamboat Springs, CO 80477
Newspapers: *Steamboat Pilot* (weekly) and *Steamboat Today* (daily), PO Box 774827, Steamboat Springs, CO 80477
Airport: Yampa Valley Airport, with year-round service by commuter airlines and express service to Denver Airport
Bus: local service is provided by Steamboat Springs Transit, and Greyhound will get you to Denver and Salt Lake City

STEAMBOAT SPR.	Jan.	Apr.	July	Oct.		Rain	Snow
Daily Highs	30	52	82	60		26	60
Daily Lows	01	24	41	24		in.	in.

NEVADA

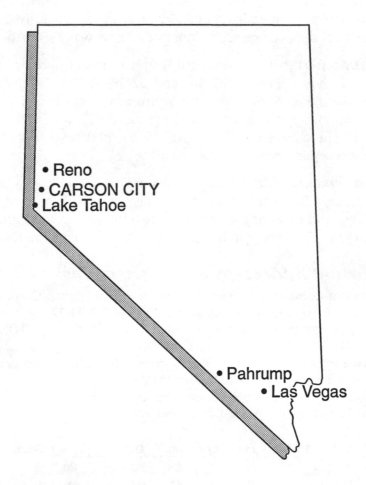

- Reno
- CARSON CITY
- Lake Tahoe

- Pahrump
- Las Vegas

B ecause a high mountain range, the Sierra Nevada, extends along the California-Nevada border cutting off rain-bearing winds from the Pacific Ocean, Nevada is the driest of the Southwestern states. Extensive deserts cover most of the land, with most residents choosing to live in or near one of Nevada's major towns. In fact more than half live in the vicinity of Las Vegas or Reno. Measuring both rain and melted snow, the average precipitation is only nine inches in northern Nevada, around Elko, while the southern part, around Las Vegas, receives about four inches. Most rain falls in the spring, at which time barren deserts become a riot of color with the blossoms of cactus, sagebrush, and wild iris.

Of all the Western states, Nevada most represents the "old west" to me. Sparsely settled, yet growing with new settlers arriving daily, Nevada feels like a frontier, a place of new beginnings. Something about Nevada's wide-open spaces stimulates a spirit of adventure and go-for-broke attitudes. It's a place where string ties, boot-top jeans and snakeskin boots feel like natural apparel, a place where you might even be tempted to wear a Stetson hat, confident you won't look downright foolish.

Perhaps a hangover from an era of frontier gambling and gold rushes, a definite atmosphere of excitement hovers over Nevada. Gambling casinos are everywhere, and slot machines are strategically located in gasoline stations, drug stores and supermarkets. Sometimes you'll even find them in restrooms; the gambling syndicates don't want to miss a bet. This is a state where lucky gamblers made a stake and lucky miners made fortunes. This is evident today: prospecting for precious metals is a big hobby in Nevada. There's always that chance that the next rock you crack open with a hammer will expose a gleaming streak of gold. (I've broke open many a rock myself in Nevada.)

Nevada is the country's fastest-growing state, by the way, with a 5.4-percent increase in population every year. And, there's plenty of room to grow, since 87 percent of the land is public property, owned by the United States government. Newcomers aren't strangers here, because their neighbors come from all over North America, just as you do. In Nevada casinos, you'll notice blackjack dealers, bartenders and security guards traditionally wear name tags that tell you where they came from. Sometimes without names, just their hometowns. According to my figures, only 386 Nevada residents are native Nevadans—the rest come from somewhere

119

else. (I can vouch for the accuracy of these figures, since I made them up myself.)

Gambling fever used to be a reason for not retiring here, and still is, if you are a compulsive gambler. Sometimes people are surprised to discover they are compulsive. After a lifetime of not having a problem, the overpowering temptation of large casinos— packed with slot machines, dice and card games—hooks them, but good. Today however, most areas in the country are infected by legal gambling, either by state governments running lotteries and numbers games or by legalizing casinos. By the way, Nevada casinos set the odds so they can rake off 10 to 20 percent for overhead and profit. But state lotteries stiff you for 40 to 60 percent—maybe even more. So, you really can't figure you're gambling when you buy state lottery tickets; you're being robbed.

But should you know that you, or your spouse, has a tendency to go overboard on gambling and succumb to the irresistible fever of chance, then forget Nevada. Go around it, fly over it or go the opposite direction. The round-the-clock excitement is just too much for some folks. They end up throwing their household money on the tables in increasing amounts in a desperate attempt to recoup their losses. The sad thing is, if they do hit a lucky streak and win a bundle, the fever won't let them quit. They'll play until they are broke again.

Nevada
"The Grand Canyon State"
"Sagebrush State" / "Silver State"
36th state to enter the Union
October 31, 1864

State Capital: Carson City
Population (1990): 1,206,152; rank, 39th
Population Density: 11 per sq. mile; urban: 85.3%, rural: 14.7%
Geography: 7th state in size, with 110,561 square miles, including 667 square miles of water surface and 7,000,000 acres of forested land. Highest elevation: Boundary Peak, 13,140 feet; lowest elevation: Colorado River at southwest corner of state, 470 feet. Average elevation: 5,500 feet.
State Flower: Sagebrush
State Bird: Mountain Bluebird
State Tree: Single-leaf Pinon
State Song: Home Means Nevada

On the other hand, many retirees handle gambling quite well, taking advantage of all the freebies and bargains the clubs offer to lure customers inside. Some never put even a nickel in the machines but have a great time anyway. Buffet tables, laden with salads, entrees and deserts, offer unlimited visits for three or four dollars. Prime rib dinners can be as low as $5.50. Lounge entertainment, with music, dancers and comedians, is free, although you're encouraged to buy a drink. Some casinos even present free circus acts, complete with animals, high-wire performers and clowns.

One reason many give for considering Nevada retirement is that the state collects no income tax. Of course, this is an advantage only if your income is substantial and your tax liabilities will be large. But there's another tax angle that encourages other folks to retire here: Nevada doesn't collect, and won't allow other states to collect, "source taxes" from Nevada residents.

What's a source tax? It's a state income tax on a pension or annuity which comes from a former employer based in a state where you used to live. Retirees are often surprised and outraged to discover that they owe income taxes to a state where they no longer live, where they can't vote and where they derive no benefits. Thirteen states have Source Tax laws on the books and three states vigorously enforce this law at the moment: California, New York and Vermont. These states contend that if you qualify for a pension because you once worked there, then you owe taxes on the pension, no matter when you receive it, no matter where you live! In some cases, you have to pay taxes to both states on the same pension! Furthermore, the pension is taxable at the rate of the source state, which could be higher than the income tax where you now live (in the case of Nevada, that's zero percent). I know of one California retiree, unaware of the law, who moved to another state; then, 15 years later he received a California tax bill for $26,000 for back taxes and penalties! (By the way, if you are drawing a government pension, your pension could be taxed at its source to make sure you pay up. Also, if you have property in that source state, it could be attached for back taxes.)

History

In 1833, Joseph Walker's expedition followed the Humboldt River in search of new fur-trapping country. They found several different tribes inhabiting the area, basically peaceful and nomadic hunters and seed gatherers, such as the Shoshone and the Paiute. The Washo lived in the west near Lake Tahoe. Today, about 14,000 Native Americans live in Nevada, more than half of them on reservations. The largest reservations are Pyramid Lake, in Washoe County; Walker River, east of Carson City; and Western Shoshone, on the Nevada-Idaho border.

The first road across Nevada followed the Humboldt Trail blazed by Joseph Walker and became part of the Gold Rush–era California Trail. It followed the Humboldt River, which provided water for wagon trains as they crossed this dry region. Today this trail is called Interstate 80.

Nevada's early history was largely the story of its mining discoveries, booms and busts. The discovery of the Comstock Lode and other deposits in 1859 started a 20-year boom, followed by a 20-year depression in the industry. Then, around 1900, another boom boosted Nevada with silver and gold strikes at Tonopah and Goldfield and the development of copper mining at Ely. Between the two World Wars, another decline in mining activity depressed the economy.

Although minerals and mining play an important part in Nevada's present-day economy, a new, non-mining economy has finally emerged, largely due to the state's fabulous year-round gambling industry. Casino gambling started this economy rolling, and it seems to be continuing with great success even though gambling casinos are no longer the monopoly of Nevada.

Ghost Towns and Prospecting

A favorite pastime among Nevada retirees is exploring historic relics of Nevada's past and visiting nearby mines that once supported the towns. Ghost towns are fun places to search for old purple-glass bottles and other treasures discarded by yesterday's miners. It's not difficult to go one step further and try your hand at prospecting for valuable minerals yourself. This is not only fun, but it's healthy outdoor recreation that doesn't require special athletic skills or investment. Because the desert and mountain terrain is usually free of vegetation, prospecting is an easy matter. Classes in mineralogy are available in Reno's adult education classes and at the local university to prepare you for some serious rock hunting and prospecting.

Don't think prospecting for valuable minerals is just a dreamy fantasy. It's still possible to strike it rich (not probable, just possible). Most Western silver mines were abandoned back in the 1930s when silver dropped to 25 cents an ounce, and gold mines were closed during World War II on orders of the federal government. After the war, mining activity never regained its momentum; gold and silver mines were left to revert to nature. With today's higher gold and silver prices, prospects once passed over because of low returns could now be valuable. A case in point: my brother, an amateur prospector on a weekend outing, stumbled across a lead-silver outcropping in Death Valley that turned out to be the state's largest silver producer for the 16 years it yielded ore.

Some ghost towns are marked by shells of buildings, roofless and disintegrating with time. Others are found only by studying maps and looking for old dumps and traces of foundations. The dumps, incidentally, are the best places to find old bottles and artifacts.

Not all ghost towns wasted away to true "ghost" status. Many held on to a percentage of their population, partly because folks couldn't sell their real estate and partly because these old towns are fascinating places to live. Today, some old mining towns are making a comeback, and it turns out these are great places for retirement for a certain type of retiree. Ghost towns appeal to those fascinated by history who don't mind living in a rustic, isolated town, with few neighbors or community facilities. If you've read this far, maybe the notion of ghost town retirement is an appropriate one to pursue. Frankly, it's not something I or my wife would consider, but there are those who retire in ghost towns and love every minute of it.

Places like Ely (pop. 4,800), Tonopah (pop. 2,700), and Goldfield (pop. 3,600) never died out completely and will never completely make it back to former glory. Other places, even smaller, such as Austin (pop. 400) or Eureka (pop. 800), are worthwhile investigating, if only as a tourist. But I can't emphasize too strongly that you must be specially suited for living in a place that time has left behind. This is not a situation where you can invest impulsively and expect to sell out quickly and move on if you find out you've made a mistake. The reason for so many vacant houses is that it's neither a seller's market, nor a buyer's market!

NEVADA TAXES

Nevada Dept. of Taxation, Capitol Complex, Carson City, NV 89710
702-687-4892

Income Tax
Nevada does not levy a personal income tax.

Sales Taxes
State 6.5%; **County** 0.25–1.0% (maximum)
Combined Rate in Selected Towns Las Vegas: 7.0%; Reno: 7.0%; Carson City: 6.75%
General Coverage Food for home consumption and prescription drugs are exempt.

Property Taxes
All property is subject to local tax. Some intangibles are subject to taxation. In relation to personal income, property tax collections are in the lowest third among the 50 states.
Tax Relief for Homeowners and renters, aged 62 or older, who lived in primary residence since July 1 of preceding year; income ceiling $19,100; max. benefit 90% of tax owed, up to $500.
Blind $3,000 assessed value ($8,571 market value).
Widows, Orphans and Veterans $1,000 assessed value ($2,857 market value).
Disabled Veterans Up to $10,000 assessed value ($28,570 market value).
Deferral Program None.

Estate/Inheritance Taxes
Nevada does not impose an estate tax or an inheritance tax. It imposes only a pick-up tax, which is a portion of the federal estate tax and does not increase the total tax owed.

Licenses
Driver's License Required within 45 days of establishing residence. A written, vision and driving test are required upon surrender of old driver's license. Fee $20.50, valid four years.
Automobile License Registration and title fee of $50. Annual tax based on value of car. Tax on a car valued at $12,000 would be around $250 yearly.

Las Vegas

I figure that with all these Las Vegas casino buffets, low-cost restaurants and 99-cent breakfasts, I'll never have to cook again! I plan on pulling those damned burners out of my kitchen stove and replacing them with potted geraniums!
                                                              —June Land

Once mainly a glittering entertainment focal point for Los Angeles high-rollers, Las Vegas is gaining a national reputation as much more than a gambling center. Today it's a virtual boomtown, said to be the fastest-growing city in the nation. About 60,000 new residents a year arrive—many of 'em retirees—and they're spreading the city farther out into the desert every day. To accommodate newcomers, 12,000 houses sprout up annually.

Because of this vigorous growth, retirees easily find part-time work if they so desire—and often times more than just minimum-wage jobs. Casinos, restaurants and other tourist businesses need part-time help, and the area leads the nation in employment growth with a rate of 9 percent. As in Reno, casinos tend to give special consideration to hiring senior citizens. Well that is, except for the cocktail waitresses, who tend to be young, peachy-cheeked and bosomy. Clearly, this is age discrimination, but you probably wouldn't care to run around half-naked, delivering booze to a bunch of gamblers in the first place, would you?

Many retirees who normally might have chosen Phoenix for retirement are trying Las Vegas instead. When asked why, they give various reasons, with the excitement of casinos, absence of state income taxes and proximity to southern California heading the list. (Las Vegas is a 5-hour drive to Los Angeles, compared to Phoenix's 7–8 hours.) There's talk of a privately financed super-train that will link Las Vegas and southern California, moving millions of visitors at a fantastic 250 miles per hour!

Other taxes in the state are low, because about 50 percent of all state tax revenues come from the resort, tourism and casino industry. Because of this bountiful source of income, Nevada doesn't depend on corporate-income or personal-income taxes, and its property taxes are among the lowest in the West.

Those questioned about their choice of Las Vegas as a retirement destination usually include weather as a factor in one form or another. Make no mistake, summers in Las Vegas are hot, yet those who retire here maintain that they love it that way. (Everything is air-conditioned, so what do they know about hot weather?) Winters are delightful, except for a few windy days now and then, and an occasional flash flood that takes out a casino or two.

Because of low humidity and the absence of freezing weather, mobile homes are quite practical and a source of lower-cost housing. Inexpensive evaporative coolers do a fine job during the hot months. Mobile home parks present a wide choice of options, from inexpensive to super-luxurious. During the winter, RV parks fill with cold-weather fugitives, who, as expected, depart for cooler climes come the summer. Nevertheless, retirees in Las Vegas form a steady, year-round population as opposed to the second-home group found along the Colorado River and in southern Arizona.

Las Vegas has several active senior citizens groups as well as the usual volunteer organizations like R.S.V.P. Local newspapers run regular features covering news and activities of interest to retirees. Because this is a city instead of a town, senior citizens centers aren't small and intimate as you might expect in a smaller place, but they certainly offer a wide range of activities to keep active folks busy and happy.

Recreation and Culture   As in most heavily populated

tourist towns, golf, tennis and swimming facilities are quite common. Golf in Las Vegas is too big a subject to cover here. Suffice to say that courses are famous, numerous and challenging. Tennis players will find many municipal courts scattered about town, which are augmented by countless tennis courts at resorts and casinos. Fishing and boating on Lake Powell and Lake Mead bring a water wonderland to one of the driest deserts in North America.

Las Vegas casinos promote some of the most spectacular sports events of the year. Prize fights, bowling invitationals, golf tournaments and the World Series of Poker are held in Vegas, not to mention off-road racing, rodeos and softball championships.

Las Vegas' nightlife is legendary, with Hollywood headline stars appearing with hopeful newcomers in all sorts of revues, musicals and concerts. Many of these presentations are expensive but other shows have a two-drink minimum instead of a cover charge. Lounge shows, with up-and-coming entertainers are both enjoyable and inexpensive, since buying a drink is all that's expected.

Several Las Vegas cultural centers present concerts, plays and dance programs. Free concerts by the Nevada String Quartet are regularly given in the Flamingo Library auditorium. The University of Nevada stages classic and contemporary theater throughout the year, as well as symphony and ballet, directed by internationally known artists. And unlike in many cities, where lack of library funding is a perennial issue, Las Vegas retirees have a huge new city library to meet their literary needs.

Real Estate Housing activity keeps up with this influx of new-comers, in fact, it has more than kept up. From its inception, Las Vegas has tended to over-build; optimistic developers keep supply ahead of demand, keeping housing costs under control. Two- and three-bedroom homes can be found at prices half that of other parts of the country. Apartments are plentiful, with high vacancy rates.

Medical Care Surprisingly, Las Vegas' level of medical care is only adequate instead of superb, as is the case in Phoenix or Los Angeles. Las Vegas has a couple of good-sized hospitals, but for the population, the town has far fewer hospital beds, general practitioners and medical specialists than the national average.

When Grandkids Visit There's not many places to take them that don't charge a hefty entrance fee. That's the way it is in tourist towns. However, Red Rock Canyon is one place, and it's the next-best desert trip to a long drive to Death Valley. The 13-mile scenic road takes you by the 3,000-foot-high Red Rock Escarpment, and you stand a chance of seeing wild burros and possibly even big horn sheep. Another idea is to visit the Circus Circus casino; yes, kids are allowed in to watch highwire gymnastics and circus acts. There's also a large video arcade where you can leave the kiddies with a pocket full of quarters and let them shoot down space invaders while you make a surreptitious visit to a blackjack table.

Important Addresses and Connections

Chamber of Commerce: 2301 E. Sahara Ave., Las Vegas, NV 89104
Senior Services: 450 E. Bonanza Rd., Las Vegas, NV 89106
Daily Newspaper: *Review-Journal and Sun*, 1111 W. Bonanza Rd., Las Vegas, NV 89106
Airport: McCarran International
Bus/Train: Citizens Area Transit buses serve the area (and give senior discounts), and Greyhound and Amtrak provide out-of-area transport

LAS VEGAS	Jan.	Apr.	July	Oct.	Rain	Snow
Daily Highs	56	77	105	82	4	1
Daily Lows	33	50	76	54	in.	in.

Pahrump

We love the desert. As often as we can, we drive our jeep into the hills and prospect for gold. We haven't found any yet, don't really expect to, but that's not the point. Most of the fun is just getting out there in the wild, surrounded by desert plants and mysterious animal tracks.
— Barbara and Terry Briggs

A fast-growing star in Nevada's retirement communities is the town of Pahrump, 63 miles west of Las Vegas and about the same distance east from Death Valley. The setting is pure desert as Pahrump sprawls in a long valley with the Spring Mountain range on one side and the Nopah mountains on the other.

When I first visited Pahrump several years ago, it consisted of little more than a couple of small taverns, a handful of stores and some cotton farms. Today it's grown into a small city. Complete with a senior citizen center, a library, a medical facility, a bowling alley and a community center (with swimming pool), Pahrump has moved from the category of crossroad settlement to a viable retirement community. In fact, about 40 percent of the residents are retired. The town has grown at an astounding 15 percent per year for the last four years to its present size of 17,000.

The major drawing cards in this valley are sunshine, mild weather, low-cost land and friendly neighbors. Pahrump ranks just below Yuma, Arizona, as one of the places with the most sunny days in the United States. Its low humidity makes even the hottest days feel bearable, if not comfortable. The mountains surrounding Pahrump act as effective barriers to moisture-laden storms which traditionally drift in from the Pacific Ocean. Therefore you can count on very few overcast or rainy days. The average rainfall is only four inches, and the relative humidity about 29 percent, making this one of the driest localities in the nation. Yet water supplies are not a problem because Pahrump sits on the third-largest underground supply of water in the United States.

Travelers are often unaware they've entered the town of Pahrump, because its inhabitants are scattered over an area of 25 square miles. A feeling of spaciousness is enhanced by homes sitting on large parcels of land, mostly one acre in size—sometimes 10 to 20 acres—and as far off the main highway as possible. Since desert land is inexpensive, folks see no need to crowd themselves next to the neighbors. Pahrump also lacks a compact, traditional downtown center so characteristic of other communities its size. Like residential homes, businesses tend to locate on large pieces of land, spaced apart from competitors. There's never a problem finding a parking space here! Several small shopping centers host a collection of stores grouped about a supermarket, but with plenty of open space between the complex and other businesses. Since everyone drives a car here, sidewalks are absent, adding to the rural feeling of Western desert living.

Recreation and Culture
As you might expect, fishing, boating and waterskiing aren't all that great around Pahrump. But outdoor sports enthusiasts will enjoy two golf courses, and rockhounds and amateur prospectors have a ball with all that open country to wander around in.

Although cultural activities are understandably limited in a desert community, the Oasis Writer's Guild is quite active, as well as the Visual and Performing Arts Council which has great things planned. The Community College of Southern Nevada offers evening courses at Pahrump Valley High School.

Several small casinos provide gaming excitement for those who enjoy exercising by way of pulling slot machine handles or tossing ivory cubes across a green felt table. Since these places are small and tourists scarce, the bulk of the patrons are Pahrump residents, so the sterile, impersonal air of Vegas casinos is absent here. Local folks enjoy meeting here for a social evening of dancing and entertainment by local bands. I might mention that the one time I hit a jackpot in a Pahrump casino, the bartender immediately hung an "out of order" sign on the machine.

The Pahrump Valley Harvest Festival and Fair had its beginnings 30 years ago. It's grown from an unofficial weekend of relaxation for farmers after the harvest, into a three-day event attracting over 20,000 people from the surrounding desert towns and villages. For 1995, the plans are to deep-pit barbecue 6,000 pounds of beef to feed the throngs. A rodeo, stock car races and dancing under the stars are also on the program.

Real Estate
The town of Pahrump straddles the dividing line of Nye and Clark counties. You know when you cross into Nye County, because the architectural styles change. At one time, Nye County had no strict building codes, so homeowners built any way they pleased. It made for some interesting and innovative build-

ings. However, this is changing as Nye County is adding building inspectors to enforce the Nevada State Building Code.

Because desert land is so plentiful, acreage is inexpensive. Large tracts in town are becoming scarce nowadays as owners are tempted to break them into acre-size parcels and get more money. The price of typical three-bedroom homes ranges from $70,000 to $140,000. Rentals are usually scarce, starting at $700 a month for the occasional vacancy. This will change, as several apartment and townhouse developments are underway. Mobile homes are big here and are a great option for low-cost housing on your own acreage. Many folks start off with an inexpensive mobile while they construct their more substantial housing.

Medical Care One drawback about living in a small town far from a metropolitan center is that you'll have a long way to go to get to a full-service medical facility. However, two small clinics take care of emergencies, and a 24-hour emergency center is due to open soon. Doctors here are accepting new patients.

Home Health Services of Nevada (HHSN), a non-profit home health agency, has been in Pahrump for 20 years now. According to the local manager, "The cost for HHSN to visit a patient in the home for a month is less than for a patient to stay in the hospital for two days." While this care isn't free, most patients are covered by Medicare, Medicaid or private insurance companies.

Crime and Safety Pahrump presents a rural, hometown atmosphere, and like similar places of this size around the country, it enjoys low crime rates. Even though homes may be spaced farther apart than in conventional, non-desert locations, neighbors watch out for surrounding homes. People know each other in a small town like Pahrump and become uneasy when they see strangers who may not belong on a neighbor's property. This is not a place where burglars feel comfortable plying their trade.

When Grandkids Visit Be sure to take them to Death Valley, about an hour's drive away. Pahrump also has a historical museum that's good for a short visit. Cathedral Canyon, 14 miles to the southeast, is another place for hiking paths and unusual displays of sculpture. For things to do in town, there's the Valley Fun Park with go-cart rides, a bungee jump and a miniature golf course. (You might inquire to see if senior citizens are entitled to discounts on the bungee jump.)

Important Addresses and Connections

Chamber of Commerce: P.O. Box 42, Pahrump, NV 89041
Senior Services: 1300 W. Basin, Pahrump, NV 89041
Newspapers: *Death Valley Gateway Gazette*, Pahrump, NV 89041; *Valley Times*, 2160 Calvada Blvd., Pahrump, NV 89048
Real Estate Agent: Hafen & Hafen, 1321 S. Hwy. 160, Pahrump, NV 89041
Airport: nearest is Las Vegas, but there's no shuttle service
Bus: none—you'll need an automobile here

PAHRUMP	Jan.	Apr.	July	Oct.	Rain	Snow
Daily Highs	56	77	103	81	4	1
Daily Lows	32	59	75	54	in.	in.

Reno

There's something comfortable about Reno, something old fashioned, relaxed, yet Reno can be as fast-paced as you'd ever want, whenever you want.
—John Burt

Traditionally, Las Vegas and Lake Tahoe are formal and glitzy places, while Reno tends to be informal and relaxed. Western wear and work clothes are Reno's style. Still, the town has changed, with large Las Vegas– and Lake Tahoe–style casinos cropping up all over the place. But some older establishments, especially in the downtown center, still cater to those in bluejeans and workshirts. Including the adjoining city of Sparks, the population is about 180,000, making it a good-sized city. The Reno area has all the facilities necessary for good retirement: hospitals, colleges, cultural events and community services.

Reno is an old town, with a deliberately preserved Old West atmosphere. This is a town proud of its rowdy gold- and silver-mining past, a picturesque setting with a backdrop of snow-fringed peaks looming in the distance. Originally, Reno's major business was supplying the booming mining camps that flourished nearby. About the time the mines played out, a new industry arose in the form of quickie divorces. As other states liberalized their divorce laws, legalized gambling became the leading industry. Ironically, today Reno has become a quick marriage center, with wedding chapels scattered around town like fast-food restaurants. Today, marriages in Reno outnumber divorces by ten to one.

Although Las Vegas construction imitates southern California modern style—stucco, sprawling ranch houses and tile roofs—Reno prefers old-fashioned houses built of honest red brick. The older neighborhoods are of solidly built, no-nonsense homes—a settled, mature city. Las Vegas is an Eastern-style glamour girl, adorned with mink and diamond bracelets; Reno is pure Western, a cowboy with a string tie and Stetson hat.

Folks here are proud of Reno's self-bestowed title of "The Biggest Little City in the World." The 24-hour entertainment and glitter is one reason many retirees are drawn here. This is why you'll see so many local people around downtown gaming tables or dining in the casinos' bargain restaurants. Tourists tend to go to the fancy casinos farther away from the center of things. This hometown feeling was deliberately cultivated when gambling was legalized during the depression days. Harold Smith, founder of "Harold's Club," decided to go after local money instead of depending upon tourists. He instituted the practice of giving free drinks and double odds on craps tables. He cashed paychecks without charge and tried to make people feel at home. Harold's Club also started the practice of preferential hiring of local people and senior citizens. That policy remains in force today, with retirees working at everything from dealing blackjack to making change.

As a retirement center, Reno is one of our favorites. Because of the large number of retirees, services for senior citizens are plentiful. Retiree clubs and organizations are unusually active. Thirteen apartment complexes specialize in assisted housing for elderly, handicapped and disabled, plus there are three large full-service retirement facilities. Programs such as Meals on Wheels and Care and Share are active, as well as several city, county and state programs. They operate a senior citizens employment service and a senior citizens law center, providing free assistance with wills, Social Security, leases and things of that nature.

Some choose Reno retirement for excitement, but everybody like its extraordinary climate. The 4,440-foot altitude and very low humidity keep the weather pleasant year-round despite its apparent low temperatures. For those who cannot stand hot summer weather, Reno is perfect. Expect to enjoy about 300 sunny days each year in Reno. Even though July and August midday temperatures usually approach 90 degrees by mid-afternoon, you will sleep under an electric blanket every night; the thermometer always drops into the 40s. Even in the middle of winter the high temperatures are about the same as summer lows!

A light jacket or sweater feels warm in this dry climate, even when the temperature is below freezing. I am always surprised to walk out of a casino in my shirt-sleeves, feeling perfectly comfortable, and then notice a thermometer announcing that it is 38 degrees! Air conditioning is unknown in residential properties, and low electricity rates keep winter heating bills reasonable.

Living Costs and Real Estate
Reno's cost of living is not cheap. Living costs here are 12.3 percent above national average, even a bit higher than Las Vegas. The only expense that's considerably below average is utility rates. The area has been undergoing a tremendous expansion, both in growth of business and in the number of new homes under construction. The desert around the city seems to be sprouting subdivisions. Economical homes start around $95,000, with the median price closer to $120,000. Condos and apartments have experienced some of the housing boom, but have barely kept up with demand, and as a result are slightly higher priced than average for a city the size of Reno.

Recreation and Culture
Reno's weather encourages a wide variety of outdoor activities. Skiing at numerous resorts in the Sierra Nevada is a matter of less than an hour's drive. This same country is wonderful for warm-weather fun. There are lakes and streams for fishing and camping, and the hiking trails are seemingly unlimited. Rockhounds, gold panners and amateur prospectors enjoy the marvels of Nevada's mineralized districts, some within an hour's drive from the city. Reno is also famous for annual events, like its famous National Air Races, the Reno Rodeo and balloon races. Because of an appreciable Basque influence in western Nevada, a Basque Festival is celebrated here every year.

Crime and Safety
Reno's gambling and excitement attracts folks from all over the country, and as you might expect, a percentage are predictably unstable. As they lose their money, they turn to crime to recoup their loses. Therefore, like all gambling centers, Reno has more than its share of crime. But the majority of the transgressions are crimes like shoplifting and stealing things from automobiles. Retirees report that they feel perfectly safe in their residential neighborhoods.

Medical Care Reno is the medical center for the western Nevada–eastern California area. Washoe Medical Center has an important cardiac rehabilitation facility and is the hospital where other hospitals send patients when serious problems arise. St. Mary's and four other hostpitals serve the Reno area.

When Grandkids Visit If they're old enough to appreciate a museum of antique, classic automobiles, take 'em to the National Automobile Museum. Not as big as Harrah's famous collection (now gone), the display of 200 cars nevertheless makes an interesting tour.

Important Addresses and Connections

Chamber of Commerce: 4590 S. Virginia St., Reno, NV 89502
Senior Services: Sutro & 9th, Reno, NV 89502
Daily Newspaper: *Reno Gazette-Journal,* 955 Kuenzli St., Reno, NV 89502
Airport: Reno Airport, with connections to major airlines
Bus: city buses, Greyhound and Amtrak serve the area

RENO	Jan.	Apr.	July	Oct.		Rain	Snow
Daily Highs	45	63	91	70		8	24
Daily Lows	20	29	48	31		in.	in.

Lake Tahoe

We bought a place here years ago, just for investment. We used it for vacations, occasionally, but mostly we rented it out. But when retirement time came around we got to thinking about how nice Lake Tahoe is, and we decided to move here permanently.
—Mr. and Mrs. G. LaFrance

A short drive from Carson City—up the mountainside along a wide, four-lane highway—a bustling, fast-growing community clusters around one of the country's most famous lakes. Many consider the Lake Tahoe area a prime place for retirement, despite its drawbacks of heavy tourism and crowded streets. What most people refer to as "Lake Tahoe" is actually a sprawling collection of small cities that group near the lake and sometimes straddle the line between Nevada and California. A majority of retirees live on the California side; all of the gambling is on the Nevada side. Also on the Nevada side are some folks who have enough income that California state income taxes could hurt.

Well-known for luxurious hotels and gambling casinos, Lake Tahoe is also celebrated for beauty; it sits next to one of the most gorgeous lakes in the world. After a while you become numb trying to take in all of its delights. Mark Twain had this to say about Lake Tahoe, in his book *Roughing It*:

> Three months of camp life on Lake Tahoe would restore an Egyptian mummy to his pristine vigor and give him an appetite like an alligator. I do not mean the oldest and driest mummies, of course, but the fresher ones. The air up there in the clouds is very pure and fine, bracing and delicious. And why shouldn't it be? It is the same the angels breathe. Lake Tahoe must surely be the fairest picture the whole earth affords.

Snow is an important part of Tahoe's winter. If there isn't at least a six-foot pack on the ski slopes, skiers feel cheated. From anywhere in town it is a matter of minutes to a ski lift, a joy to those who enjoy the sport. The snow typically falls in isolated, heavy storms that dump up to three feet in one night; then the weather turns sunny for days or weeks until the next snow. From my perspective, the best thing about Lake Tahoe snow is that it takes only a 20-minute drive to be out of it. You can be skiing at Incline Village in the morning and wandering through Carson City in shirt-sleeves that same evening.

Why would folks consider retiring here? "Living here is like being on permanent vacation," says a friend of ours who owns a lakefront cottage near North Shore. Like many residents, he bought his home several years ago, in anticipation of retirement. He rented out his place by the day or week at premium rates to regular visitors—vacationers, skiers and gamblers—and by the time he was ready to retire, a good portion of his retirement home had been paid off. The deductions and depreciation as a rental also helped ease his tax burdens. Long-term rentals, however, are usually available at rates one would expect to pay in most California urban areas. That can be expensive and worth it only if you cannot consider living anywhere else because you love Lake Tahoe so much. Many people living there feel just that way.

Recreation and Culture
Outdoor recreation is superb, since Tahoe sits smack in the middle of national forest wonderland, with high lakes, rivers and streams—not to mention the beautiful,

blue Lake Tahoe itself. It goes without saying that skiing around the lake and places like Squaw Valley is world famous. Golf courses are plentiful, and most are open to the public because they were originally built to service tourists.

Since the Lake Tahoe economy is basically tourist oriented, many normal cultural and entertainment activities are lacking. For example, to the best of my knowledge, there aren't any traditional senior citizen centers other than three nutrition programs. But the lack of organized recreation is more than made up by the top-notch talent presented by the casinos. Hollywood stars and entertainers regularly appear at the gambling emporiums, often at a fraction of the entrance fees you'd expect in a non-competitive economy.

In addition, the area is served by Lake Tahoe Community College, which offers various courses oriented toward seniors, from computers to exercise classes.

Living Costs and Real Estate The cost of living here is clearly higher than in nearby Reno or Carson City. With tourist dollars floating around freely, you can expect that prices will float with them. Housing is expensive, as well. But for many, a higher cost of living is a reasonable trade off for the quality of the surroundings and the excitement of the lake area with its outdoor wonderland.

Medical Care One major hospital, Tahoe Forest, serves the medical needs of the Lake Tahoe area. The facility is equipped to handle most cases, but when the staff gets in over its head, they have quick transportation to either University of California hospital at Davis, near Sacramento, or to the Washoe Medical Center in Reno.

When Grandkids Visit Consider the Ponderosa Ranch in Incline Village, on the Nevada side of the lake. If they've watched re-runs of the "Bonanza" show they'll enjoy this theme park which features the original Cartwright ranch setting. The park includes a museum, a petting farm, a mystery mine, and a saloon (thank God).

Important Addresses and Connections

Chamber of Commerce: Crystal Bay Chamber, 969 Tahoe Blvd., Incline Village, NV 89451

Senior Services: 885 Hwy. 50, Zephyr Cove; or write: P.O. Box 1771, Zephyr Cove, NV 89448

Daily Newspaper: none, but see the Reno and Carson City papers

Airport: Tahoe Airport, with connections to major airlines
Bus: a local bus serves South Lake Tahoe, while shuttles get you to and
from the airport, and Greyhound passes through the area as well

LAKE TAHOE	Jan.	Apr.	July	Oct.	Rain	Snow
Daily Highs	42	61	86	67	18	60
Daily Lows	16	24	49	34	in.	in.

Carson City

*We decided on Carson City because of the views from our house,
clean air, inexpensive housing, and not last or least, because
there's no state income tax. Since we don't gamble, that's not a
problem.*
—Kent and Olive Tumblin

Nevada's state capital is Carson City, the state's fifth-largest city,
even though it has a population of less than 48,000. The downtown's old buildings give you a feeling for Carson City's historic
past and rich Western heritage. The old State Legislature and the
Courthouse probably look much the same as they did back in the
days when Mark Twain worked in nearby Virginia City.

There's been an explosion of population growth here, just as in
most other Nevada cities, but the growth has been outward, into
the desert, rather than upward with tall casinos. Tourist demand for
large, luxurious casinos hasn't hit Carson City as it has Reno and Las
Vegas, so the funky old downtown has changed little over the
years. This is one of the city's charms: a comfortable, slow-paced
and non-touristy atmosphere. Subdivisions fan away from the city
with both upscale and moderate construction. All neighborhoods
enjoy views of nearby mountains, and the clear air seems to mag-
nify their presence. The altitude here is 4,697 feet, approximately
the same as Reno. Carson City shares Reno's cool, dry climate.

The senior citizens center here is exceptionally active, with a
long list of services from health programs to Social Security counseling. Volunteering is an important part of the center's structure,
with over 200 volunteers working on various projects.

Don't expect much help from the chamber of commerce here.
In response to my request for retirement information for this book,
the chamber sent a pamphlet with an order blank for a packet of
information, at $12.50 plus tax.

FBI statistics aren't available for Carson City, but presumably they would be similar to Reno's crime rates. That is, they would fall into a middle range. I would suspect that since Carson City is a much smaller place, with a lesser concentration on gambling, that crime rates might even be somewhat lower here.

Recreation and Culture Carson City's location, in the desert yet close to the mountains, gives easy access to year-round sports and recreation opportunities. Within a 30- to 90-minute drive, there's an impressive concentration of world-class ski resorts. Trout fishing in mountain streams or alpine lakes is the best imaginable, with rare golden trout lurking in the higher altitudes. Big-game hunting includes elk, antelope deer and bighorn sheep in the mountains and deserts (hopefully shot with cameras, not automatic weapons). Both amateur and professional golfers will appreciate Carson City's championship golf layouts. Eagle Valley offers two challenging 18-hole courses.

Despite what some may believe, cultural events in Carson City do not involve cards, dice or roulette wheels—not always. The Brewery Arts Center receives multiple use with a variety of visual and performing arts. The Center also houses the Nevada Artists Association Gallery, and a broad range of arts and crafts classes are available. There's also the Carson City Chamber Orchestra, the Carson City Community Band and the Carson Chamber Singers, all of whom present musical, theatrical and dance productions at either the Brewery Arts Center, the Carson Community Center or at Western Nevada Community College. The college also has a variety of community service classes which may be of interest to retirees.

An interesting side trip, and a possible place for retirement (for the right people) is nearby Virginia City. Known as the "Queen of the Comstock," this is probably one of the best-preserved ghost towns in the West. At one time Virginia City had 30,000 residents, a hundred saloons, banks, theaters and elegant hotels, the likes of which couldn't be matched between Denver and San Francisco. Today the population is a mere 800. This is where Mark Twain and Brett Harte got their start as writers. Many buildings from those boom days are still inhabitable, and many have been refurbished and used as residences, bed and breakfasts or shops. Virginia City has a special place in my heart, because that's where my grandfather worked deep within the Comstock Lode and where he died back around 1910.

Living Costs and Real Estate Carson City's cost of living is slightly lower than Reno's, but still about 8 percent over the national average. The only category which falls below normal is utilities, at the 95th percentile. However, this is more than offset by exceptionally high health-care costs of 30 percent above average and housing at 10 percent above.

The housing market reflects the growing interest in the Carson Valley. New homes, with all amenities, are selling from $110,000 to $250,000, depending on size and location. Since Carson City is expanding at such a rate, many choose to look in Gardnerville or Minden, which are centered about smaller downtown areas, but also with adequate shopping and amenities. Older homes in Carson City, closer to downtown, sell for way under average, but you'll need to investigate the neighborhood and condition of the home carefully.

Medical Care Although not far from large-scale medical facilities in Reno, Carson City has a 116-bed hospital. The Carson-Tahoe Hospital also offers nutritional counseling, wellness programs and hospice services. The hospital recently completed an $8.5-million expansion and remodeling project.

When Grandkids Visit Try to visit the Nevada State Railroad Museum. On display are more than 26 pieces of equipment that once were used on the Virginia and Truckee Railroad. This line carried silver ore from the famous Comstock Lode mines in Virginia City for years. If you time it right, you and the grandkids can catch a ride on the train pulled by a working steam-engine.

Important Addresses and Connections

Chamber of Commerce: 1900 S. Carson St., Suite 100, Carson City, NV 89701
Senior Services: 901 Beverly Dr., Carson City, NV 89706
Daily Newspaper: *Nevada Appeal*, 200 Bath St., Carson City, NV 89703
Airport: Reno Tahoe International, local general aviation airport
Bus: Greyhound service, airport shuttle to Reno, no city bus service

CARSON CITY	Jan.	Apr	July	Oct.	Rain	Snow
Daily Highs	45	63	91	70	8	24
Daily Lows	20	29	48	31	in.	in.

NEW MEXICO

• Taos

• SANTA FE

• Albuquerque

• Ruidoso
• Truth or Consequences
• Silver City

• Las Cruces   • Carlsbad

The state of New Mexico is shaped like a big rectangle, bounded on the north by Colorado and on the south by Mexico and Texas, with Arizona bordering the west. On New Mexico's eastern border are Texas and the tip of Oklahoma's Panhandle. At New Mexico's northwest corner you'll find the only point in the nation where four states meet—New Mexico, Colorado, Arizona and Utah. This is the famous "Four Corners" area. It's a state big on land—the nation's fifth-largest (after Alaska, Texas, California and Montana). Yet, with only about 1,500,000 residents, it's lightly populated (fewer people live in the state than in the metropolitan area of Denver), so there's plenty of room for newcomers.

With its inventory of scenic deserts, lush forests and high mountain ranges, New Mexico clearly lives up to its nickname: the Land of Enchantment. The state has a partly dry to dry climate, not particularly different from other Southwestern arid regions. A combination of low humidity, high altitude and abundant sunshine makes this a pleasant and healthy place to live. Summer days are hot, but nights in New Mexico are always cool. Many localities commonly find that temperatures may register 90 degrees on a sunny day and then fall to 50 degrees in the evening. Although daytime air conditioning may be popular in some areas, most of the time you'll sleep under blankets at night. Precipitation (including snow) varies from eight inches per year in some places to as much as 24 inches in some mountainous areas. Yearly snowfall ranges from almost nothing to as much as 300 inches near Ruidoso.

About a third of New Mexico's population consider themselves to be Hispanic and are quite proud of their heritage. Hispanics were the first white settlers in this area, the early Spanish explorers and colonists. The founders were farming and building towns and villages in New Mexico a full generation before the first Pilgrim ever set foot on Plymouth rock. By the way, don't make the mistake of calling New Mexico Hispanics "Mexican-Americans," or you'll run the risk of dirty looks and sarcastic replies. After all, their ancestors were living here more than three centuries before there even was a Mexico! People here converse in an archaic form of Spanish, the cultured manner of speaking that was in vogue back in the 16th and 17th centuries; some words in their vocabulary wouldn't be understood in Mexico. They've been isolated so long that their customs, cooking and worldviews are very different from Mexico. And, although New Mexico shares a border with Mexico, no highways, railroads or connections with Mexico exist along the desolate southern frontier other than one minor border crossing at Columbus. Historically, Mexican immigration (legal and illegal) bypassed New Mexico, moving into California, Arizona or Texas instead.

For some retirees the good news about New Mexico is that the state legislature passed a law to protect retirement income coming from other states from being taxed by those other states. This prevents other states from swooping in on New Mexico retirees and collecting a "source tax" on retirement money from that state by attaching property or placing liens. (This is explained in the section about Nevada, which also has laws against collecting source taxes.) However, since New Mexico taxes retirement income anyway, in many cases it would be a wash. As regards state income taxes for residents, New Mexico is a mixed bag. For those with low income levels (less than $15,000 a year), New Mexico income taxes are lower than most other popular retirement states. For those earning over $95,000 a year, tax rates are higher. However, a legislative task force is looking into possible retirement-income relief measures.

> **New Mexico**
> "Land of Enchantment"
> The 47th state to enter the Union
> January 6, 1912
>
> **State Capital:** Santa Fe
> **Population (1990):** 1,521,779; rank, 37th
> **Population Density:** 12.5 per sq. mile; urban: 72.1%, rural: 27.9%
> **Geography:** 5th state in size, with 121,666 square miles, including 254 square miles of water surface. Highest elevation: Wheeler Peak, 13,160 feet; lowest elevation: Red Bluff Lake, 2,817 feet. Average elevation: 5,700 feet.
> **State Flower:** Yucca
> **State Bird:** Road Runner
> **State Tree:** Pinon
> **State Song:** Oh, Fair New Mexico

History

Like many Southwestern areas, ancient pueblo ruins and cliff dwellings show that the region was inhabited long before Europeans discovered America. Many were abandoned a couple of centuries before Spanish Conquistadores explored what is now New Mexico as early as 1536. Inexplicably, some ancient Indian towns remained populated—remnants of the early civilization—even when the Spaniards arrived.

One example of this is Acoma, the so-called "sky city," in Cibola County. Continually inhabited for unknown centuries, the village sits atop a sheer cliff that rises 357 feet above the plain. Multi-roomed, three-story, adobe buildings impressed early explorers so much that Francisco Coronado thought he had found one of the legendary Seven Golden Cities of Cibola when he discovered the pueblo in 1540.

The first Spanish settlers moved into New Mexico in 1598 and 12 years later established a political capital and governorship in Santa Fe. Native Americans living in the area were peaceful farmers when the Spanish first encountered them, raising crops and engaging in peaceful trade. Even the Apache tribes, later to gain fame as warriors, lived along river bottoms in small villages, tranquilly growing corn, beans and pumpkins—and minding their own business. However, as so often happened when white men moved into Native American territory, squabbles broke out over who owned the land. Fighting escalated over the years and didn't cease until almost 300 years later, when the last Apache war chief, Geronimo, signed a peace treaty with the U.S. government in 1896.

Isolated from the Spanish vice royalty in distant Mexico City, the territory developed slowly and quite independently from other colonial possessions. People developed a culture which is called "Hispanic." In 1821, after Mexico won its independence from Spain, the province came under Mexican rule, which meant little to the Hispanics here, because Mexico was so far away.

About this time, Americans started entering the territory by way of the Santa Fe Trail, which Capt. William Becknell had traced across the Great Plains from Missouri in 1821. Then, in 1846, during the Mexican War, Gen. Stephen Watts Kearny seized the province for the United States. The change of government wasn't supposed to have had much of an impact on the Hispanic residents, since the Treaty of Guadalupe-Hidalgo guaranteed their lands, their language and customs and granted full citizenship in the new country. Not to worry. Later, as many of the treaty's provisions were ignored or overturned, many injustices occurred, always in favor of the newcomers. Yet, because New Mexico was predominantly Hispanic and politically astute, they escaped many of the injustices wrought against the original landowners in California.

In 1862, during the American Civil War, the Confederate flag flew over Santa Fe for a time, when the city was occupied by Confederate troops from Texas. They were driven back into Texas later in the year. The Apaches and Navajos took full advantage of this conflict between white soldiers, going on the warpath against their enemy. In 1864 Union troops defeated the Navajo warriors, forcing them to accept confinement within a reservation. But it took another 20 years to get the upper hand against the Apache.

From that time until after World War II, New Mexico developed rather slowly. The Hispanics were left pretty much to their old, traditional and laid-back ways. Then suddenly, between 1950 and 1960, the population of New Mexico increased by more than a third. Then things slowed down, and during the next ten years (1960-70) the state's population increased by only 6.8 percent. Another decade of growth then increased the state's population by more than 20 percent—nearly three times the national growth rate. For the foreseeable future, the prognosis is more growth to come.

NEW MEXICO TAXES

Dept. of Taxation and Rev., P.O. Box 630, Santa Fe, NM 87504; 505-827-0700

Income Tax

Single		Married Filing Jointly	
Taxable Income	Rate	Taxable Income	Rate
First $5,500	1.7%	First $8,000	2.2%
$5,501 - $11,000	3.0%	$8,001 - $16,000	3.2%
$11,001 - $16,000	4.7%	$16,001 - $24,000	4.7%
$16,001 - $26,000	6.0%	$24,001 - $36,000	6.0%
$26,001 - $31,200	7.1%	$36,001 - $48,000	7.1%
$31,201 - $41,600	7.9%	$48,001 - $64,000	7.9%
Over $41,600	8.5%	Over $64,000	8.5%

Standard Deductions Same as Federal.
Additional Deductions Over 65 or blind: maximum $8,000; exemption decreases as income increases.
Public/Private Pension Exclusion None.
Social Security/Railroad Retirement Benefits Taxed same as Federal.
Federal Income Tax Deduction None.
Other Refundable credit for 3% of out-of-pocket prescription drug costs, up to a maximum of $150 per individual or $300 per return. Also, rebate up to $220 depending on income (maximum $14,000) and number of exemptions.

Sales Taxes

State 5.0%; **County** 0.125–.8125%; **City** 0.125–1.4375%
Combined Rate in Selected Towns Albuq.: 5.8125%; Las Cruces: 6.312%
General Coverage Food and prescrip. drugs taxed; new cars, 3% excise tax.

Property Taxes

All real or personal tangible property is subject to local tax. Taxes on a typical $100,000 home would be about $1,200.
Tax Relief for Homeowners and renters, age 65 or older, with income less than $16,000; max. benefit: $250.
Homestead Credit Up to $2,000 assessed value ($6,000 market value); veterans: $4,000 assessed value ($12,000 market value).
Deferrals None.

Estate/Inheritance Taxes

No estate tax nor inheritance tax, only a pick-up tax, which is a portion of the federal estate tax and does not increase the total tax owed.

Licenses

Driver's License Required within 30 days of establishing residence. Fee $10 for four years. A written and vision test is required upon surrender of old driver's license, as is a three-hour alcohol-driving prevention course.
Automobile License New residents must register vehicle within 30 days. Certificate of title: $5.30; reg. fee depends on weight and age, from $18 to $44.

Albuquerque

When I retired in Hawaii, I realized I couldn't possibly get by there, not with my house payments and high cost of living. We bought a place in Rio Rancho for a third of what we sold our Hawaiian place for. And it's a bigger house, too.

—Chris McEwen

High in the middle New Mexico desert, sitting on the east bank of the Rio Grande, Albuquerque is a fast-growing city that's highly praised by many retirees. Its combination of 5,000-foot altitude, dry air and mild temperatures provide exactly what many people look for in a place to live. Summer temperatures rarely get out of the 90s, and winter almost never sees zero degrees. With low humidity, the weather seems even milder than charts might indicate. In July, the hottest month, the average daytime temperature goes into the 90s, but you'll almost always be wearing a sweater at night.

For most retirees, good weather is what Albuquerque retirement is all about. Rainfall is a scant eight inches per year, which means lots of brilliant, sunny weather. And the best part is that the winter months of December and January are the sunniest. It's a four-season year, with about 11 inches of snow expected every winter. It doesn't stick around for long, though, because winter days usually hit 50 degrees by noon.

Muggy days and long, drizzling spells are just about unknown in Albuquerque. Summers can become quite dry, however, causing the mighty Rio Grande to dwindle to a muddy trickle. Once, when will Rogers was giving a talk in Albuquerque, he cajoled: "Why, you folks ought to be out there right now irrigating that river to keep it from blowing away!"

The city has taken pains to preserve its historic sector. Preservation was possible partly because the coming of the railroad in 1880 moved the "downtown" away from the original plaza, thus sparing it from development. Today the area, now known as Old Town, offers interesting restaurants and shops and maintains the historic flavor of the Old West, with its venerable adobe buildings and museums.

The downtown section is clean, modern and prosperous looking; everything seems polished and tastefully designed. A pedestrian mall completes the picture of a pleasant city center. The rest of the metropolitan area is also pleasant, with a mixture of Western ranch-style homes and pueblo-adobe style, with huge shade trees in the older areas of town.

Almost any direction from the city leads to interesting day trips to historical, cultural and scenic marvels. The snowcapped 10,000-foot Sandia Mountains tower on the east and a chain of extinct volcanoes on the west. The Turquoise Trail (Highway 22) to the north takes you through the old mining towns of Golden, Madrid and Cerillos. To the south on Mission Trail (Highway 14) are the pueblos of Gran Quivira, Abo and Quarai. Several Zuñi pueblos are within easy visiting distance; Mescalero and Jicarilla Apache and Navajo reservations are not far away.

The metropolitan hub of New Mexico, Albuquerque is also a high-technology center of the Southwest. As such, it attracts people from all over the country to work and live there. There's no getting around the fact that Albuquerque is a big city; more than half a million live within the city limits and several large developments and communities circle the city. And, as you might expect from a big city, the crime rates here aren't low, but neither are they particularly out-of-hand. The city ranks slightly below average in personal safety on our crime charts.

People looking for retirement have the choice of numerous neighborhoods. In the city proper, one of our recommendations would be around the campus of the University of New Mexico, in the southern part of the city (east of downtown). This neighborhood is typical of the pleasant, livable areas in and around Albuquerque. Mature trees shade the streets, and most homes are of tasteful brick-and-frame construction. A similar type neighborhood, known as Taylor Ranch, is in the northwestern sector of the city. As an illustration of an upscale community—one built around 27 holes of golf—visit Tanoan, a gated community with luxury homes and prices to match.

Rio Rancho
As an sample of Albuquerque retirement away from the city congestion, let's look at Rio Rancho, 20 minutes from downtown Albuquerque and 45 minutes from Santa Fe. It's a comfortable, safe area of mixed new and older homes. Originally started as a mail-order retirement scheme to sell parcels of worthless desert landscape, Rio Rancho targeted New York residents, and as a result, many residents come from that state. Some folks were skeptical about the project, but they were surprised when the project actually took off, and it hasn't stopped since.

Today, about 40,000 people live on ranch land that 25 years ago supported less than 200 cows. Rio Rancho is one of the fastest-growing communities in the country. Although many retirees are buying new and older homes there, a recent Intel Company facility is bringing high-tech workers from all over the world. It's a great place for retirees, but it's basically a multi-generational community.

With a 27-hole golf course and panorama of the Sandia mountains in the distance, Rio Rancho is a blend between Southwest desert and middle-class suburb. A word of caution about driving in Rio Rancho: it's famous for speed traps. When you encounter a 25-mile-an-hour speed limit, even in a rural area with nothing but empty fields about, don't even think of going 26!

Real Estate In Albuquerque, over 70 percent of the dwellings are single-family homes. Housing prices are about 5 percent over the national average. According to local real estate brokers, three-bedroom homes in nice neighborhoods cost between $60,000 and $80,000. More upscale areas run upwards of $130,000, and truly exclusive neighborhoods start in the mid-$150,000 range. However, at the time of our last visit, we could have purchased an excellent three-bedroom home for less than $80,000. Older ones are advertised as low as $45,000. Mobile home park and apartment rents are moderate.

Newly constructed Rio Rancho homes are being offered from $95,000 to $118,000. Homes ten years and older sell for less, often below $50,000, and we've seen virtual dream homes listed here for $120,000.

A particularly beautiful residential area is out of town, near the Sandia Peak Tramway, the longest continuous aerial tramway in the world. The houses are constructed with nature in mind, each designed to fit in with the gnarled juniper trees, rocks and boulders, and look as if they grew naturally rather than being built by humans. There's also a great view of the city. Prices aren't cheap, starting at $150,000, but the homes are worth it. Condos or town houses can be bought for $90,000 and up.

Recreation and Culture Skiers have the choice of 11 downhill complexes within striking distance of Albuquerque. Sandia Peak (15 miles northeast of Albuquerque) has lifts that rise over 10,000 feet. Hunting, fishing, prospecting and rock-hunting are all great outdoor pastimes. But all outdoor activities don't require going into the wilderness. Horse-racing fans will find seven race tracks within driving distance of Albuquerque, with the season starting in January at the Downs at Santa Fe.

The University of New Mexico (25,000 enrollment) contributes to the rich cultural offerings of the city. There's a full calendar of lectures, concerts, drama and sporting events. The school offers numerous classes of interest to senior citizens.

Medical Care High-quality health care is available from major medical centers in Albuquerque, including urgent care centers and top quality hospitals. The nearest hospital to Rio Rancho is St. Joseph's, a 128-bed facility located 15 minutes from the furthest point in Rio Rancho.

When Grandkids Visit The Rio Grande Zoological Park has an astounding number of animals for your enjoyment. You'll find 300 species represented by 1,300 animals, including African gorillas, Indian tigers, polar bears and even sea lions.

Important Addresses and Connections

Chambers of Commerce: P.O. Box 25100, Albuquerque, NM 87125; or, 1463 Rancho Drive, Rio Rancho, NM 87124

Senior Services: Meadowlark Senior Services, 4330 Meadowlark Lane SE, Rio Rancho, NM 87124

Daily Newspaper: *Albuquerque Journal,* 7777 Jefferson St. NE, Albuquerque, NM 87109; weekly: *Rio Rancho Observer,* 1594 Sara Rd., Suite D, Rio Rancho, NM 87124

Real Estate Agent: Onorio Colucci, Century 21, 4425 Juan Tabo, Albuquerque, NM 87111

Airport: Albuquerque City Airport, with major airline connections

Bus/Train: a city bus system, Greyhound, and Amtrak all serve the Albuquerque area

ALBUQUERQUE	Jan.	Apr.	July	Oct.	Rain	Snow
Daily Highs	47	71	93	72	8	12
Daily Lows	22	40	65	43	in.	in.

Carlsbad

We live in a nice neighborhood where we always feel safe and secure. You don't have to worry when you leave. Property is reasonable and taxes are low.
—Joe and Mary Garner

Tucked away in the southeastern corner of New Mexico, on the banks of the slow-moving Pecos River, Carlsbad sits at an altitude of 3,200 feet and enjoys a mild, four-season climate. It's a pleasant city of 27,000 inhabitants who swear by Carlsbad's peaceful, quiet location. They unanimously endorse the weather, as well. With only 12 inches of rain a year, the residents enjoy an average 340 days of sunshine, warm days and cool nights, which add up to a comfortable climate for retirement living.

The local chamber of commerce actively solicits retirees and works hard to bring its story to the retiring public. However, local boosters also concentrate on bringing in light industry, particularly high-tech companies. This means mixed, multi-generation neighborhoods rather than predominantly retirement groupings. Over 400 new retiree households were established in the community over the past three years.

For its size, Carlsbad has impressive services for retirees, with two senior centers, and the active Senior Recreation Center. Three retirement communities offer services from independent living through full care.

The city has no bus service, but taxis give seniors a discount. A major problem for some retirees would be Carlsbad's isolation from the nearest big towns, El Paso and Albuquerque. If you don't need access to major shopping and big-city amenities, that may not be a problem. Carlsbad is self contained for shopping and commerce.

Living Costs and Real Estate With low housing costs (the chamber of commerce says apartment rents start at $200 a month) and taxes ranking at the bottom of the scale, Carlsbad could be a possibility for those who want economical retirement and who don't need a big city nearby. The average selling price of a home in early 1995 was reported to be $57,267, with some listed as low as $35,000 and others as high as $135,000. Nice places in town sell for around $60,000 to $70,000. For places with acreage suitable for keeping horses, you'll find something for $100,000 to $200,000.

Medical Care Carlsbad has a good-sized medical center (144 beds) which offers all services except invasive cardiology and neurosurgery. Patients requiring assistance in these two areas are flown by helicopter to Lubbock. Otherwise all other medical services are available, and doctors are accepting new patients.

Recreation and Culture The Pecos River runs through town and forms a nearby lake for boating and fishing year-round. According to local fishermen, "catfish is king in Carlsbad." The slow-moving river waters, warm and rife with protected holes, brush piles and undercut banks, make the river a natural haven for channel catfish. Other fish that thrive in the river and nearby lakes are white and black bass, crappie and walleye. Fishermen occasionally hook trout in the colder waters in winter. Hunters go after deer, squirrel and game birds, often not far from the city limits.

Two 18-hole golf courses and a lighted nine-hole, par-three course are open year-round for play. A seniors annual golf pass is available at a nice discount. The local country club, with its 18-hole course, charges a $50 initiation fee and $95 per month for a family membership. A lighted tennis complex offers nine courts plus three handball/racquetball layouts.

The Carlsbad Community Theater presents four quality dramatic presentations each year. Two colleges, College of the Southwest at Carlsbad, a four-year institution, and New Mexico State University at Carlsbad, a two-year branch of the school, offer many community interest classes. The schools give Carlsbad a sort of university town flavor.

Carlsbad Museum has exhibitions of Native American crafts, pottery, jewelry, the Hollebeke Collection of historical artifacts and Tarahumara tribal artifacts from Northern Mexico.

When Grandkids Visit Don't miss the opportunity of visiting world-famous Carlsbad Caverns. One of the largest caves in the world, you have a choice of several tours. One trail descends the equivalent of 79 stories below the main cavern level. Don't panic, you don't have to climb back up; an elevator whisks you to the top.

Important Addresses and Connections
Chamber of Commerce: P.O. Box 910, Carlsbad, NM 88221
Senior Services: 1112 N. Mesa, Carlsbad, NM 88220

Daily Newspaper: *Carlsbad Current-Argus*, 620 S. Main, Carlsbad, NM 88220
Real Estate Agent: Century 21, 1205 Pierce, Carlsbad, NM 88220
Airport: commuter airline service, with 26 flights a week to Albuquerque and Dallas
Bus: no city bus, but Greyhound does serve the area

CARLSBAD	Jan.	Apr.	July	Oct.	Rain	Snow
Daily Highs	58	80	96	79	12	4
Daily Lows	28	47	67	48	in.	in.

Las Cruces

We settled on Las Cruces because of the friendly people, the good climate and the advantages of the University's cultural and entertainment activities. The sun shines so much, I don't know what we'd do without it.

—Charles and Ruth Boyce

In Spanish, Las Cruces means "the crosses." The town's name derives from a group of crosses marking the graves of victims of an Apache attack, back in 1830. The entire area is steeped in history. This was the home of the earliest human inhabitants known on the continent—the Clovis and Folsom cultures—and nearby cliff dwellings are among the oldest structures found in the United States. Spaniards settled the valley before the Pilgrims landed on Plymouth Rock. Famous outlaws, lawmen and gunfighters contributed to the valley's history. Billy the Kid was tried for murder here, sentenced to hang and then escaped. Later he was cornered and shot just outside Las Cruces by the county sheriff, Pat Garrett.

Today, Las Cruces consistently earns high ratings as a retirement location and a quality place to live from publications like *Money* magazine. Although the largest town in southern New Mexico, Las Cruces' population is less than 67,000. It's a city, but not a metropolis. For big-city shopping and special needs, El Paso is only 45 miles away via fast-moving Interstate 10. However, as one local booster put it: "Don't move here if you expect Las Cruces to stay small and quiet. We're the second-fastest-growing city in America!"

Nestled in the fertile Mesilla Valley, which draws irrigation water from the Rio Grande, Las Cruces is the center of a prosperous farming district, producing cotton, pecans and chili peppers. Because it sits on a large natural underground water reservoir, the town isn't troubled by water shortages as are some desert cities.

Architecture here reflects the region's multi-cultural history by blending Native American, Spanish and modern into a distinctive Las Cruces style. Newer neighborhoods clearly suggest a Santa Fe "pueblo" influence. Quiet, earthen tones predominate, yet manage to avoid a regimented, stiff adherence to style. Contrasting pastels and bright colors are interspersed with muted browns and tans so characteristic of Santa Fe.

Mountains surround Las Cruces, rising to over 9,000 feet to block most northern winter winds. This results in a mild, low-humidity winter. Summers are warm, not hot, with 94-degree highs in July and August; residents are proud of the area's high number of sunny days. The combination of 4,000 feet in altitude and low humidity guarantees that the temperature will drop as soon as the sun sets. Instead of air conditioners, most folks rely on inexpensive evaporative coolers (swamp coolers). Even during the coldest winter months, afternoon temperatures usually climb into the 60s, enabling you to spend time outdoors year-round.

Recreation and Culture Mild weather permits fishing every month of the year in nearby Elephant Butte and Caballo reservoirs, with trophy-sized striped bass upwards of 50 pounds lurking in the depths. Las Cruces has two public golf courses and a private country club. Eighteen lighted tennis courts make for comfortable play on warm summer evenings. For horse racing, there's Sunland Park Racetrack about 30 miles to the south.

For those many sports fans addicted to duck racing, you'll have to travel to Deming, some 50 miles distant. However, if ostrich races, camel races or pig races are among your favorite spectator sports (or participant sports, for that matter), you'll have to travel to Alamogordo, 70 miles east. (I'm not making this up.)

New Mexico State University exerts a considerable influence on the community's cultural life. The school brings the community together by inviting participation in activities and presenting a theater and a symphony orchestra. Its cultural and entertainment events are a definite plus. Seniors are welcome to take regular courses or occasional classes at the "Weekend College." A new pro-

gram just for seniors offers scholarly mini-courses on subjects ranging from local history to opera appreciation. A community college
with 3,600 students completes the continuing education opportunities with more than 100 unusual community education courses,
many specifically designed for retiree participation.

For a town its size, Las Cruces has a large selection of cultural
activities. The Doña Ana Lyric Opera stages several full-scale musicals each year, including traditional operas as well as lighter
Broadway musicals. The Las Cruces Chamber Ballet performs a
Christmas "Nutcracker" program as well as traditional ballet in the
spring. Old and foreign movies are presented by the Mesilla Valley
Film Society, with senior discounts.

Living Costs and Real Estate Las Cruces ranks below
national cost-of-living averages in all categories except housing,
which is about 2 percent above the norm. Utilities are almost 10
percent below average and health care about 7 percent below.

We looked at a display of exceptionally imaginative homes of
elegant, Old-West style. They were set on low-maintenance landscaped lots that incorporated natural shrubs and cactus. We
guessed the price at $250,000 and were surprised to learn the ask-
ing price was just over $100,000. A buyers' market prevailed in Las
Cruces at the time of our most recent visit.

Low-end, three-bedroom homes in an acceptable neighborhood sell for $70,000 and high-end at $475,000. An average three-
bedroom home rents for $750 and a two-bedroom apartment for
$600. According to local real estate people, good home rentals are
scarce, although apartments are easy to find. Mobile homes for sale
are also heavily advertised, at seemingly bargain prices.

Medical Care Medical care here is exceptional, with one of
the best-equipped hospitals in the state, the 286-bed Memorial
Medical Center. Las Cruces is the medical hub of a five-county
region. Even larger medical facilities are in nearby El Paso, just a
short drive down the interstate. As in many localities in the U.S.
some doctors are reluctant to accept new Medicare patients. Most
will take on new patients if the first few visits are paid in cash, with
Medicare reimbursement going to the patient.

Crime and Safety Like all sunbelt cities, Las Cruces has its
share of crime, but compared to larger cities, this is a safe place to
live. Property crimes such as burglary and auto theft are above

average for towns of similar size. However, better areas report fewer problems. Crimes of this nature can be avoided through common sense and awareness. Don't leave valuables in your car and don't park in dark, isolated areas. Locked doors, windows, security alarms and good relationships with your neighbors keep burglars away.

On the other hand, Las Cruces police chief Peter Hampton points out that the crime rate here is below average in violent crime. Since most violent crimes are connected with drugs and gangs, and because senior citizens rarely get involved in drive-by shootings and cocaine deals, they are relatively safe. Police Chief Hampton says, "I know of only one senior citizen–related homicide in the last nine years."

When Grandkids Visit Drive on down to El Paso and cross the Rio Grande into old Mexico for a cultural experience in another nation. It's less than an hour's drive. There, in Ciudad Juarez, the kiddies can load up on wonderfully tasteless curios such as green-and-purple penguins, imitation leather goods and disgusting stuffed and varnished frogs. Meanwhile, you can shop for tax-free rum or onyx chess sets.

Important Addresses and Connections

Chamber of Commerce: 750 W. Picacho, Las Cruces, NM 88005
Senior Services: 975 S Mesquite St., Las Cruces, NM 88001
Daily Newspaper: *Las Cruces Sun News*, 256 W. Las Cruces Ave., Las Cruces, NM 88001
Real Estate Agent: Sunstate Realty, 1240 S. Telshor, Suite A, Las Cruces, NM 88001
Airport: Las Cruces International Airport, served by Mesa Airlines; El Paso International Airport is a 45-minute drive
Bus: local bus system gives seniors 50% discounts, and Greyhound serves the town as well

LAS CRUCES	Jan.	Apr.	July	Oct.		Rain	Snow
Daily Highs	59	79	96	76		9	3
Daily Lows	27	42	63	44		in.	in.

Santa Fe

We love knowing that almost every day, when we get out of bed,
we're going to see incredibly blue skies and brilliant sunshine
That's only the beginning of the day.

—Todd and Susan Baldwin

Fifty-nine miles northeast of Albuquerque, the town of Santa Fe sits like an antique jewel in the picturesque Sangre de Cristo mountains. This is high desert country, lofting at an altitude of 7,000 feet, which means cool summers and crisp (but dry) winters. An awesome sense of history pervades the streets and byways of Santa Fe, the oldest capital city in the United States. It's been an important seat of government for over 375 years. When the Pilgrims set foot on Plymouth Rock, Santa Fe had been a bustling commercial center for several years. The oldest private home in the United States is here. A prized landmark is the Palace of the Governors, the oldest public building in the country. The Palace became General Kearney's headquarters in 1846, when his troops captured Santa Fe during the Mexican-American War. Incidentally, this was the first foreign capital ever captured by U.S. armed forces.

Santa Fe, with a population of 62,000, is not only a town steeped in history and culture, but its residents work hard at keeping it that way. Strict building codes insist that all new construction be of adobe or adobe-looking material; all exteriors must be earth tones. This preserves the distinctive Spanish pueblo style for which Santa Fe is famous. Occasionally, one sees a home that was built in the days before zoning codes, and the blue or white building sticks out like the proverbial sore thumb. At first the shades of sand, brown and tan can seem a bit somber, but after while, one grows to appreciate the way they complement the setting.

Art impacts the everyday life of Santa Fe residents, with literally thousands of working artists and more than 150 galleries exhibiting their treasures. The old plaza in the heart of the city is often lined with street artisans displaying jewelry, paintings, leather goods and all kinds of quality artwork. Local Native Americans bring intricate silver and turquoise jewelry to sell in the plaza.

Santa Fe is about tied with Albuquerque for percentage of sunshine; around 300 days each year are guaranteed to be at least partly sunny. Santa Fe gets more rain, 14 inches a year, and there's three times as much snow, about 33 inches annually. This keeps Santa Fe greener. You'll find a true four-season year with very pleasant summers. Be prepared to wear a sweater on summer evenings—the temperature typically drops to below 50 degrees at night.

Recreation and Culture A rodeo every summer attracts those who enjoy outdoor sports, and of course, the thoroughbreds race at famous Santa Fe Downs from May to Labor Day. Two public golf courses and 27 tennis courts receive year-round play because of Santa Fe's mild climate. White-water rafting is just an hour away, and there's trout fishing in nearby rivers and lakes. A nationally famous race track adds to the outdoor recreational opportunities.

The Santa Fe Ski Area is but a 30-minute drive from downtown. Sitting at an elevation of over 12,000 feet, this is one of the nation's highest ski areas. With an average of 225 inches of snow a year, you aren't likely to be disappointed.

A highly regarded opera company performs in a unique outdoor theater. Fortunately, with its light precipitation, Santa Fe's weather seldom interferes with the performances. A year-round calendar of events include concerts by the Orchestra of Santa Fe, the Chorus of Santa Fe, the Desert Chorale, the Santa Fe Symphony, as well as Native American fiestas, festivals and celebrations. Numerous theater and drama presentations come from the New Mexico Repertory Theatre, the British American Theatre Institute, the Armory for the Arts, the Santuario de Guadalupe, the Community Theatre and the Greer Garson Theater. The Santa Fe Community College offers a wide range of classes designed for seniors, and three private colleges plus the University of New Mexico's Graduate Center provide educational opportunities.

Living Costs and Real Estate Santa Fe is one of those places where folks who can afford to buy a second house anywhere buy their second homes. That should tell us something about Santa Fe's quality of life. It also tells you something about the cost of living here, the highest in the state, at 126 percent of the national average. A bright spot on the cost-of-living landscape is the cost of utilities, about 15 percent below average. But that's more than offset by housing costs at 57 percent above average, among the highest in the nation. The only place in the state more expensive is nearby Los Alamos, where a preponderance of Ph.D. scientists earning very good money jack up the local housing costs.

The problem is Santa Fe has such a reputation as a retirement and art center that outsiders have bid up real estate to an unusual level. "It's getting so that we natives can't afford to live here anymore," lamented one hometown resident. Yet, housing is curiously mixed in price. Generally, it's much more expensive than Albuquerque, particularly for nicer housing. But there are also some inexpensive places. Economical housing can be found for a little over $100,000 per unit (occasionally), even though the median price of a city home is $181,000. But the average sales price is well over $200,000, which tells you that many homes are selling in the half-million-and-up range. Several high-end developments are under way, at least one with a private golf course.

A couple of attractive full-care retirement residences are located in Santa Fe; one of them (the Ponce de Leon) is unique in that it doesn't charge endowment or entrance fees. You pay a monthly fee for an apartment, take meals in the dining room if you wish and receive weekly housekeeping and maid service. Be aware that there could be a waiting list.

Santa Fe is a retirement possibility for people with moderate to affluent means, those with deep interests in art and culture, and those who like cool, crisp, sunny weather. It offers a great ambiance for writers or artists who need the company of kindred souls.

Medical Care and Senior Services
Four hospitals and many private practitioners make Santa Fe an excellent place for health care. The 265-bed St. Vincent Hospital is prepared for almost any contingency, and large-scale facilities at Albuquerque are but an hour's drive away.

Four different senior citizen centers serve the city, with services such as adult protection and health care. An active senior citizen program, Open Hands, offers services and an opportunity to volunteer for satisfying and worthwhile community projects. The city furnishes transit services to seniors for grocery shopping, doctor and social service agency appointments. The city also offers taxi coupons for 75-percent discounts off the standard fare. The local bus system, with new, clean-burning, natural-gas engines, services main routes that cover most of the city and offers 25-cent fares for senior citizens.

Crime and Safety
For some reason, the city of Santa Fe isn't covered in the FBI Uniform Crime Report. My feeling is that the crime rate may be a bit higher than average. Many homeowners have installed security systems, and there are a number of private

security companies that patrol neighborhoods on a regular basis. It's suggested that you discuss with the police the likelihood of burglary in the particular areas you are considering. Our own observation is that overall it's a safe place to live.

When Grandkids Visit   Take a drive to one of the nearby pueblos. Eight different villages invite visitors to enjoy a rare opportunity to experience cultures that date back centuries, well before foreign settlers came here. Each village is unique, with its own art, dances, ceremonies and some even speak different languages.

Important Addresses and Connections

Chamber of Commerce: 333 Montezuma, Santa Fe, NM 87504
Senior Services: 520 Onate Pl., Santa Fe, NM 87501
Daily Newspaper: *The New Mexican,* P.O Box 2038, 202 E. Marcy St., Santa Fe, NM 87501; weekly newspaper: *Santa Fe Reporter,* P.O. Box 2306, Santa Fe, NM 87504
Real Estate Agent: Melanie Peters Real Estate, Ed. Reid, 125 East Palace Ave. Santa Fe, NM 87502
Airport: Shuttle to Albuquerque Airport
Bus/Train: the vicinity is served by Greyhound, a local bus system and Amtrak

SANTA FE	Jan.	Apr.	July	Oct.	Rain	Snow
Daily Highs	40	60	82	63	14	32
Daily Lows	19	35	57	39	in.	in.

Silver City

When I retired from my New York City job, I wanted something out West, and I decided that Silver City is in the position where Santa Fe was several years ago, before it started to grow larger and more expensive.
                                                              —Tom Moreau

For a thousand years the area around Silver City has been a source of valuable minerals. Early Native Americans mined outcrops of copper to fashion ornaments and spear points. In the 1790s, Spanish miners worked the copper deposits, loading the ore on the backs of burros and trekking south into Chihuahua for smelting. But Silver City itself wasn't established until returning

California 49ers discovered silver ore a few miles north of the present town site. This kicked off a typical mining boom scenario, with a tent city being replaced by substantial brick buildings and optimistic expansion. When silver mines gave up the last of the bonanza, Silver City would have turned into a typical Western ghost town except for miners turning their attention to the enormous copper deposits nearby. Two large companies operate open pit mines to this day, 24 hours a day, providing steady employment for thousands of residents.

For years, Silver City was well-known to El Paso residents for something other than minerals: pleasant summer weather. Like nearby Ruidoso, this area became popular as a summer "getaway" location, a haven to escape scorching west Texas and southern New Mexico weather. Silver City's 6,000-foot altitude provides cool, dry weather and beautiful, forested mountain vistas. It seemed only natural that when retirement time rolled around, these vacationers would begin thinking about Silver City for retirement. Today, west Texas retirees are being joined by others from all over the country who seek quality living in a mild climate at affordable prices. With a population of 12,000, Silver City is large enough to supply most services, but still small enough to escape big-city crowding, crime and pollution.

The town's architectural style clearly reflects the time frame when Silver City developed. Downtown buildings are influenced by the town's ranching and mining background, rich with Victorian brick buildings so popular in Western mining towns during the last century. In fact, Silver City's historic district boasts the largest concentration of Victorian homes in southern New Mexico.

Silver City is some distance from the nearest interstate, but motor traffic along the highway to Interstate 10 is almost non-existent, so it is an easy drive of 110 miles to Las Cruces, the nearest large town; two and a half hours to El Paso, and a little over three hours to Tucson.

The presence of Western New Mexico University takes Silver City out of the category of an ordinary mining town and protects it from the boom and bust nature of mining business cycles. The school brings stability to the community as well as adding a background of intellectual and cultural diversity to Silver City. In the process of expanding, the university recently added a nursing curriculum which is proving very popular.

The university is also responsible in part for inspiring a fast-growing artists' colony in Silver City. An astonishing number of galleries, studios and workshops welcome art lovers, either regularly or by invitation. Dozens of artisans display their works here and some offer lessons. At the rate the art community is growing here, it promises to become one of the premier art centers in the state.

A fascinating place a few miles above Silver City is an even older mining town called Pinos Altos. Not quite a ghost town today, Pinos Altos is worth a visit, possibly as a place to live for those who want the peace and quiet of a village. Pioneer buildings, a famous saloon and old opera house are still standing, as well as Ft. Cobre, which is now a sort of museum. Here is where the famous Apache war chief, Mangas Coloradas, was captured and murdered by U.S. soldiers in the 1880s when he attended a peace conference. Tourism here is light, so residents aren't overwhelmed by traffic.

Recreation and Culture Western New Mexico University provides a variety of cultural and sporting events. A wide variety of learning opportunities are available to the community. According to the school registrar, a considerable number of over-50 students are always registered here. The university is famous for its collection of prehistoric pottery and ancient jewelry.

Surrounded by the 3.3-million-acre Gila National Forest, outdoor enthusiasts will find much to do within a short distance from Silver City. Five fishing lakes offer good catches of bass and crappie, plus rivers and streams with trout. Two hours away is Elephant Butte Lake, New Mexico's largest body of water, where fishing for lunker bass can be a memorable experience. Hunters find one of the few places in the nation where seven species can be stalked in a single season. Skiing is four hours away at Ruidoso. Five tennis courts and an 18-hole golf course augment the ten parks and two swimming pools in Silver City.

Western history buffs might be interested that Silver City is where Billy the Kid grew up, went to school, committed his first known crime, was arrested for the first time and made his first of several escapes from jail. By the way, according to local historians, Billy the Kid's first known crime was not killing a man in Silver City when he was 12 years old, but robbing clothes from a Chinese laundry when he was 15.

Real Estate Affordable real estate is one of the attractions that draw retirees here. In nearby Tyrone, the Phelps Dodge company decided to move some of its company housing by marketing the workers' homes as retirement locations. Homes were refurbished and sold starting at $40,000. Now that these are gone, executive housing is going on the block, starting around $80,000.

Most Silver City neighborhoods are quite comfortable looking, with homes priced from $60,000 to $90,000. $155,000 will buy a very nice home on three-quarters of an acre with an impressive view. For exceptionally low-cost housing, several mobile home parks fill the bill.

Medical Care Gila Regional Medical Center, one of the newest and most modern multi-service facilities in the state, serves residents in a 100-mile radius. The center boasts a staff of more than 450, including over 40 physicians and dentists. With a 24-hour emergency room, full-service radiology and a home health and hospice program, the hospital provides ambulances strategically located to serve the county.

When Grandkids Visit Be sure and see the Gila Cliff Dwellings about 44 miles up Highway 15. Discover how prehistoric cultures developed and browse through 42 walled rooms in five caves in this 13th-century citadel. Camping facilities are located nearby. Here you can hike through fields of spring wildflowers, follow meandering streams to waterfalls, set up your tent under the stars or backpack into high mountain meadows. It's all free. Another educational experience is a visit to the Santa Rita copper mine, the oldest active mine in the Southwest.

Important Addresses and Connections

Chamber of Commerce: 1103 N. Hudson St., Silver City, NM 88061
Senior Services: 1016 N. Silver St., Silver City, NM 88061
Daily Newspaper: *Silver City Daily Press*, 300 W. Market St., Silver City, NM 88061
Real Estate Agent: Mimbres Realty, 315 S. Hudson #13, Silver City, NM 88062
Airport: Grant County Airport offers commuter flights on Mesa Airlines
Bus: no local bus, but there's Greyhound and a shuttle service to Las Cruces and Amtrak, 45 minutes away

SILVER CITY	Jan.	Apr.	July	Oct.		Rain	Snow
Daily Highs	48	70	85	71		15	12
Daily Lows	22	40	66	47		in.	in.

Taos

*I'm not normally superstitious, but there's a legend here that
sometimes I almost believe. That is, if the mountains don't want
you to be in Taos, you leave. But if they want you to stay, you'll
stay. Even if you try to move away, you'll return.*

—Margaret Romero

Seventy miles north of Santa Fe, another famous New Mexico
artists' colony has been attracting painters, writers, musicians and
artisans for over a century. Taos sits in a high mesa valley, perched
at an altitude of 7,000 feet at the foot of the Sangre de Cristo mountain range. The scenic drive up the Rio Grande Valley is worth it
even if you have no intention of retiring here. You watch the river
change from a meandering, flatland stream into a rushing current
that cuts a canyon 650 feet below the plain, a not-so-miniature
Grand Canyon.

Bustling tourist village, quiet retreat, art colony and ski resort—
these are but a few of the many descriptions that fit Taos. Its 55 art
galleries and numerous art programs emphasize the large number
of artists and art lovers in residence. Like its sister city, Santa Fe,
Taos is a well-known creative center for painters, writers, weavers,
musicians and artists of all categories. Nationally recognized artists
in Taos have made a profound mark on the U.S. art scene. Because
of the small population (about 4,100), resident artists tend to form
a closely integrated group. The successful and well-known mingle
with the unsuccessful and amateurs much more freely than they do
in large-scale Santa Fe. One resident said, "We permanent residents
of Taos achieve social equality that you seldom find elsewhere.
Some very wealthy, successful people I know prefer to drive rusty
pickups instead of Mercedes and wear blue jeans and boots instead
of city dress. I've attended cocktail parties where starving artists,
multi-millionaires and local business people mix as if they were at
class reunions."

Picturesque adobes, narrow winding streets and the ancient
Pueblo village on Taos' outskirts provide awesome inspiration for
the artist set, but there are three other parts to the equation: winter
skiers, summer tourists and seasonal residents.

Skiing at nearby Ski Valley draws snow enthusiasts beginning
at Thanksgiving. Ski Valley averages 321 inches of snow each year,
so the season lasts into the middle of April. Then, just when ski traffic thins out, camera-toting tourists take up the slack. They come to

photograph the village of Taos as well as the nearby 1,000-year-old Taos Pueblo—one of the most-photographed sites in the West. World-famous photo opportunities and museums are bonanzas for tourists. However, the one main complaint you'll hear from permanent residents is about tourist traffic and the business community's dependence upon tourism for survival. Part-time residents are divided between wealthy folks who can afford a summer home, or perhaps a winter ski home, and those who come to rent a condo for a few months to experience the magic ambience of the area.

The county's ethnic composition may be of interest. New Mexican Hispanics make up 65 percent of the population, with Anglos 27 percent and Native American seven percent. What about Taos as a retirement location? For those who are drawn here, either by the "magic mountain" or by the ambience, Taos can be a dream retirement home. However, it's easy to become disappointed, to wonder what the fuss is all about should you not "fit in" or if you should find a small town boring, far removed from large-scale shopping and city conveniences. For example, there are only two regular grocery stores to serve the area, plus two natural food stores. It's difficult to comment on crime and personal safety in the Taos area, because FBI statistics aren't available. A surprising number of people in the county live at below poverty level (if that means anything), but residents we interviewed expressed no particular concern in this area.

Well, what about retirement here? In short, a special sort of person will adore Taos, others will enjoy it only as a tourist attraction and move on. Do yourself a favor, at least see Taos and the surrounding countryside; it's very interesting.

Real Estate Property falls into two categories here. Most desirable real estate is surprisingly expensive, partly because Taos is a popular place—and the rest of the properties look substandard, probably not the kind of housing most retirees would choose. In the town of Taos, few real estate listings are under $95,000, with $150,000 and up more common, sometimes for postage-size lots. Homes in nearby Ranchos de Taos have larger lots and some larger sales prices as well. Land is also surprisingly expensive. Most of the town's surrounding acreage belongs either to the Pueblo Indian Reservation, the U.S. Bureau of Land Management or the Forest Service, so the supply is finite. According to the Taos chamber of commerce, land prices have appreciated 31 percent per year during the past three years! Rentals seem to be plentiful, starting at $450 for a small place near the village's main plaza and going up quickly for larger digs.

Strict deed restrictions insist upon new buildings being of adobe, or at least looking like adobe, to blend in with the very old, the sort of old and the look-like-old buildings already there. Local residents feel that anything out of place would disturb the charm and quaintness. I suppose they're correct, but it's a bit jarring to see gasoline stations, hardware stores and plumbing shops disguised as ancient adobes. You'll even see an occasional mobile home, sides plastered with earth-tones and wooden vigas protruding at the roofline, trying desperately to fit into the ancient Pueblo style. However, research clearly demonstrates that the ancient Pueblos rarely constructed their mobile homes of adobe brick.

Recreation and Culture

There's prime skiing at Taos Ski Valley, considered one of the premier winter sports areas in the Southwest—at 9,200 feet, with 72 ski slopes. Another ski resort can be found, with a little more driving, at Angel Fire Mountain; it's not quite as high as Taos, so the season probably doesn't last as long.

Golf nuts needn't worry about neglecting their swing; they can check out the Taos Country Club, with 18 holes, four miles from Taos Town Plaza. The club also offers three-acre homesites on or near the course.

Cultural interests are served by several museums and intense focus on artistic endeavors. The Taos Institute of Arts is one example. A branch of the state university system is currently enlarging its campus to handle 1,300 students.

Medical Care

A new hospital recently went into Taos, a 45-bed acute care facility. Local people say the quality of doctors at the hospital is high, because they like to move here because of the skiing in the winter time. The hospital states that physicians are always available, so it's okay to get sick during ski season.

When Grandkids Visit

Be sure to visit the Taos Pueblo, just a couple of miles from the center of the Taos Plaza. Even after 400 years of Spanish and Anglo presence, the Native Americans in this incredibly ancient pueblo maintain their village much the same as when Spanish explorers found it four centuries ago. To this day they refuse to accept such civilized amenities as running water or electricity. This may be the oldest continually occupied town in the

United States, and it has the tallest buildings of any pueblo, some five stories high!

Important Addresses and Connections

Chamber of Commerce: P.O. Drawer 1, Taos, NM 87571
Weekly Newspaper: *The Taos News*, P.O. Drawer U, Taos, NM 87571
Real Estate Agent: Century 21, 829 Paseo del Pueblo Sur, Taos, NM 87571
Airport: shuttle to Albuquerque's airport on demand
Bus: shuttle services to Taos Ski Valley, Santa Fe and Albuquerque

TAOS	Jan.	Apr.	July	Oct.	Rain	Snow
Daily Highs	40	63	86	66	12	35
Daily Lows	9	29	51	32	in.	in.

Truth or Consequences

This area is ideal for retirement, with its gentle climate, unhurried pace and a multitude of recreational opportunities. A low tax rate, clean air and readily available housing add to the desirability.
—Connie Siffring

If you're old enough to remember when Truth or Consequences received its name, you are either retired or ready to retire. It happened back in 1950 when Ralph Edwards, host of the popular "Truth or Consequences" radio program, was looking for a way to celebrate the show's 10th anniversary. As a joke, he wondered if some town might change its name to Truth or Consequences. It just so happened that residents of a little town in New Mexico—a place called Hot Springs—were looking for ways to publicize their wide spot in the road. They decided to make a deal with Ralph Edwards. They offered to change the name of the town if he would come there to broadcast a show.

The deal was consummated at what was probably the height of the town's silly season. But it worked. Newspapers and magazines all over the nation boosted the event with invaluable publicity. Everyone tuned into the radio show that night. (I know I did.) Changing its name literally put the town on the map. From that time on, road maps listed the town of Truth or Consequences, and tourists detoured to see the place. The additional commerce enabled local business to expand until the stores now offer everything one might need without making a trip into Las Cruces or Albuquerque.

Over the years, many retirees ventured a look at this strange-sounding place and discovered a pleasant community with a comfortable, small-town atmosphere. Today, an astounding 53 percent of the town's residents are retirees! Since most folks come from somewhere else, local residents welcome newcomers with exceptional friendliness. Realize, however, the emphasis in Truth or Consequences is on "comfortable" rather than "elegant," so don't expect another Santa Fe. Truth or Consequences has an abundance of older mobile homes and tired-looking frame houses belonging to retirees more interested in getting to the lake for a day of fishing rather than doing gardening or painting. To give you an idea, at the time of our last visit, there were several mobile homes priced at and below $20,000, including the lot.

Because Truth or Consequences sits at a fairly high elevation (4,260 feet), summers are quite pleasant. It occasionally snows in the winter, but local boosters claim this is "very unusual," and snow usually melts off the same day it falls.

The entire downtown area of Truth or Consequences sits above a system of hot springs. Hot mineral water, ranging from 80 to a bottom-scorching 115 degrees, can be pumped from wells or pools. It's used for heating as well as saunas and hot tubs.

FBI crime statistics aren't available for the area, but my guess would be that personal safety is excellent. At the recreation center for seniors there are dances nearly every night in addition to the usual shuffleboard, cards, dominoes. The pace here is slow; because there is only one stoplight in town, traffic is easy to manage. For major shopping, Truth or Consequences' positioning on Interstate 25 makes the 73-mile drive to Las Cruces and Interstate 10 an easy chore.

Recreation and Culture

A special fiesta commemorating the re-naming of Hot Springs to Truth or Consequences is held the first week of every May. Another important date on the calendar is the "Geronimo Days" festival. Apaches entertain with native dancing, music and story telling. There's also a display of local arts and crafts and wine tasting.

Golf is played year-round at two public golf courses and tennis buffs have four facilities. A new bowling alley and two city parks

with trap shooting, tennis courts, softball fields and exercise courses complete the recreational roster.

Nearby Elephant Butte is an extension of the retiree neighborhoods here. The lakeside village offers a variety of services, including restaurants, lounges, motels boat storage, fishing supplies and
sports equipment. Elephant Butte is one of two large lakes, formed
by damming the Rio Grande, which supply great fishing and which,
truthfully, is why most retirees come here. Elephant Butte Lake,
largest in New Mexico, also has a state park with camping and picnic sites; Caballo Lake has a state park as well. Unexpected in the
middle of the desert, these lakes provide welcome water-sport
recreation and year-round fishing for bass, walleyes, northern pike,
blue catfish, bluegill, crappie and perch.

On the educational front, Western New Mexico University
holds extension classes here, and a community college, New
Mexico Tech, also offers classes for senior citizens.

Living Costs and Real Estate
Most housing is single-
family homes, modest and affordable, but there are also lots of
mobile homes and some rentals. According to local real estate people, three-bedroom homes in an economical neighborhood start at
$60,000 and go as high as $175,000 in the best areas. Home rentals
can be found for as low as $450 and apartments for $350. Mobile
homes are a popular form of housing, with numerous parks around
town as well as units on privately owned lots.

Medical Care and Senior Services
The local hospital
is a 43-bed medical/surgical facility with a full complement of inpa-
tient and outpatient services. For a small town, medical care is
above average, and the hospital does accept Medicare assignments.
The local senior center has a Meals on Wheels program, housekeeping assistance and adult protective services as well as the usual
senior citizen services. There's also a senior transport service to
make sure folks get around town when they need to.

When Grandkids Visit
Take 'em to the Geronimo Springs
Museum for displays of prehistoric pottery and artifacts. There's
also a historical exhibit depicting the valley's mining and ranching
industries. In case you're interested you'll also find mementos of
Ralph Edwards' Truth or Consequences radio show.

Important Addresses and Connections

Chamber of Commerce: 201 Foch St., Truth or Consequences, NM 87901

Weekly Newspaper: *The Herald,* 517 Main St., Truth or Consequences, NM 87901

Real Estate Agent: Century 21-Howell Assoc. 376 S. Foch St., Truth or Consequences, NM 87901

Airport: Albuquerque Airport, a 95-minute drive, or Las Cruces, 50 minutes away

Bus: Greyhound, local bus transportation for senior citizens only

TRUTH OR CONS.	Jan.	Apr.	July	Oct.	Rain	Snow
Daily Highs	54	75	92	75	12	6
Daily Lows	27	44	66	47	in.	in.

Ruidoso

My husband and I came to Ruidoso on our honeymoon, and we've been coming back every year. When we retired, we knew exactly where we wanted to live.
                                                        —Charlotte Seitz

Ruidoso bursts upon travelers as an absolute surprise; it's a setting you don't expect from New Mexico. Almost magically, the landscape changes from hot desert, covered with brush and patches of carrizo grass, into a gorgeous, winding river canyon graced with tall, majestic evergreens perfuming the air. Cool mountain air and lush vegetation make Californians imagine they're at Lake Tahoe. Easterners might recall Maine forests or Canadian mountain vistas.

Of course, this isn't news to West Texans; they knew about the Ruidoso Upper Canyon for decades, as an excellent place to escape blazing Texas summers. The crystal clear river cascading through the tree-shaded canyon made for a wonderful escape and family fun. Summer cabins sprang up among the large ponderosa pines and along the small river. By the way, "Ruidoso" in Spanish means "noisy," an apt description of the sound of cascading water.

With the opening of the racetrack at Ruidoso Downs in 1947, people started thinking of Ruidoso as a resort instead of merely a summertime mountain getaway. About 32 years ago, the Mescalero Apache tribe, with the help of a Texas oil man, developed a ski run high up on Apache Peak, a part of the Mescalero Reservation. They called it Ski Apache and established Ruidoso's second career as a winter resort. The 12,000-foot ski run immediately attracted the attention of ski buffs from all over the country. This is the southernmost place to ski in the Southwest, and because of its exceptionally high location, skiing lasts long after many other areas have closed down, providing some of the best warm-weather powder skiing in the world. The January 1994 issue of *Ski* magazine rated Ruidoso as one of the ten best ski towns in which to live.

Skiing did more than simply bring tourists and increase employment opportunities, it brought visitors and allowed them to observe the area under winter conditions as well as summer. Visitors were pleasantly surprised to discover relatively mild winters here and to learn that fall and spring are delightful seasons as well. This launched Ruidoso upon yet another career as a center for year-round residence and retirement.

Summer cabins were enlarged and larger homes started springing up for both retirees and working families. This continuing growth provides employment for even more new residents and encourages more businesses to open. Today Ruidoso has blossomed into a pleasant town of about 7,500 inhabitants and is still growing. The county population is pushing 12,000. However, the area supports many more shops, stores, restaurants and businesses of all kinds than you might expect of a town this size. Since Ruidoso draws visitors and tourists all year long, small businesses flourish, and you'll find an astonishing selection of excellent restaurants, serving almost any kind of cuisine imaginable, from French to Chinese, from prime rib to Indian squaw bread. According to local business owners, the only slow time is in April, when they manage to squeeze in their vacation time. April, by the way, is an excellent time of the year to investigate Ruidoso as a retirement destination. You'll not only find less traffic and off-season rates for motels, you'll experience Ruidoso's spring, one of its best seasons.

At first, the vast majority of the retirees here came from Texas, but this is changing rapidly. Ruidoso now draws folks from all over the United States and even foreign countries. Some expensive homes belong to wealthy Mexican families, who enjoy the novelty of skiing, a sport somewhat rare in sunny Mexico. At least one family is said to have retired here from Canada.

Recreation and Culture A combination of tourism and local community spirit keeps culture going all year, with art shows, chili cookoffs, parades, golf tournaments and so forth. Local folks say it seems as if there's never a week or weekend without something happening.

You can play golf locally at one of the highest courses in the world. Because of the heavy tourist traffic, the area maintains three courses of high-altitude play. One boasts an island fairway and has been listed in the top 25 golf courses in America. There are also several public and private tennis courts.

Ruidoso Downs has earned a national reputation for its top-rated quarter horse facilities. The world's richest quarter horse race, the All American Futurity, boasts a purse averaging two million dollars. The track also hosts the Southwest's finest thoroughbreds.

Three hundred miles of trails wind through the county, inviting hiking, horseback riding and mountain biking, with most trails on U.S. Forest Service land. Rainbow and German trout lurk in streams and small lakes to thrill fishermen, and wild game such as elk, deer, quail, dove and turkey challenge hunters.

Ruidoso also boasts the largest uphill lift capacity of any ski area in New Mexico. The run has a vertical drop of 1,900 feet and averages more than 300 inches of exceptionally light powder snow annually. The abundance of sunshine and stunning vistas, created by the juxtaposition of alpine slopes and harsh desert landscapes, makes this a popular skiing destination.

The community has plenty of cultural happenings to keep retirees from boredom. The Ruidoso Arts & Film Commission is working on ambitious plans to attract jazz, bluegrass, mariachi and country-western festivals to use its perfect setting for outdoor performances. The county's spectacular surroundings make perfect subjects for artists; more are moving here all the time. Of intercultural interest, the Mescalero Apache reservation celebrates the Fourth of July with a Native American Rodeo and ceremonial puberty rites for young Apache maidens with singing, dancing and traditional food.

A branch of East New Mexico University provides continuing education opportunities for seniors. Small in size, the school offers many courses of interest to senior citizens. One example is a special course, "Computers for Seniors," another is a class in basic fly-tying given by a well-known fishing guide. For indoor sports fans there's a class called "Resort Town Casino Gaming" which teaches the fine art of blackjack, bingo and video poker. Tuition is drastically reduced for New Mexico residents over 62.

Real Estate The tall forest makes a proper setting for Ruidoso real estate, with homes shaded by a thick green canopy, casually located in a somewhat hodgepodge way. Elegant homes can sit next door to small cottages, log cabins and, often, a mobile home. The higher end of the housing scale is also at the highest elevation, at the northern edge of town. Trees are higher here, as are selling prices. One example is Alto, a private golf community where homes range between $145,000 and $165,000 and occasionally up to $500,000. Midway down the canyon, three-bedroom places average $95,000 to $105,000, with mobile homes on individual lots selling for much less.

The most affordable housing is a few miles down the canyon in the community of Ruidoso Downs. Sitting 400 feet lower than Ruidoso proper, Ruidoso Downs demonstrates the dramatic difference altitude can make in the environment. Trees here are plentiful, but of a different species, smaller and tending to spread out rather than grow tall and slender. This doesn't detract from the beauty of the area, however; it's just different. Nice three-bedroom houses start at $75,000 to $85,000. Some places are even less expensive, and perfectly livable mobile homes tucked away on tree-shaded lots sell for as little as $40,000.

Medical Care Medical facilities here are adequate, with a 42-bed hospital, the Lincoln County Medical Center, providing full diagnostic lab and X-ray capabilities as well as an intensive care unit and emergency room service. The facility was recognized in 1994 in a national, independent study, "100 Top U.S. Hospitals—Benchmark for Success." The hospital's motto is "Small town hospital, big city care." There's also a nursing home with 85 beds and a home health care service.

When Grandkids Visit Take a day hike along the Crest Trail, which snakes along the divide between Bonito and Eagle Creek Watersheds. A destination for the hike might be the Mon Jeau Fire Lookout. Should your feet rebel against this suggestion, you could tour the fascinating Museum of the Horse. This museum's collection includes everything of and about horses, from a Russian sleigh to an authentic 1860 stagecoach.

Important Addresses and Connections

Chamber of Commerce: 720 Sudderith Dr., Ruidoso, NM 88345
Bi-Weekly Newspaper: *Ruidoso News*, 104 Park Ave., Ruidoso, NM 88345
Real Estate Agent: Gary Lynch Realty, 419 Mechem Drive, Ruidoso, NM 88345
Airport: shuttle to Alamogordo airport
Bus: no local bus, but there is Greyhound service

RUIDOSO	Jan.	Apr.	July	Oct.	Rain	Snow
Daily Highs	50	65	81	67	21	44
Daily Lows	17	28	48	31	in.	in.

TEXAS

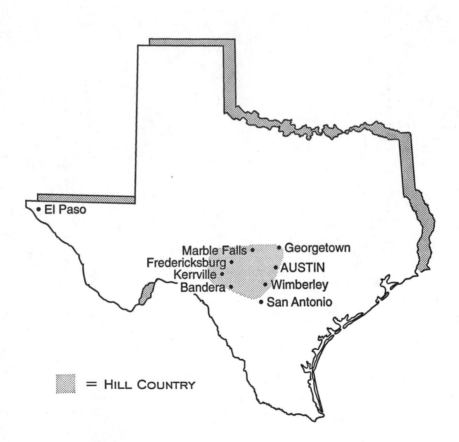

• El Paso

Marble Falls •   • Georgetown
Fredericksburg •   • AUSTIN
Kerrville •   • Wimberley
Bandera •   • San Antonio

= HILL COUNTRY

The largest state in the Union—that is, until Alaska came along and rudely shouldered it aside—Texas is larger than most sovereign nations in the world. In fact, for a brief interlude, it was a sovereign nation between the time it won independence from Mexico until it joined the United States. Texas covers more territory than the total area of five Midwestern states—Indiana, Illinois, Ohio, Michigan and Wisconsin.

Texas is also number two in population, recently passing New York as the nation's second most populous state. And the population is growing larger every day, with 356,000 people moving into the state in 1994, bringing the population to 18.4 million. Before long, Texas will push California out of first place, becoming the most populous in the nation. Ironically, part of Texas' growth comes from Californians who are moving to Texas to retire. (Don't feel bad, California, plenty of folks move there from Florida, too.)

Several things make Texas attractive for retirement. For one thing, Texas is the closest Southwest location to Eastern and Midwestern states. Many folks, considering moving away for retirement, hesitate to relocate in Arizona or Nevada; that's too far away from the grandkids and the children who live in the East. Texas is a compromise, not so far away that visiting back and forth would be out of the question.

The fact that Texas has no state income tax is very attractive for those with the enviable misfortune of making lots of money in retirement. The downside is that Texas sales taxes and real estate taxes are among the highest in the nation. This isn't surprising; the money to run the state has gotta come from somewhere. If you're among those unfortunate folks who make too much money, and your sole motive for moving to Texas is to avoid taxes, you need to sit down with a calculator and figure out whether you'll be saving money or not. After all, if you pay an extra $2,000 a year in property taxes to save $2,000 a year in state income taxes, you're not moving very far ahead financially.

Another consideration is climate. That's not to say that all of Texas has a livable climate. But the places critiqued here all enjoy mild winters and dry, bearable summers. The bonus is cheerful spring and colorful fall seasons. Deliberately excluded are places with world-class blizzards, tornadoes and baseball-size hail. Few places east of the Sierra Nevada are exempt from the above, but it's my understanding that they occur less in the Texas places

175

described in this book than in the open plains area, with its continental climate of cold winters and hot summers. Quick temperature changes are common in this area, one of the causes of tornadoes and hailstorms.

Even though this book only covers West Texas, that's still a lot of ground. Hundreds of cities, towns and crossroads in the state may feel insulted that they weren't honored by being discovered as enchanting places for retirement. There's no disputing that many people indeed retire in these communities and no doubt live happily ever after. No law says a town has to be recommended by some retirement writer for it to be a good place to live, now does it?

Apologizing in advance for possible hurt feelings, I'm going to forge ahead with my listing of Texas places for retirement using three criteria. First, the section only includes places where a significant number of folks retire, preferably coming from other states. Next, these locations should have access to a large shopping area within a reasonable driving distance. And finally, each of our recommendations has some special appeal over and above the average West Texas plains town. Not to insult Texas, but after driving through hundreds of towns, too many begin to look exactly alike. Were it not for automobile license plates, the average Texas town could be the average Kansas, Iowa or Oklahoma town—not much different from thousands of communities around the United States.

A sad fact of modern-day life is that throughout the country, commerce and shopping have shifted to the outskirts, to strip malls, abandoning the downtown to second-hand stores, gift shops and antique dealers. Out on wide stretches of multi-lane highway—accessible only by automobile—multi-acre parking lots accommodate shoppers at Wal-Mart, Piggly-Wiggly and rows of predictable,

---

Texas
"Lone Star State"
The 28th state to enter the Union
December 29, 1845

State Capital: Austin
Population (1990): 17,059,805; rank, 3rd (currently 2nd)
Population Density: 63.9 per sq. mile; urban: 79.6%, rural: 20.4%
Geography: 2nd state in size, with 266,807 square miles, including 4,790 square miles of water surface. Highest elevation: Guadalupe Peak, 8,751 feet; lowest elevation: sea level at the coast. Average elevation: 1,700 feet.
State Flower: Bluebonnet
State Bird: Mockingbird
State Tree: Pecan
State Song: Texas, Our Texas

name-brand, fast-food drive-ins of colorful red-and-yellow plastic construction. Of course, this sameness doesn't mean they're unsuitable places for retirement. But it does raise the question: why bother to change your retirement residence if one town is a near duplicate of the other?

With this in mind, you'll notice that only two parts of West Texas will be discussed as possible retirement locations. One is at the state's extreme western tip, around the city of El Paso. This is chosen partly because of the large number of retirees living there, both civilian and military, and partly because El Paso has a certain Southwest desert charm. The second area covered here is the West Texas Hill Country between and around the cities of San Antonio and Austin. The hills, with their extra rainfall and lush surroundings, seem curiously out of place in West Texas, and this unique setting encourages out-of-state folks to retire here.

History

The name Texas comes from a Caddo Indian word meaning "friends" or "allies." Spanish explorers pronounced the word "tejas" and gave this name to the area. Texas belonged to Spain for 300 years, dormant, its riches undeveloped and its population limited to a few missions and military outposts. When Mexico became an independent country in 1821, one of its priorities was to develop Texas. To populate the vast area, Mexico encouraged new settlers from the United States to move here and become Mexican citizens. Immediately, a large influx of American colonists—mostly Protestants from southern states—began building homes, farms and villages. They became Mexican citizens, but retained their own culture and brought with them African slaves, and with the Mexican government located so far away in Mexico City, the settlers had to deal with the Mexican army instead of regular political processes. This led to the well-known story of the Texas revolution and eventual defeat of the Mexican army.

After a successful war of independence against Mexico, Texans raised the Lone Star flag over the Republic of Texas in 1836. The flag flew for nine years, until 1845 when Texas accepted annexation by the United States and was admitted to the Union as the 28th state. Elated at being United States citizens once more, residents discarded their Mexican sombreros in favor of ten-gallon hats and started wearing pointy-toed, high-heeled boots and wide belts with Lone Star Beer buckles enameled in red, white and blue.

TEXAS TAXES

Comptroller of Public Accounts, Capitol Station - LBJ State Office Building, 111 East 17th St., Austin, TX 78774; 512-463-4600

Income Tax
Texas does not levy a personal income tax.

Sales Taxes
State 6.25%; **County** 0.5–1.0%; **City** 0.5–2.0%
Combined Rate in Selected Towns Austin: 8.0%; Houston: 8.25%
General Coverage Food and prescription drugs exempt.

Property Taxes
All real and tangible personal property is subject to local tax. Some intangibles are subject to taxation. In relation to personal income, property tax collections are in the highest third among the 50 states.
Tax Relief None.
Homestead Exemption/Credit General population: $3,000 assessed value for county taxes; $5,000 assessed value for school taxes. Age 65 or older, or disabled: $3,000 assessed value for county taxes; $15,000 assessed value for school taxes; $3,000 assessed value for local taxes. Additional local option of up to 20% of assessed value. There is also an assessment freeze on school taxes for senior citizens.
Disabled Veterans Up to $3,000 assessed value in addition to other exemptions.
Deferral Program Homeowners age 65 or older may defer all property taxes on their homestead.

Estate/Inheritance Taxes
Texas does not impose an estate tax nor an inheritance tax. It imposes only a pick-up tax, which is a portion of the federal estate tax and does not increase the total tax owed.

Licenses
Driver's License Texas requires a driver's license within 30 days of establishing residence. A written and vision test is required upon surrender of old driver's license. Fee $16 for four years.
Automobile License Title change $28, license depends on weight and age of car, from $40.50 to $58.50.

Texas Hill Country

The picture most of us have of West Texas is flat or rolling stretches of eternity, sparsely covered with prairie grass or low brush that extends to meet the distant horizon. Sometimes wheat replaces grass; occasionally a lethargic steer can be seen munching cactus. Nothing moves except the up-and-down rocking of oil pumps or perhaps a distant windmill. Texas flatlands do indeed flow pretty much undisturbed by mountains, except for the extreme western portion, where the Rocky Mountains march southward through Big Bend National Park.

This bleak picture is more or less accurate, with a notable exception: the Texas Hill Country. A geological formation known as the Balcones Fault has pushed the land a thousand feet above the surrounding plains, creating a mini-mountain range. This not only changes the geography of Texas, it also profoundly affects the state's climate. Moisture-laden breezes from the Gulf of Mexico can't easily lift over the Hill Country, so they release their rain on the southeastern part of the state and leave the western part arid. You can easily see this, for the great Southwestern Desert begins on the other side of the Texas Hill Country.

This special part of Texas is a wonderland of large, limestone cropped hills—not quite large enough to be called mountains—mostly wooded and intersected by half a dozen clear rivers, spring-fed creeks and lakes. Perhaps half a hundred small, friendly towns and cities scatter through the lightly populated countryside, many of them holding great retirement potential. Because much of the Texas Hill Country is rocky, with high concentrations of limestone and caliche, the soil isn't suitable for extensive farming operations. Therefore, customarily the land is left in its natural state. Most acreage is covered by juniper thickets, wild cherry, gnarled oak, native pecan and mountain laurel trees. Along the slow-moving rivers, magnificent cypress and elms shade the banks and provide cover for wild creatures. Cattle and sheep share the wilderness with whitetail deer, turkey, javalina (wild pigs) and imported Russian boar.

The Texas Hill Country is as different from our usual view of Texas as can possibly be. Long considered one of the better living areas in the state, the region has been enjoying nationwide attention through retirement publications. One thing that makes it so different from other parts of West Texas is its year-round rainfall. The

Hill Country receives more than 30 inches of rain each year, several times that of many Southwest locations. This accounts for its green, sometimes lush vegetation. The rain falls every month of the year, helping to keep things fresh looking.

Hill Country's southeastern edge starts near the city of San Antonio and fans out northeast to include Texas's state capital at Austin, then west for about 150 miles. The area immediately west of Austin has a picturesque chain of lakes formed by damming the Colorado River as it stair-steps downstream. Lakes and rivers throughout this area provide abundant fishing and boat recreation as well as creating a pleasant background for retirement living.

Originally this area was settled between the 1840s and 1860s by immigrant German families, who brought their customs, language and architecture with them. An interesting bit of history: during the Civil War, the Germans remained staunchly loyal to the Federal government, refusing to pledge allegiance to the Confederacy. They abhorred the notion of slavery and rebellion. Because of this, other Texans persecuted them. One group of 65 volunteers tried to join with Union forces in the East, but were waylaid and slaughtered by Confederate troops as they tried to cross the Nueces River. A monument to the victims is found in the town of Comfort, the only tribute to Union sympathizers to be found in Texas, probably the only such monument in the entire South.

Those settlers who came to Texas later on ignored the Hill Country; they preferred to farm the more level, richer agricultural lands so plentiful in other parts of the state. Therefore, the Hill Country developed at a more leisurely pace. This permitted German colonists to maintain their old-country customs well into this century. To this day some residents still speak German on special occasions, obviously quite proud of their heritage.

Fredericksburg

This is a community where retirees have fun volunteering. Everyone pitches in, and things get done. The library, hospital and museum couldn't get by without them.

—Becky and Armand Lindig

Fredericksburg, with its setting of scenic hills covered with junipers and low-growing oak trees, is the Texas Hill Country's most famous pioneer town. Almost a century and a half ago, in 1846, a group of German immigrants reached the banks of the

Perdernales River and decided this was where they would settle. The group's leader was a German nobleman, Baron Ottfried Hans von Muesebach (who later became plain John Muesebach once the town was established). The settlers decided to name the village after Prince Frederick of Prussia, and set about constructing homes similar in style to those they left behind in Germany. Abundant limestone made quality construction both possible and practical.

However, the newcomers were not alone. At night, in the hills surrounding the town, Indian campfires cast ominous glows. Comanche warriors carefully observed the strange activity below. To quiet their children's concern, pioneer women explained away the flickering lights as cooking fires of Easter Rabbits, who were simply boiling Easter eggs. (They didn't mention that the Easter Bunnies were equipped with tomahawks.) But through the leadership of John Meusebach, a peace treaty was signed with the Comanches in 1847, one of the few Indian-White treaties that was never broken. The town celebrates this treaty signing with the traditional "Fredericksburg Easter Fires." On Easter eve, campfires glow on the hills around the town. Another celebration soon to come, Fredericksburg's 150th anniversary, promises to be a big one.

The pioneers did their best at replicating a village reminiscent of those in Germany's Black Forest. Sturdily constructed pioneer churches, businesses and homes weathered the passage of time quite well. Many are in everyday use after more than a century, looking as if they're good for another hundred years.

Modern-day residents recognize this treasure and, determined to preserve their heritage, have put it to full advantage as a tourist attraction. An old-fashioned horse and carriage ride and period-style restaurants along Main Street help foster this old-time German village ambience. Fredericksburg attracts tourists from all over the nation, many of whom give serious thought to retirement here.

One old tradition is the tolling of church bells when a church member dies, one peal for each of the years the person lived on this earth. Church bells ring before weddings and after funerals and, of course, always on Sunday mornings as a call to worship.

Fredericksburg's population today is almost 7,000, and supports a thriving business community aside from tourism. The town is conveniently located ninety minutes' drive from either Austin or San Antonio for big-city shopping or airline transportation. Regularly scheduled buses pass through town on their way from

Kerrville to Austin. The cost of living here is about average. Utility costs, however, are unusually low, partly because the city operates both electricity and water utilities and is said to do a great job of recycling profits into improving the system.

Recreation and Culture An interesting concept in outdoor recreation started here 20 years ago, something called Volksport, which is apparently gaining popularity around the nation. Volksport is best categorized as "non-competitive" sporting events such as walking, biking and swimming. Group events are conducted over pre-determined routes or courses, but points and awards are given for completion of the event rather than how speedily you covered the course. You only compete against yourself. Older people find this an excellent way to join in the sociability of healthful exercise without pushing their capabilities or feeling overwhelmed by competition. "I didn't start biking until I was 50," said one lady, "and I never would have started if it hadn't been for Volksport." Fredericksburg just happens to be national headquarters for the American Volksport Association.

The town has facilities for competitive sports as well. The Lady Bird Johnson Municipal Golf Course is a popular 18-hole layout, and you'll find tennis courts throughout the area. The Hill Country area claims to have 11 of the top 50 golf courses in Texas (this is counting several courses in Austin and San Antonio).

A satellite campus of Austin Community College holds classes here, but mostly giving conventional educational courses for those with a precise academic goal. Somewhere down the line, there'll be continuing ed classes for seniors. But for the moment, the local school district offers some interesting adult education classes. Some residents participate by teaching their specialties and sharing their knowledge. "My husband and I just finished taking a computer class," said one retiree, "and before that we enjoyed studying early Fredericksburg history."

Medical Care The privately owned Hill Country Memorial Hospital is the pride of the region. With 61 beds and 35 physicians, the facility is completing its second expansion in only a few years. Also, Gillespie County Emergency Medical Services employs a paid and volunteer staff for 24-hour medical care and assistance.

Real Estate Fredericksburg is loaded with old, historic homes. Some have been painstakingly restored and put to use as bed-and-breakfasts or other commercial enterprises. Others are used as residences by proud owners. Because of the area's growing popularity, the real estate market has been moving steadily upward. Several well-heeled Hollywood personalities recently purchased estates and game ranches near Fredericksburg which contributed to push prices upward. Yet, in town, it's still possible to find satisfactory three-bedroom homes in the $65,000-$75,000 range. Most properties are selling at an average of $90,000. Really grand places have commanded prices approaching $500,000.

When Grandkids Visit Treat them to a little history of World War II (the Big One, remember?). The Admiral Nimitz Museum of the Pacific War pays homage to the two million Americans who served along with the admiral in the South Pacific. The museum depicts the four years of fighting and the final surrender of the Japanese military on Nimitz's battleship. Nearby is a four-acre display of tanks, airplanes and weapons used in Pacific battles. The Nimitz family hotel, built by Nimitz's grandfather in 1850, houses the museum and is staffed by local volunteers.

Important Addresses and Connections

Chamber of Commerce: 106 N. Adams, Fredericksburg, TX 78624
Senior Services: The Golden Hub, 1009 N. Lincoln, Fredericksburg, TX 78624
Daily Newspaper: *Kerrville Daily Times*, 429 Jefferson, Kerrville, TX 78028
Real Estate Agent: Fredericksburg Realty, 217 East Main, Fredericksburg, TX 78624
Airport: the nearest is in Austin or San Antonio, a 90-minute drive
Bus: no local bus system, but the Kerrville Bus Co. travels through Fredericksburg to Austin, with connections to Greyhound

FREDERICKSBURG	Jan.	Apr.	July	Oct.	Rain	Snow
Daily Highs	62	79	92	81	30	–
Daily Lows	39	59	72	59	in.	

Kerrville

This is one of the premier retirement areas in the United States.
We've got a good climate, good medical facilities and are proud
to live in such a scenic and beautiful place.
                                                              —Ben Peek

Kerrville, not far from Fredericksburg, is often considered the "capital" of the Hill Country since it's the largest city in the hills and centrally located among them. With a population of almost 19,000, Kerrville is also Fredericksburg's major shopping destination. Being close to Interstate 10, many residents find it convenient to commute to jobs in San Antonio, about 45 minutes away. Thus Kerrville fulfills two roles: as a retirement community and as a bedroom community.

Kerrville shares in the Hill Country's panoramic views and is further blessed by the Guadalupe River flowing softly through the heart of town. Kerrville's location at 1,600 to 1,800 feet above sea level—the Hill Country's highest—contributes to its good climate, providing cooler summers and more clearly defined seasons than Austin or San Antonio. Local people are happy with July and August days, always several degrees cooler than the lowland cities. One source of retirees stems from those who customarily visit here for the pleasant summer weather and later decide to move to the Hill Country when embarking on new careers as retirees.

Because of the area's growing population of retirees (almost 30 percent of county residents are over 65), many Kerrville social and business events focus on seniors. The local chamber of commerce is one of the few we've seen that really goes all out for retirees and deserves high praise. An interesting example is the annual Senior Job Opportunity Fair which the chamber of commerce conducts. This year, local businessmen and more than 200 seniors joined together in a half-day seminar to explore employment possibilities. Together they worked out ways to create a large number of part-time and permanent jobs for retirees and supplied valuable employees for area businesses.

One of the premier events of the year is when retiree volunteers have great fun staging a "Senior Prom" dance. The dance is preceded by an election for a "prom queen" to reign over the celebration. Seniors dance the evening away to the sound of big-band music while juniors and sophomores look on in unabashed envy.

The crime rate here, like all Hill Country towns, is low. Kerrville ranks in the top 30 percent of towns for high personal safety, according to the FBI's crime reports.

Kerrville holds a reputation as the Hill County's preeminent art colony. The picturesque surroundings naturally encourage artistic development and act as a magnet to draw working artists, many of whom display works in local galleries and boutiques. One of Kerrville's galleries, the Cowboy Artists of America Museum, is the nation's only museum whose exhibitions are restricted to America's Western and cowboy artists. The architectural design of the museum's building is also a work of Southwestern art, combining Moorish and Spanish architecture in a fortressed hacienda style.

Recreation and Culture

While Fredericksburg has its Volksport, Kerrville's claim to recreational fame is the Kerrville Senior Games. Started five years ago, the original intent was to simply promote active, healthy lifestyles and good fellowship among Kerrville's senior citizens. But the games surprised everyone by becoming a major tourist event in their own right. Planned and executed entirely by Hill Country volunteers, the Senior Games lure close to a thousand participants, some traveling from states as far away as Illinois, Montana and California. Unlike Volksport events, Senior Games are truly competitive, with clearly defined winners and losers. However, we get the feeling that winning isn't the important thing. One contestant at this year's contest traveled from Houston to compete with his team in the volleyball event. When asked, "How did you do?" he smiled proudly. He replied, "We did great! Well, we lost every game, but we played great!"

For golfers, there's the Scott Schreiner Municipal Course, a public 18-hole layout, as well as the Riverhill Country Club, also with 18 holes. Two excellent golf courses can be found in nearby Bandera, a short drive down the road.

The Hill Country Arts Foundation is located just west of Kerrville. A non-profit organization, it is dedicated to furthering visual and performing arts hereabouts, enriching the lives of residents for three decades by presenting theater, art instruction and exhibitions. More than 30 intensive art classes and weekend workshops are presently underway at the foundation's facilities. Topics range from water colors and ceramics to digital art on computers. The Foundation's Point Theatre features a summer outdoor season of musicals, comedy and drama.

Another popular cultural presentation is the annual Kerrville Folk Festival in the late spring. Residents and tourists enjoy 18 days of musical events which include original works performed by artists in an outdoor theater, evening concerts around campfires and a songwriter's competition.

Kerrville is also fortunate in having a dynamic community education system. The administration is constantly searching for innovative classes and interesting people to teach them. If a retiree comes up with an idea of something he or she would like to learn, the school looks for more students and an instructor. Crafts, languages, dancing, tennis, investment programs and cooking classes are just a few of the subjects up for grabs here. A "salons redux" series is designed to bring scholars and professionals out of their classrooms to engage in in-depth conversations with the people of the community. The discussions range from classical novelists to philosophy to movies.

Real Estate Not much property can be found at giveaway prices anywhere in the Hill Country; it's too desirable for that. But value for your dollar is high. In Kerrville, three-bedroom homes in nice neighborhoods usually sell for $80,000 to $130,000. With persistence and a sharp eye for bargains, you can beat these prices. Average three-bedroom homes rent for $700, two-bedroom apartments for $600. As in most Hill Country locations, Kerrville has few condos. Rentals aren't too plentiful either; folks tend to stay here year round. We were told that taxes on a $100,000 Kerrville home are estimated at $2,180 a year—expensive compared with other parts of the nation—but the quality of surroundings makes higher taxes endurable.

Medical Care In keeping with its dominant position as the Hill Country's only real city, Kerrville has the largest and probably the best medical facilities. The Sid Peterson Memorial Hospital is a 148-bed, acute-care, not-for-profit hospital. It provides a comprehensive range of medical and surgical services and operates a 24-hour emergency clinic. The hospital foundation operates five other non-profit facilities in the region, which include nursing and home care units, a radiation therapy center and a cardiac rehab facility.

When Grandkids Visit You might consider an innertube float trip on the lazy sections of the Guadalupe River. You can rent tubes for the day and arrange to be picked up at the end of the journey. You'll find places to dawdle along the way, swimming holes with rope swings to drop you in the middle of the river, and grassy banks for a picnic. No, you won't look foolish floating in an inner-tube; you'll have plenty of company, because tubing is a popular sport here. You might look foolish in a swimming suit, but that's a different problem.

Important Addresses and Connections

Chamber of Commerce: 1600 Sidney Baker, Kerrville, TX 78028
Senior Services: The Dietert Claim Senior Citizen's Center, 617 Jefferson St., Kerrville, TX 78028
Daily Newspaper: *Kerrville Daily Times*, 429 Jefferson, Kerrville, TX 78028
Real Estate Agent: Coldwell Banker, 1712 Sidney Baker, Kerrville, TX 78028
Airports: nearest airports are in Austin or San Antonio
Bus: no local bus system; the Kerrville Bus Co. travels to Austin, connecting with Greyhound

KERRVILLE	Jan.	Apr.	July	Oct.	Rain	Snow
Daily Highs	60	78	90	80	30	–
Daily Lows	32	51	66	52	in.	

Bandera

We're only a hop, skip and a jump from San Antonio, but for all practical purposes, we're a million miles away. It's green, peaceful, and the only noises we hear are birds and the neighing of our horses.
—Mr. & Mrs. James B.

Perhaps too small to be included under its own section—its population is under a thousand—yet Bandera is too nice to ignore. It's become a retirement haven for San Antonio residents who are familiar with the area and probably will draw retirees from other parts of the country, once Bandera becomes better known. Just a 26-mile drive from Kerrville, this community is one of the nicest, greenest and most comfortable of all. Situated on the Medina River, surrounded by oak-covered hills laced with winding creeks, Bandera has long been a favorite of San Antonio residents as a weekend getaway.

The town's carefully preserved main street is pretty much the same as it must have appeared in the last century, recalling memories of the days back in the 1870s when Bandera was known as the "Cowboy Capital of the World." This was a staging area for Texas cowboys and their cattle herds to join up with drives traveling north along the Western Trail to Kansas and sometimes on to Montana. It's easy to imagine the "Lonesome Dove" crew moving their herd through here on their way north.

This historic Western tradition lives on in Bandera, and if you feel up to it, you can try your hand at herding longhorns at one of the nearby dude ranches. (This sport was popularized in the recent movie "City Slickers.") On the other hand, if you're like most of us broken-down old travel writers, you'll be more likely to enjoy betting on horses than sitting on horses. So, stop off at Bandera's famous race track and place your bets; this thoroughbred and quarterhorse track draws throngs who pilgrimage here for the privilege of throwing money away on pari-mutuel betting. I understand there's going to be a track in San Antonio before long, but that won't detract from Bandera's charm.

Love of horses goes beyond watching them race. Many residents maintain stables on their property and exercise their animals on the many miles of horse trails in the 5,000-acre Hill Country State Natural Area. This happens to be Texas' largest state park open to horseback camping. Having a stable on your property is a good way to ensure good resale value, too.

Bandera has yet another historical tradition: country-western and dance music. The Cabaret Dance Hall on Bandera's Western-style main street brings in music fans from all over the region. The list of past performers at the cabaret reads like a Who's Who in Texas country music.

This is very much the rural community, despite the sophistication of the racetrack and many sumptuous homes. Residential property tends toward large lots and privacy.

Medina and Camp Verde

For those who enjoy truly small town living, a similar town is Medina, not far from Bandera and 37 miles from Kerrville. It's slightly larger, but quieter, without the country music aspect of Bandera.

Another interesting place is Camp Verde, in between Bandera and Kerrville, a location curiously connected with camels. Back in the 1850s, the U.S. Army experimented with camels for transportation. They established a camel route from Camp Verde that stretched all the way to Yuma, Arizona. And no, I am not making this up.

BANDERA	Jan.	Apr.	July	Oct.	Rain	Snow
Daily Highs	62	78	92	79	30	–
Daily Lows	35	54	73	54	in.	

Marble Falls

My husband and I came here expecting to stay a year. It's been four years now. We'll probably stay for the rest of our lives.
—Mona and John Wefler

At the northern edge of the Texas Hill Country, the Colorado River feeds a series of seven lakes that work their way southeast through the city of Austin. This water wonderland provides hundreds of miles of waterway, offering every type of lake recreation imaginable. This area is known as the Highland Lakes district and also shares the Hill Country's scenic wonders, peaceful surroundings and pleasant weather. A number of excellent retirement locations are found here.

The largest town on this chain of lakes is Marble Falls, with a population of 5,300 (about 13,000 within a ten-mile radius). Marble Falls takes its name from a spot where the Colorado River roared as a 20-foot waterfall said to have been created by a ledge of marble. Early settlers called it "Great Falls" and dreamed of a manufacturing center that could be powered by the rush of water. Today the falls are covered by the waters of Lake Lyndon B. Johnson, and Marble Falls has been spared the ugliness of mills and factories. Instead, tourists and retirees power the town. In fact, the number of over-65 residents is more than double the average Texas community's.

Some say the marble ledge of the falls was actually granite, maybe the same color as the huge stone monolith called Granite Mountain which looms on the town's western edge. When Texas decided to build a state capitol building in Austin, Granite Mountain's owner convinced the state to use Texas granite in the construction rather than imported limestone. His donation of all the granite needed was a very convincing argument, so the state accepted. The use of convict labor and imported workers from Scotland stirred the ire of labor unions, but work proceeded anyway. When completed, the building was second in size only to the

National Capitol Building in Washington D.C. A visit to the capitol in nearby Austin provides eloquent testimony to the workmanship of that day in distinctive red and pink stone. And after 100 years of continuous quarrying, the mountain still looks virtually intact.

By and large, Marble Falls is a comfortable place with a traditional downtown area. The quaint, old-fashioned Main Street has seven antique shops that can keep antique lovers busy for hours on end. Several historical sites in the downtown area also have been carefully preserved.

Marble Falls is unique among small cities in that it has two assisted-living apartment complexes. Neither of these require a "buy-in," that is, you don't have to come up with a large payment to become a resident. You merely get on the waiting list and move in, making monthly payments of about $1,500. This includes three meals and lots of organized activities. If you don't like it, you can always leave without forfeiting an upfront payment.

Most of the Marble Falls area is in modest to expensive housing. Asking prices depend upon whether you're sitting on the water's edge or are some blocks away. Almost any neighborhood you look at could be appropriate for a retired family. But one interesting neighborhood that particularly appeals to retirees (particularly golf-nut retirees) is a lake-front development called Meadowlakes. This is a gated community on the western edge of Marble Falls. As you might imagine, homes around the golf course are more expensive. Although Meadowlakes appears to be part of Marble Falls, in fact it isn't. To maintain autonomy from the rest of the area, Meadowlakes formally incorporated to form its own little "town-within-a-town."

Like all Hill Country and Highland Lakes communities, crime is low and personal safety high. Burnet County (site of Marble Falls) reported 40 percent fewer crimes than the national average. Many folks here claim that they seldom lock their doors. However most refused to give me their addresses so I could go and check. The cost of living is also similar to surrounding towns, which is to say, low.

Recreation and Culture

Outdoor recreation, of course, centers around the lakes. Bass fishing, boating and sailing bring people from all over the region and encourage them to retire here when the workdays become permanent vacation days. White-tail deer and wild turkey are said to be plentiful for hunters.

Seven beautiful, all-weather golf courses are within a 20-mile radius. Three of them are Robert Trent Jones layouts at Horseshoe Bay, however the golf course and tennis courts here are restricted to residents and guests of Horseshoe Bay Resort. The 18-hole course at Meadowlakes and a nine-hole course at Blue Lake are open to public play for a fee.

The Highland Arts Council is the umbrella organization for six arts councils in the lake area. Most have permanent galleries, which are kept open by volunteer members. Workshops, classes and demonstrations are given at the Marble Falls location on Main Street. The population hereabouts just isn't large enough at present to support a community college. Although a few adult ed courses are taught at the high school, the nearest place for continuing education classes is in Austin.

I've never been quite sure whether a chili cook-off qualifies as a cultural event or a dangerous contact sport, but in any event, Marble Falls is home to Howdy Roo, the fourth-oldest chili cook-off in the state.

Real Estate According to local real estate professionals, the market in and around Marble Falls is vigorous, with homes selling for 93 percent of the asking price. Three-bedroom homes, away from the lake shore, go for $80,000 to $85,000. Being on the water raises prices another $20,000 to $30,000, although we've seen some going for much higher. Meadowlakes homes tend to be pricey, just as you would expect from a gated, golf-course community. Beautiful homes here range between $80,000 and $120,000, but on the golf course the range climbs to $150,000 to $180,000. Waterfront homes add $50,000 for the privilege. All property isn't high-priced in Marble Falls, however. Some rather modestly-priced neighborhoods offer homes starting at the $50,000 level.

Medical Care The hospital serving the lake district is in Burnet, about 19 miles north of Marble Falls and 13 miles east of Buchanan Dam. The Highland Lakes Medical Center provides urgent care 24 hours a day and a full medical staff. In Marble Falls itself there's a volunteer group called Emergency Medical Service (EMS) that operates an ambulance and in emergencies offers medical procedures. The area is served by two helicopters that rush patients to either Austin or San Antonio. In Marble Falls, the Hoerster Clinic opened offices in October 1994 with two full-time physicians. An office of Revis Home Care is also located in Marble Falls.

Buchanan Dam   Around both Lake LBJ and Lake Buchanan you'll find several small communities appropriate for retirement. Buchanan lake is the largest and also the highest in altitude. The resort and retirement community of Buchanan Dam takes its name from the construction site that created Buchanan Lake. The population here is about 3,800, many retired. Buchanan Dam is known for arts and crafts, having the oldest co-op gallery in the nation. Open year-round, the gallery exhibits original paints, weavings and a variety of crafts. The Highland Lakes Golf Course at nearby Inks Lake State Park is open to the public.

Other nearby locales are Granite Shoals, Sunrise Beach and Kingsland. Roads circle the lake giving access to homes, RV parks and rental properties.

Horseshoe Bay   Another popular, upscale retirement locale is Horseshoe Bay, about seven miles from Marble Falls. Situated on 8,500 acres, Horseshoe Bay features three 18-hole golf courses, 20 tennis courts, a marina and its own 6,000-foot airstrip. It isn't a gated community, but it does have its own police and fire department as well as an emergency medical service to take care of its 1,500 full-time residents. Since this is the most luxurious of the upscale communities around here, real estate is priced accordingly. Older condominiums, away from the golf courses start around $50,000. Conventional housing starts at $100,000 and ranges up to $8 million. Homes on the golf course range between $250,000 and $300,000; on the water, count on $400,000 and up. Other upscale resort-retirement locations in the area are Blue Lake and Deer Haven.

When Grandkids Visit   An interesting side trip would be to Longhorn Cavern. Always a comfortable 64 degrees, the historic cave offers a level and easy walk through a natural wonder. It takes about an hour and a half to walk the mile-long round trip. Fossil remains found in the cave indicate a variety of beasts of prey used the cave as a dining room, and arrowheads and spear points show that Indians lived here, at least temporarily. According to legend the famous Texas outlaw, Sam Bass, used the cavern as a hideout, and it was a Confederate stronghold where gunpowder was manufactured during the Civil War.

Important Addresses and Connections

Chamber of Commerce: 801 Hwy 281, Marble Falls, TX 78654
Senior Services: 1200 7th St., Marble Falls, TX 78654
Weekly Newspapers: *The Highlander*, 206 Main St., Marble Falls, TX 78654; *The Picayune*, 905 W. Third, Marble Falls, TX 78654
Real Estate Agent: Joe Dockery, NGD Real Estate, 511 Hwy. 281, Marble Falls, TX 78654
Airports: shuttles available to Austin or San Antonio airports
Bus: no city bus services, but Burnet County community buses link various towns with connections to Austin

MARBLE FALLS	Jan.	Apr.	July	Oct.	Rain	Snow
Daily Highs	59	79	96	81	30	–
Daily Lows	40	59	73	59	in.	

Wimberley

Wimberley used to be thought of as a place for retirement, but in the last five years more and more families with youngsters are moving in. The second-largest group coming here nowdays are artists. This makes a nice mixture of neighbors. —Lorie Witten

Wimberley is another Hill Country town that's been basking in the warm light of national publicity as a new "discovery" in retirement destinations. Its photogenic qualities make wonderful color layouts for magazines. This is where the clear, cool waters of Cypress Creek join the warmer waters of the slow-moving Blanco River, a place where large trees and old homes of native stone hark back to another era. This was a popular getaway during World War II, when rich folks from Houston and San Antonio didn't have enough gasoline to travel to their second homes in the Blue Ridge Mountains. So they built summer homes—or "camp houses" as they called them—in Wimberley. When they retired, these summer places became permanent homes, thus starting a retirement trend. As a result, Houston transplants are well represented here. It's properly called a "village," because it's never been incorporated, and folks hereabout like it that way.

Wimberley also presents many genuinely old, wonderfully preserved buildings for your amazement. The oldest are the Wimberley Mill, built in 1856, and the Winters-Wimberley House, possibly built at the same time as the mill. Many buildings here are of native stone. A walking tour of the historic area leads you to a dozen homes built from the mid-1800s to the 1920s.

The main drawback I see here is that the village of Wimberley hasn't been a very well-kept secret with tourists. They've known about it for many years. Often characterized as a "quaint little village," Wimberley clearly lives up to the reputation, and folks from all around come to see for themselves. So many come, in fact, that traffic clogs the main drag. I would characterize Wimberley as a *busy* quaint little village. It isn't all that small, either—the population is a little under 9,000. This is a shopper's paradise for the artsy-craftsy crowd, with art galleries, craftwork and gift shops, antique stores and a couple of stained-glass craftsworkers. A couple of fairly nice restaurants feed the crowds and an old-fashioned ice cream parlor supplies walking-around goodies.

Located equal distances from either Austin or San Antonio, 15 miles off Interstate 35, Wimberley sits about 500 feet lower in altitude than other towns in the Hill Country. This doesn't seem to significantly affect the weather. The nearest small city is San Marcos, 12 miles distant; that's where most heavy-duty shopping is done. San Marcos is exceptionally popular with some shoppers because that's the nearest place to purchase wines or liquors. (Some local restaurants do serve wines and cocktails by the drink, but you must buy a "membership" card for $3 before they'll serve you.) Another reason for San Marcos' popularity with shoppers is it's the location of one of the largest and best-designed factory outlet centers we've ever seen. By the way, San Marcos is a nice-looking little city. For a time, we considered covering it as a retirement recommendation even though it isn't really in the Texas Hill Country proper.

Wimberley sits at an altitude of 1,100 feet—twice as high as Austin—and therefore enjoys slightly cooler summers and a few inches more rainfall. Like other towns in this part of the country, snow is a rarity. In the past two years approximately 200 families have moved in, with 65 percent of the newcomers retirees. A summer community tradition, from Memorial Day through Labor Day, is an outdoor movie theater. Residents come to watch the latest flicks under the stars. Most bring a lawn chair or blanket—as the seating area may be full.

Although there is no Greyhound bus service, the county sponsors a service called CARTS, which takes disabled and senior citizens to medical appointments, and even into Austin for shopping and special medical needs.

Recreation and Culture

For continuing education, people drive to San Marcos, the location of Southwest Texas State University. The school's music department gives concerts in Wimberley several times a year. Other local events are an annual Crawfish Boil and the Lions Club Market Day, which is held every Saturday from April to December, with 400 booths offering everything from arts and crafts to antiques. Many offer goodies from the backs of their trucks or auto trunks.

The Wimberley Players, a little theatre group, have over a decade behind them; their season usually consists of four productions. They use the Greenhouse Theatre at Woodcreek resort which seats 77 theatregoers.

One of the sports quite popular with Hill Country residents is rafting and innertubing on the many rivers that traverse the region. Unfortunately, this is not to be in Wimberley. For some reason the state sets property lines in the middle of the Blanco River, which means the entire river is privately owned. Therefore you aren't allowed access to the river without a property owner's permission. Bummer.

Real Estate

Property in and around Wimberley sells for less than national averages, but considerably higher than in San Antonio or Austin. This seems to be the case in many Hill Country communities. However, this isn't a fair comparison of costs, because few neighborhoods in Austin or San Antonio are remotely similar in quality to those in the Hill Country. Homeowners choose among properties on rivers and hills, on city-size lots or acreages with homes. Properties range from $70,000 to as much as you can pay.

A few minutes north of Wimberley is Woodcreek, a planned community with an 18-hole golf course, tennis courts, clubhouse and other amenities. Homes here start around $90,000. A new section of Woodcreek is under development, which means another 18-hole golf course to go along with it. Unlike many planned communities, Woodcreek has no formal social planning structure.

Occasionally a few rentals can be found in Woodcreek, mostly two- or three-bedroom townhouses. Otherwise, rentals in Wimberley are almost impossible to find, since there are no apartments, just single-family homes. However, there are 29 overnighters in the area and reportedly 90 bed-and-breakfast rooms with accommodations ranging from a palace with an indoor swimming pool to a log cabin with indoor plumbing. You'll have a place to stay while looking the area over.

Medical Care The Family Clinic, a branch of the Texas Medical Center in San Marcos, operates with family practice doctors on duty daily. Wimberley has no hospital of its own, but trained volunteer ambulance teams rush emergency cases to the hospital in nearby San Marcos. They have two ambulances available, one of them a mobile intensive-care unit. In San Marcos, there's the Central Texas Medical Center's 109-bed hospital. For exceptional cases a helicopter can whisk patients to Austin. Wimberley does have a 120-bed nursing home and a small assisted-living facility.

When Grandkids Visit You might want to visit the 7-A Pioneer Town about a mile and a half from the Senior Center on R.R. 12. This is a replica of an early-day Texas village, complete with the obligatory shoot-outs with blank cartridges and a ride on a genuine train.

Important Addresses and Connections

Chamber of Commerce: Ranch Road 12, PO Box 12, Wimberley, TX 78676
Senior Services: (on R.R. 12) P.O. Box 678, Wimberley, TX 78676
Weekly Newspaper: *Wimberley View*, Ranch Road 12, Wimberley, TX 78676
Airports: you must use either Austin or San Antonio
Bus: no local bus or taxi service

WIMBERLEY	Jan.	Apr.	July	Oct.	Rain	Snow
Daily Highs	53	79	97	81	37	–
Daily Lows	40	58	75	59	in.	

Georgetown

After spending much of my life in Houston, living in Georgetown is like stepping back in time. It's a breath of fresh air and a slower lane of traffic.
                                        —Fannie Vaughn

Another pioneer town—founded July 4, 1848 by George Washington Glasscock—sits on the banks of the San Gabriel River.

In its early days, Georgetown was a wild and woolly frontier town, a watering place on the famous Chisholm Trail, where cowboys herded longhorn cattle through the center of town.

Georgetown is proud of its history and delights in its wealth of Victorian architecture. The centerpiece is old, historic Courthouse Square, with antique stores and boutiques. Residents take great care in the restoration and preservation of this historic town, with 180 homes and commercial structures designated as having historical significance. Some are now in use as restaurants and bed and breakfasts.

Although sometimes billed as the "Gateway to the Hill Country," Georgetown's altitude is only 750 feet—not much higher than Austin—so it can't technically be considered Hill Country. That doesn't detract from its charm, however. The population here is a little over 15,000. Since it's only 27 miles from Austin on the interstate, it's within easy commuting distance from the city. This makes it convenient for those who want to visit some of Austin's attractions, things like shopping, college sports events and continuing-education opportunities. As far as personal safety goes, Georgetown ranks in the top 25 percent according to FBI statistics.

Sun City at Georgetown

As an indication of faith in Georgetown's future as a retirement location, the Del Webb Corporation is proceeding with one of its famous "Sun City" developments near here. Sun City Georgetown's 5,300-acre planned community features two scenic creeks meandering through fields of Texas wildflowers and stands of native pecans, walnuts and majestic live oaks. Del Webb's first Texas venture, this will be an active retirement community designed for those aged 55 and older.

As envisioned, 9,500 homes will be built, with 45 percent of the land remaining as open space and natural areas. Four 18-hole golf courses are planned. Other recreational facilities will include swimming pools, tennis courts and extensive hiking and biking trails.

When asked why Georgetown, Rich Vandermeer, Del Webb's Sun City Georgetown general manager, replies: "Georgetown has an interesting blend of the old and new. It's the archetypal Texas town where people know their neighbors and often greet visitors with a 'howdy' on the streets."

Recreation and Culture

For swimming, boating, fishing, hiking and camping, Lake Georgetown is about five miles from town. This 1,310-acre, bass fishing hole, with limestone bluffs and large herds of deer, has plenty of camp sites and places for picnics, plus a crystal-clear swimming area. To the east of Georgetown is Granger Lake, with four state parks; to the west, the stair-stepped lakes on the Colorado River provide even more water recreation. The town of Georgetown has two country clubs, three golf courses, 38 tennis courts, a racquet club and three swimming pools.

Southwestern University is located in Georgetown, a small liberal arts institution. The oldest active university in Texas, it has more of an Ivy League atmosphere than any other school in the state. Although the school limits enrollment to only 1,200 students, the institution has considerable impact on Georgetown's cultural climate with its many artistic and sports events. The drama and music departments are particularly active, providing the community with many enjoyable performances throughout the year.

A popular event, open to the public without charge, is the annual Brown Symposium which explores topics as diverse as the cosmology of black holes in space, symphonies of famous composers and Thailand traditional dances. Nobel Prize winners and intellectual celebrities such as Isaac Asimov and Alex Haley have participated in the symposium.

Real Estate Because Georgetown is on the interstate, and easily accessible to Austin, it's become a "bedroom community" for folks who work in the city. (The chamber of commerce director disputes this, claiming that Georgetown is a "living room" community, because people choose to live here rather than in Austin.) Real estate prices quite naturally are somewhat higher than in the true Hill Country towns. The range here for an average home begins around $75,000, compared with $65,000 in many Hill Country locations. Homes can be found for less by judicious shoppers.

Medical Care Besides excellent area medical facilities, a number of major regional providers are nearby. The Georgetown Hospital has 66 beds and over 30 active admitting physicians, and there's easy access to the VA Hospital Center and veterans' facilities at Fort Hood. Since Austin's medical community is just 20 minutes away, you can rest easy about health care.

When Grandkids Visit Check out Inner Space Cavern, just one mile south of town, next to Interstate 35. The cavern was unknown until a construction crew working on the interstate broke through the earth and made the discovery. One of only seven commercially operated caves in Texas, the Inner Space Cavern tour takes about an hour and a half. You enter by cable car and are treated to special lighting and sound effects.

Important Addresses and Connections

Chamber of Commerce: 100 Stadium Rd., Georgetown, TX 78627
Senior Services: 1704 Hart St., Georgetown, TX 78626
Twice-Weekly Newspaper: *Williamson County Sun*, 709 S. Main St, P.O. Drawer 39, Georgetown, TX 78767
Real Estate Agent: Richard Smith, Coldwell Banker, 1701 Williams Dr., Georgetown, TX 78628
Airport: Mueller Field in Austin, no shuttle connections, but within three years the local airport will have commuter connections
Bus: no local or intercity connections

GEORGETOWN	Jan.	Apr.	July	Oct.	Rain	Snow
Daily Highs	59	79	95	81	32	1
Daily Lows	39	58	74	59	in.	in.

Austin

We always thought we'd retire in Florida or California. But after we made a couple of visits to each place, we started looking for something more our style. Slower, less expensive and safe. We found it here in Austin.
—Mr. and Mrs. Frank Langley

Eighty miles north of San Antonio on Interstate 35 is Texas' capital city. Austin's population of 470,000 makes it about half the size of San Antonio, giving residents more elbow room. This also makes it more practical to live closer to the middle of town. Downtown Austin centers around an ornate state capitol building with extensive grounds and park-like landscaping. The capitol is worth a visit just to see the marvelous workmanship in rose-colored granite. If you read the section about Marble Falls, you'll learn where the granite came from.

Not as level as most Texas cities, Austin sits on the fringe of the Texas Hill Country, surrounded by a circle of low hills. Unlike San Antonio, which developed from a haphazard grouping of trails converging at a river crossing, Austin began as a carefully planned city designed to be the state's capital. The downtown section is laid out in an easy-to-follow grid instead of random happenstance as in many Texas cities. The downtown has an interesting mixture of modern buildings and older ones, creating an interesting air of informality.

Recreation and Culture Almost 20 golf courses are open to the public plus another 15 private clubs in the Austin area. Austin's mild climate permits fairway use throughout the year. Because Austin has more than 15 tennis facilities, totaling about 200 courts, *Tennis* magazine recently named this one of the 10 best tennis cities in the country.

The Highland Lakes are gathering places for sailors, windsurfers, boaters and, of course, fishermen. Austin also has a 30-mile network of hike-and-bike trails that wander through quiet meadows, past restaurants and across bridges.

The Dallas Cowboys hold a summer training camp here at St. Edwards University. More than 100,000 Cowboy fans turn out to watch practice sessions and collect autographs.

Austin is home to the University of Texas with its exceptional libraries, museum, sports activities and cultural facilities, including a world-class concert hall for the performing arts and an 18,000-seat sports arena. The LBJ Library is also located on the university campus. The university and Austin Community College offer many continuing education and personal development courses of interest to senior citizens.

Austin is becoming widely known as the second country music center of the nation, behind only Nashville. Not only country and western music but everything from jazz to reggae can be heard in the clubs around the city, particularly on Sixth Street, the renovated 19th-century historic district. The city is also proud of its reputation as a cultural center in arts other than music. Museums, theaters and art galleries are well attended throughout the city. A symphony, ballet and lyric opera complement the cultural offerings. Zilker Hillside Theatre stages very popular summer music and drama programs.

Real Estate Real estate costs are similar to San Antonio's, with many pleasant-looking neighborhoods on the fringes of the city. For a time HUD repossessions dropped prices to a giveaway level, with new four-bedroom homes going for $57,000, a five-year-old three-bedroom home for $35,000, and an older two-bedroom, two-bath house for only $27,000. These distress sales forced conventional sellers to drop their prices to be competitive. However, this depressed market recovered to a great extent, but the aftermath still keeps prices in a buyer's market.

Austin is unique in having many retirement communities, at least eight newer ones, most in the north and northwestern edge of the city. They offer retirees a range of living conditions from luxurious to economical. The services range from full care, with personal care apartments and nursing care units, to ordinary apartment-type living.

A place called Hidden Hills appears to be one of the most expensive in the area. Although not a retirement community per se, its location on Lake Travis and its 18-hole golf course designed by Arnold Palmer have attracted many retirees. Two-bedroom cottages start at $150,000, and some homes are priced at over a million bucks. For this you get high security with guarded gates and in-home security systems linked to the guard station.

Several other luxury retirement developments are connected with the chain of lakes along the Colorado River. One of the better-known places is The Island, located on Lake Travis. Monthly fees start at $1,300 for an apartment, maid service and some meals. Costs climb up to almost $3,000 for the larger units. Many other developments, not necessarily just for retirees, are sprinkled around Austin's western edge. Tennis and golf are often the central focus.

For something a little less expensive in a retirement development, Camlu Apartments is a good example. They offer two-bedroom units beginning at under $1,000 a month, with paid utilities, daily meals, weekly maid service and shopping transportation.

Medical Care Medical services are more than adequate, with a dozen hospitals and numerous specialists in attendance. Breckenridge Hospital is a teaching hospital and has the only trauma center in the area. The Seton Medical Center is also located here, the home of Central Texas Heart Institute. The Emergency Medical Services (EMS) is said to be one of the best in the nation with loads of equipment, including helicopters.

When Grandkids Visit Consider taking 'em on a half-day train ride with a genuine, 143-ton steam engine. The old 1920s-era passenger coaches roll across some of the finest scenery found in the Lone Star State. The round trip starts at nearby Cedar Park and goes to Burnet.

Important Addresses and Connections

Chamber of Commerce: 210 E. 2nd Ave., Austin, TX 78767
Senior Services: 405 E. 15th St., Austin, TX 78701
Daily Newspaper: *Austin American Statesman*, 166 East Riverside Dr., Austin, TX 78767
Airport: Mueller Field, scheduled to be replaced by a new facility at the old Breckenridge Air Force Base
Bus: there's a city bus system and Greyhound, with connections to Kerrville and other Texas Hill Country towns

AUSTIN	Jan.	Apr.	July	Oct.	Rain	Snow
Daily Highs	59	79	95	81	32	1
Daily Lows	39	58	74	59	in.	in.

San Antonio

Many military families arrange to make San Antonio their last tour of duty when they are reaching the end of their career. That's because they've already decided this is where they want to retire.
—Col. William V. Howells

San Antonio is a big city, the ninth largest in the country and third largest in Texas. It's also growing quickly, having increased its population from 785,000 in 1980 to almost a million by 1995. A good portion of San Antonio's growth can be attributed to retirees.

Normally, I don't like recommending such a large city as a place to retire, but San Antonio is a special place, and you needn't live in the heart of the city in order to enjoy what it has to offer. The city keeps expanding in an outward ring, with neighborhoods that provide a small-town flavor. I can heartily recommend these residential/commercial areas. The neighborhoods are complete in themselves. The core of the city is convenient to any part of the circle and is easy to visit for special occasions, but not at all essential for every-day living.

A major consideration of San Antonio retirement is its climate. San Antonio enjoys what weather experts call a modified subtropical climate. Summer days are hot, with highs typically in the low 90s. Yet summer evenings are delightful, with temperatures dropping into the high 60s or low 70s; just right for shirt-sleeve evenings and for sleeping without the annoyance of air conditioning. Mild weather prevails during the winter, with afternoon temperatures above 60 degrees, even in the coldest months. Snow? Almost none; every three or four years San Antonio catches enough snow to measure (although in 1985 it snowed 13 inches!). Rain? Enough to keep lawns and shrubbery green. San Antonio marks the western boundary of naturally green vegetation, with plenty of trees growing wild in the countryside. When you drive south and west of San Antonio, you'll see a dramatic dryness, the beginning of the Great Southwest Desert that stretches from here to California.

Because the city is so big, there's plenty to do and see. Shopping at the 10-acre River Center Mall, a bewildering number of good restaurants, art shows and downtown walking tours are just for starters. Also downtown you'll find San Antonio's pride and joy: the Alamo, site of the famous battle.

When white men first came here, a Coahuilecan Indian village occupied the bank of a beautiful river, the site of present-day downtown San Antonio. The river, life-giving and crystal-clear, was shaded by large poplar trees ("alamo" trees in Spanish). The Indians called the river "Yanaguana" or "refreshing waters." The Spanish settlers were so overwhelmed with the river's beauty that they chased away the natives, changed the name of the river to "San Antonio," and began polluting it.

Happily, today this river is a symbol of San Antonio's progressive fight against urban decay. The Downtown River Project is a textbook example of how to remedy central core blight. The city completely transformed the river—which was little more than a weed-choked garbage dump a few years ago—turning its banks into an elegant shopping and restaurant complex. Soaring cypress and cottonwood trees grace the riverbanks, shading shops, restaurants and hotels. Tourists and residents alike enjoy strolls, boat rides and nightlife along the riverbanks. The project revitalized San Antonio's entire downtown section. The Coahuilecan tribe would be proud of the way their river has returned to its "refreshing waters" status.

A Model Community Let's take a look at a single San Antonio neighborhood, one that is typical of several around the fringes of San Antonio. This development is called the "Great Northwest" and is home to 4,000 families, many of them retired. Although other areas are equally nice, I choose to highlight Great Northwest because it's a model residential community. An indication of this is that for two of the last three years Great Northwest has been awarded first place in quality living by the National Community Association. What this means is that like many San Antonio neighborhoods, residents maintain an active property owners' association that pulls the community together. Although this may seem merely like the neighborly thing to do, it goes much further, since a good association can greatly improve your quality of life.

Great Northwest may not have a golf course, country club, stables or lakes that some retirees might expect. But the association does provide an Olympic-size pool, several tennis courts and a 20-acre park, all maintained by residents' yearly dues. The neighborhood doesn't have gates to keep strangers out. It doesn't need gates; people look out for each other, and if that's not enough, six private patrol cars police the area 24 hours a day.

This is not an age-restricted retirement community. Not by any means. One of Great Northwest's charms is its mixed generation composition. Many residents are on active military duty; others work in San Antonio's electronics industry, and so forth. Many have toddlers, kids and teenagers living at home. Now, ordinarily, teenagers can spell trouble for a neighborhood because most vandalism, break-ins and general cussedness comes from adolescents. But an active community association will provide activities for kids, to keep them out of trouble. And, when the entire family participates in community affairs, when everybody knows their neighbors, teenagers tend to behave; their parents will hear about everything that happens. So they go to somebody else's neighborhood to make nuisances of themselves.

Neighborhood shopping is convenient, with large malls and commercial centers liberally scattered around the beltway surrounding San Antonio. Downtown is a 20-minute drive, and the largest, most complete medical facility in Texas is also 20 minutes from Great Northwest.

Military Retirement Since its beginning as a Spanish presidio almost three centuries ago, San Antonio has sustained its strong military tradition. Four Air Force bases circle the city: Brooks, Kelly Field, Lackland and Randolph, plus Fort Sam Houston, an army post. Lackland Air Force Base is famous in military circles for having one of the finest medical facilities in the country. This alone is an attraction for military retirees and would bring them here even if San Antonio weren't such a nice place to live. Our understanding is that almost 70,000 service personnel and families live in the San Antonio area and at least twice that many retirees. This may well be the largest population of ex-military in the country.

Every good-sized town has its share of retirement complexes and life-care communities. But San Antonio has several for military only. These are non-profit organizations and do not receive direct government funding. We visited one on the western edge of San Antonio, called Air Force Village. Conveniently located across the highway from Lackland Air Force Hospital, this facility provides quality apartments or cottages for a pleasant life-long environment. Residents—who must be retired Air Force officers—buy into the complex with a "founder's fee," which starts at $40,280 for a one-bedroom, one-bath unit, going up to $83,600 for a deluxe two-bedroom, two-bath, 1,100-square-foot apartment. Then, with a $500 to $1,000 fee (depending on the size of the quarters), the resident is entitled to maid service, physician visits, transportation, all utilities and meals. If it's needed, home health care and delivered food are provided, as well as 24-hour nursing care.

Real Estate San Antonio, like Austin to the north, enjoys a low cost of living, several percentage points below national averages for large cities; utility costs are particularly favorable. A buyers' real estate market has kept prices well within the affordable range. Preferred residential areas flourish on the fringes of the city, with new subdivisions popping up everywhere. The central area and older sections offer the biggest bargains in real estate, sometimes in the low $30,000s, but for heaven's sake, don't make decisions on price alone; most central areas are clearly not suitable for most retirees. Among other things, crime levels here can be somewhat elevated.

Most newcomers prefer to live in the outer ring of newer subdivisions, near one of several large shopping centers. These areas have comfortably high levels of personal safety, as opposed to the inevitable higher crime rate found closer to a city's center. Most San Antonio area homes fall in the price area of $50,000 to $90,000, with an average size of 1,400 square feet. Townhouses are priced anywhere from $45,000 to $80,000 for maintenance-free living.

One reason for the abundance of rentals and reasonable rents is the enormous military population that is continuously on the move. A few years ago, developers sized up this market and decided to increase the number of rentals. With abundant savings-and-loan money available, apartments and condos sprouted far quicker than tenants. The result was too many rentals. However, lately this happy condition of ridiculously low rents is changing, as more people move into the San Antonio area and fewer new apartments are constructed.

Medical Care Medical care in and around San Antonio is awesome. The University of Texas Health Science Center is located here, with schools in medicine, dentistry and nursing and research programs in cancer, cardiovascular problems and other problems endemic to the elderly. This is one of only six sites in the nation that is approved for patients to try experimental new cancer drugs. The South Texas Medical Center, a 700-acre complex, encompasses eight major hospitals, clinics, laboratories and a cancer research and therapy center. Also there's the world-renowned burn unit at Brooke Army Medical Center at Fort Sam Houston, which receives burn victims from all over the world.

Recreation and Culture This is the home of the San Antonio Spurs NBA professional basketball team, the San Antonio Mission baseball team, the San Antonio Racquets tennis team, the San Antonio Iguanas hockey team and the U.S. Modern Pentathalon Olympic team. The city administers 135 parks with over 6,535 acres and two municipal swimming pools. For saltwater fishing, a little more than a two-hour drive places you at the beach, in Corpus Christi or the famous Padre Islands.

San Antonians enjoy a wide variety of cultural attractions and entertainment. There are several community theaters, the Symphony Society of San Antonio, a number of museums and dance companies. Fiesta, a week-long festival, occurs every April. It was originally staged as a memorial to the heroes of the Alamo and has grown to such huge proportions that there's hardly space to move downtown. To foster tourism, the city sponsors a multitude of events, going to great bother to provide interesting things to do, events which residents happily join. There's hardly a day in the year without something special happening. They even dye the river green for St. Patricks Day. (Fish hate this and try to vacation in other rivers when St. Patricks Day rolls around.)

When Grandkids Visit They might enjoy riding on the world's tallest, fastest and steepest roller coaster. Nicknamed "the Rattler," its wooden framework clings to the side of a 100-foot-tall quarry wall in the theme park "Fiesta Texas." The Rattler begins its wild ride at the top of the cliff, then climbs an additional 70 feet into the air before dropping a record 160 feet accompanied by screams of delight and terror. Then it zooms upward, zipping through a limestone tunnel and back downward at insane speeds of over 70 miles per hour. Your grandkids will love it. But you will hate it. Maybe you should take 'em to the zoo instead.

Important Addresses and Connections

Chamber of Commerce: 602 E. Commerce, San Antonio, TX 78296
Senior Services: 107 Lexington Ave., San Antonio, TX 78205
Daily Newspapers: *San Antonio Express-News*, Avenue E at Third St., San Antonio, TX 78205
Real Estate Agent: Jim Dufour, Century 21, 5431 Timber Post St., San Antonio, TX 78250
Airports: San Antonio Municipal Airport
Bus: both city buses and Greyhound are readily available

SAN ANTONIO	Jan.	Apr.	July	Oct.	Rain	Snow
Daily Highs	62	80	96	82	28	–
Daily Lows	40	59	74	59	in.	

Western Texas

West of the wooded, brushy foothills of the Texas Hill Country, the environment changes dramatically. Instead of 30 inches of rain every year, the western portion of Texas has to survive on a third of the moisture that blesses the Hill Country and East Texas. Of course, this gives the countryside a totally different look. Plants that grow here are different, having evolved to deal with seven or eight inches of rain and having learned to conserve precious water. For that reason, you can drive long stretches of the state seeing little evidence of human habitation. The occasional towns will usually be located on a river or other source of water. That's not to say that the entire western parts of Texas are pure desert; in some areas wheat fields thrive and a few other crops do quite well.

None of the above make the sparsely populated areas of West Texas bad places to retire. In fact, many people prefer small towns and the quiet solitude of wide-open spaces. But few folks will choose to move to small towns in West Texas for retirement unless they have a particular reason. (Perhaps they have relatives living there; perhaps they don't want relatives to find them; perhaps they're in a Witness Protection program.) Look at it this way: there are usually good reasons why small towns in the semi-desert portions of Texas stay small. On the other hand, a town like El Paso has a growing population. The countryside may be no different from locations a hundred miles away, but the environment is different. In the larger population centers you have shopping choices (more than one supermarket), you have entertainment and recreation choices (more than one movie theater), and you have access to better medical care. The city of El Paso is an example of a larger city that attracts retirees.

El Paso

When I retired from my job as a printer in Canada, I went looking for a place where I wouldn't have to shovel snow and where I could learn to speak Texan. I found a part-time job in an old-fashion print shop, where they still use hand-set type, and here I'm going to stay.
—Roger Halls

Just over four centuries ago, in 1581, the first Europeans pushed their way north from Mexico and found an easy crossing, or pass, across the sometimes sluggish, sometimes wild, Rio Grande. Incidentally, Mexicans call the stream "Rio Bravo," which means "wild river," instead of "Rio Grande" as we do. Early Spanish explorers named the crossing "El Paso del Norte." When Mexico relinquished claim to the crossing, the U.S. Army established a post here to protect American settlers from marauding Comanches and to oversee the growing business of international trade between Mexico and the United States.

Over the ensuing years, El Paso grew from a dusty cow town into a modern city of half a million, the largest city on the American side of the 1,933-mile U.S.-Mexico border. El Paso has several good things going for it. First, the climate is mild, with summers far cooler than those of the lower Rio Grande Valley. You can usually get out in July or August and play a game of golf without risking sunstroke. Low humidity and a 3,700-foot elevation make a world of difference. It's also a large city, with all the inherent amenities and benefits, without feeling totally urbanized, as similarly sized cities back East do. You can live just a few minutes' drive from downtown El Paso, yet not feel the pressures of a large city.

Another attraction for retirees is Ciudad Juarez, just across the Rio Grande. Juarez is more than just another border town like Reynosa or Matamoros; it is truly a city. It's even larger than El Paso, with an estimated population nearing a million. Juarez's downtown section, situated close to the border, is a bit grungy, with honkytonks, bars, an occasional good restaurant plus the inevitable bordertown curio and souvenir shops. But when you get away from the old downtown section you'll find modern areas, with broad boulevards, nice restaurants and nice clothing stores.

Depending upon the state of the economy, shopping in Juarez can be an experience in bargains and a challenge to your bargaining skills. Some commodities are always cheaper across the border, particularly items like booze, instant coffee and some grocery items. At the time of writing, the Mexican peso has dropped significantly against the U.S. dollar, making prices extremely favorable for those with dollars in their pockets. Many retirees make weekly forays across the border to take advantage of bargains. As long as the peso-dollar relationship remains favorable, Mexico will retain its status as a world-class shopping destination.

Blending Cultures El Paso has a delightful way of blending Mexican and Anglo cultures, something that doesn't happen everywhere in Texas. Instead of rigid social lines separating Anglo-Saxons and Hispanics, maintaining a gulf between U.S. and Mexico—you'll find a congenial mixture of Texas and Chihuahua. Radio and TV announcers on both sides of the border switch between Spanish and English, never missing a beat. Restaurant menus on both sides of the border do much the same. El Paso restaurants typically offer dishes like pozole or chiles rellenos, and Juarez restaurants are famous for steak-and-lobster dinners and Chinese food. Years ago, when I worked for the *El Paso Times*, my favorite lunch-break restaurant served a great chicken-fried steak. Now traditionally, chicken-fried steak is a Texas-Southern dish, but instead of the familiar milk gravy topping the steak, it came smothered with Mexican chile con queso sauce! (That's chopped green chiles in melted jack cheese. Delicious!)

American modern and old Mexican charm blends to give El Paso neighborhoods a distinctive character. The downtown's wide streets branch out in all directions, and Interstate 10 moves traffic quickly and efficiently through the center of the city. As you move toward the outskirts of the city, you can't help but be impressed with the area's neatness and cleanliness.

An area that we particularly liked is El Paso's northwest side. Still under development, the neighborhoods here sit on the sloping foothills, with views across the Rio Grande into Mexico. Homes are newly built, well-maintained and priced economically. Of course, the state's high property taxes offset the bargains somewhat, but the quality here is superb. For example, relatively new homes, tastefully designed, start at less than $80,000 and go over $200,000, depending on the neighborhood and size of the homes.

A Military Town

That first military post on the Rio Grande established a continuing tradition of military presence in El Paso. A large number of civilians are employed at military installations here, and ex-military families make up a good percentage of El Paso retirees. The area's military installations play a big part in El Paso's everyday life and activities. Fort Bliss, in northeast El Paso, is home of the U.S. Army Air Defense Center, and contributes a huge payroll to keep the economy level. Military families and support personnel live in all sections of the city and make the population very "middle America." When retirement time rolls around, Air Force and Army personnel quite readily include El Paso in their list of retirement possibilities. They remember the cleanliness and neighborliness of the city, as well as the affordable real estate. Of course, being military, post exchange privileges and medical facilities for retirees influence their final decisions.

Santa Teresa and Horizon City

A quiet secret for El Paso retirement (one we discovered when interviewing a real estate broker who lives here) is in the El Paso suburb of Santa Teresa. Actually, Santa Teresa is located in New Mexico, even though it's just 15 minutes driving time from El Paso's center. This little community offers the best of two worlds. Because it's just across the New Mexico state line, property taxes are much lower (by as much as a third), yet it's close enough to El Paso to enjoy its cultural and sports activities. The major community in Santa Teresa is gated, with homes costing from $80,000 to $300,000. The country club in the community charges an affordable membership fee and provides two 18-hole golf courses designed by Lee Trevino, 24 tennis courts and a swimming pool. Other homes outside the gated community can be found for as little as $50,000.

Another place to consider is Horizon City. Five miles east of El Paso city limits, this is reputed to be one of the fastest-growing communities in Texas. Just incorporated five years ago, the town now has 4,000 residents. Horizon City is divided into two general neighborhoods. The first one is Horizon Manor, where houses cost between $50,000 and $90,000. The second neighborhood is Horizon Heights, with homes built around a golf course; homes on the fairway cost as much as $350,000.

Crime and Safety
Like any big town, El Paso has its crime problems. But the city seems to be getting a handle on crime. In the last five years, crime rates in El Paso have fallen dramatically. For example: burglary, the crime that affects seniors the most, has dropped by 22 percent. Overall, El Paso's crime rate is 25 percent below places like Dallas and other large Texas cities. As in any large population center, the vast majority of offenses are not the kind that involve senior citizens, and most criminal activity is concentrated in areas where retirees wouldn't want to live anyway. The nicer residential areas of El Paso appear to be as safe as most small towns.

Recreation and Culture
Why retire in El Paso? A frequent answer to this question is El Paso's mild weather and many healthy, year-round outdoor activities. Besides golf, tennis and jogging, less vigorous, spectator sports include bullfights across the river in Mexico and horse racing at Sunland park in New Mexico, only 15 minutes from downtown El Paso.

Golf is an all-year sport, with four 18-hole public courses and seven members-only layouts. The city provides an unusually large number of tennis courts, which are scattered about the neighborhoods. Twenty-five public courts in all, 18 of them lighted for night play, are joined by five private tennis courts to give El Paso residents lots of opportunity to hit the balls.

El Paso Community College—one of the largest community colleges in the nation—is even bigger than the University of Texas at El Paso, with almost 20,000 students. The school offers a variety of courses through their alternative education program tailored for senior adults and their Weekend College program.

The El Paso Symphony Orchestra Association is the longest continuously running symphony orchestra in Texas. It's joined by the El Paso Pro Musica, a concert choir and chamber orchestra. The Americana Museum maintains at least 10 exhibits a year promoting and displaying local and regional art, and the El Paso Museum of Art is the fine arts museum of the region.

Living Costs and Real Estate
The cost of living in El Paso falls five percent below national average. Partly this is due to the exceptionally low cost of housing, which is almost 15 percent below average. These low real estate prices more than offset the higher Texas property tax structure. Utilities, too, are low, as is health care, both about ten points below average.

Most single-family neighborhoods are of brick construction, ranch-style homes, with low-maintenance landscaping. In 1994, average sales prices of two-bedroom homes were $51,631; for three-bedroom homes, $78,050. These figures could be misleading, because they average in homes in exceptionally low-priced neighborhoods, places where many retirees might not want to live.

In El Paso's newer sections, away from downtown, you'll find a proliferation of apartment buildings; there are over 100 apartment complexes throughout the city. Like many Texas cities that participated in the Savings-and-Loan jubilee, condo and apartment construction was overly enthusiastic, resulting in an over-supply. However, like many Texas cities, this bonanza for renters isn't quite as plush as it once was. New apartment construction has halted, and rents have crept up, almost to a normal level. Still, apartments are easy to find and relatively affordable.

Medical Care
El Paso is well supplied with medical facilities, with 13 private hospitals and one public hospital. The William Beaumont Army Medical Center is one of the largest U.S. Army general hospitals in the nation, with 479 beds for area military personnel and veterans. This is also home to a campus of Texas Tech University School of Medicine, a full-time teaching facility for third- and fourth-year med students. The city and county also have a well-organized public health services program, with branches in various parts of the city.

When Grandkids Visit
This might be an appropriate time to do some military museums, since the military figures so prominently here. The Fort Bliss museum has a reproduction of the way the fort looked in the 1850s. You'll see how soldiers lived back in the frontier days. Then, visit the Army Air Defense Museum, also on

Fort Bliss grounds, which has a slide show, films and display of anti-aircraft weapons and the history of air defense.

Important Addresses and Connections

Chamber of Commerce: 10 Civic Center Plaza, El Paso, TX 79901
Senior Services: El Paso Senior Opportunities & Services, 100 N. Oregon St., El Paso, TX 79901
Daily Newspaper: *El Paso Times*, Times Plaza, El Paso, TX 79900
Real Estate Agent: Patti Olivas, RE/MAX, 230 Thunderbird, El Paso, TX 79912
Airports: El Paso Airport, a major transportation hub
Bus: the area is well served by a city bus system and Greyhound

EL PASO	Jan.	Apr.	July	Oct.	Rain	Snow
Daily Highs	58	79	96	79	8	6
Daily Lows	30	49	70	49	in.	in.

UTAH

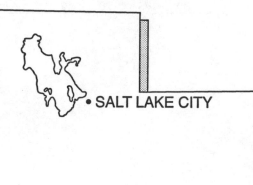

• SALT LAKE CITY

• Cedar City

• St. George

Of all the Southwestern states, Utah is the most desert-like, with seemingly endless stretches of barren land dotted with sagebrush. Sometimes alkaline flats stretch as far as the eye can see; occasionally, the landscape is crusted with pavement-like salt surface. The Great Salt Lake, actually an inland sea, embodies water so loaded with salt that most ocean fish would die if they tried swimming here. The climate's quite dry because the lofty western mountains of the Sierra Nevada rob the prevailing winds of their moisture. For example, parts of the Great Salt Lake Desert receive less than 5 inches a year. The state isn't all dry, though; the high, north-central region of the state receives considerable rain, sometimes up to 40 inches a year. But the part where most people live and tend to retire is dryer—fifteen inches per year on average.

Should this sound like a boring landscape, be aware that Utah also offers some of the nation's most spectacular landscapes, with fantastic canyons carved in brilliant red stone, lush mountain forests teaming with wildlife and sapphire lakes brimming with trout. Few if any places in the entire world can compete with Utah when it comes to sheer beauty. Zion and Bryce Canyon National Parks in the southern portion of the state will absolutely take your breath away, while Capital Reef and the Canyonlands up north are unmatched for sheer desert and mountain beauty. Anyone contemplating a motoring trip out West will never be disappointed by detouring through these areas. And although most of the state is desert, wildlife is surprisingly plentiful, including ducks, deer, elk and mountain lions. Although these areas are beautiful beyond description, few are developed to the point where most folks would consider living there, much less retiring. The most scenic locales are often isolated—with just a few scattered farms and an occasional rural village.

It's true that small-town Utah—for those of us who are not Mormons—can be a lonely place indeed. In fact, my hesitation against unconditionally recommending Utah as a place to retire is Utah's closely knit society that entwines itself with religion. Among themselves, Mormons are wonderfully warm and loving, with deep concern for one another's welfare. But outsiders are outsiders. As an indication of how religion permeates life, 90 percent of the state's politicians are active members of the Church of Jesus Christ of the Latter-Day Saints (also known as the LDS or Mormons). The vast majority of Utah's towns list only one church, the LDS. Occasionally, there'll be an alternative, perhaps a Baptist or Catholic denomination in a town—and larger cities will have several churches, but in all cases, non-Mormons are in the minority.

Having said this and emphasizing that this negative sentiment is strictly my bias, I can also say that many non-Mormons affirm that they haven't found religion much of an obstacle. "It's only a problem if you let it be a problem," said one newcomer to St. George. "We've had no trouble making friends, and our neighbors are quite gracious." And, the larger the town or city, the larger percentage of the residents who are not LDS members.

Are non-Mormons discriminated against? I've heard yes and no on this question. One member of the church I interviewed denies any discrimination and explained it this way: "What many folks don't understand is that being a member of our church isn't just a 'Sunday' thing. Our everyday activities often involve the church. So, when the Mormon families in the neighborhood all get on a bus to go a church activity, the uninvited neighbors could feel left out. But we don't mean to ignore our neighbors. It's just that they don't join in our church affairs any more than we participate in their church activities."

Utah

"The Beehive State"
The 45th state to enter the Union
January 4, 1896

State Capital: Salt Lake City

Population (1990): 1,727,784; rank, 35th

Population Density: 21.3 per sq. mile; urban: 84.4%, rural: 15.6%

Geography: 11th state in size, with 84,899 square miles, including 2,826 square miles of water surface and 16,234,000 acres of forested land. Highest elevation: Kings Peak, 13,498 feet; lowest elevation: Beaver Dam Wash at southwest corner of state, 2,180 feet. Average elevation: 6,100 feet.

State Flower: Sego Lily

State Bird: Seagull

State Tree: Blue Spruce

State Song: Utah, We Love Thee

In this chapter, we'll take a look at three Utah areas for retirement. These aren't the only places that might make good retirement homes, but they are the only places I'm aware of where a substantial number of people from other states actually do retire and where non-Mormons aren't complete rarities.

Most Utah communities present a pleasant, old-fashioned look, neat as a starched shirt. Whether or not Utah's high percentage of Mormon Church followers is the cause of the state's exceptionally low crime rate may be up for debate, but the fact is peace and quiet are the norm in most Utah locations.

History

In 1540 a Spanish expedition from Mexico brought the first white men to explore what is now Utah. Sent by Francisco Coronado to search for the "seven cities of Cibola" and its reputed strongholds of riches and gold-clad buildings, the trek yielded no gold. They did find three Native American tribes inhabiting the region—Utes, Shoshones and Paiutes—nomadic, living by hunting small animals and gathering seeds. Utah obtained its name from the Ute tribe.

More than 200 years later, in 1776, two Franciscan priests, Francisco Silvestre Velez de Escalante and Francisco Dominguez, resumed exploration of southern and central Utah. Part of the route they blazed became known as the Old Spanish Trail. Yet, the country remained relatively unexplored until 1824, when hardy fur trappers moved into northern Utah in search of rich hunting territory. Later, a few emigrant wagon trains made their way across the territory on their way to California, but it wasn't until after 1843, when John C. Fremont and Kit Carson explored the Salt Lake area that settlers began to consider Utah.

Even then, most early pioneers pushed on through Utah, their sights fixed on good pastures and timbered lands to be found in the lush lands of Oregon and California. The canyons and deserts of Utah offered little promise.

The settlement of Utah's bleak regions began in earnest when a group of persecuted Mormons, driven into exile from their Midwestern homes, loaded their covered wagons and plodded west to seek lands no one else wanted. Looking for some place where they could worship in their nontraditional way, on July 24, 1847, a group of 148 pioneers chose a spot at the foot of the Wasatch mountains as their promised land. Heroically, the disciplined and self-sufficient group turned the desert into a garden, virtually overnight.

The hardy Mormon colony spread north and southward from the original site, until in 1850 Utah's population was about 11,000. By 1880 it had multiplied more than 12 times. The Mormon church directed this development, and almost all immigrants were church members.

In 1869, when the first transcontinental railroad was completed at Promontory, Utah, the state began to see a steady influx of non-Mormons. More non-Mormons (known as Gentiles) began immigrating with the introduction of manufacturing by the end of the century. However, even today about 70 percent of the state's people are active members of the Church of Jesus Christ of Latter-day Saints. In smaller towns it's not uncommon to have 100 percent Mormon populations. An active social and political force in Utah, the church owns much property and manages many cooperative enterprises.

The desolate land that so many pioneers passed by as worthless and unyielding today produces a wealth of minerals, agricultural products and manufactured goods. Large cities, comfortable towns and small villages dot the landscape where once nomadic tribes felt lucky to find a few handfuls of seeds. Yet, some things haven't changed much from early pioneer days: water is still scarce, and religion remains a part of everyday life.

UTAH TAXES

State Tax Comm., 160 East 300 South, Salt Lake City, UT 84134; 801-530-6088

Income Tax

Single		Married Filing Jointly	
Taxable Income	Rate	Taxable Income	Rate
First $750	2.55%	First $1,500	2.55%
$751 - $1,500	3.50%	$1,501 - $3,000	3.50%
$1,501 - $2,250	4.40%	$3,001 - $4,500	4.40%
$2,251 - $3,000	5.35%	$4,501 - $6,000	5.35%
$3,001 - $3,750	6.25%	$6,001 - $7,500	6.25%
Over $3,750	7.20%	Over $7,500	7.20%

General Exemptions 75% of federal personal exemptions, not age-dependent.
Public/Private Pension Exclusion $7,500 retirement income, reduced as income increases.
Social Security/Railroad Retirement Benefits Federal amount.
Standard Deduction Federal amount.
Medical/Dental Expense Deduction Federal amount.
Federal Income Tax Deduction 50% deductible.

Sales Taxes

State 4.875%; **County** 1.0%; **City** None; **Special District** 0.25%
Combined Rate in Selected Towns Provo: 6.125%; Salt Lake City: 6.125%
General Coverage Food is taxed; prescription drugs are exempt.

Property Taxes

All property is subject to taxation.
Tax Relief for Homeowners and renters, age 65 or older, surviving spouses; income ceiling $18,400; max. benefit $475 non-refundable credit.
Disabled Veterans Up to $30,000 assessed value ($44,118 market value), if income is less than $30,000.
Blind Persons Up to $11,500 assessed value ($16,912 market value).
65 or Older, or Disabled Local option to abate 50% of tax, up to $300, if total household income is less than $18,400.
Deferral Program Local option for taxpayers age 65 or older, or disabled, with household income below $18,400.

Estate/Inheritance Taxes

No estate tax nor inheritance tax. Utah imposes only a pick-up tax, which is a portion of the federal estate tax and does not increase the total tax owed.

Licenses

Driver's License Required within 90 days of establishing residence. Written and vision test required upon surrender of old license. Fee $15 for five years.
Automobile License Registration of car within 90 days of establishing residence. Title change $6. Local tax on value of car. Plates $12 yearly.

Cedar City

We were planning on retirement in Southern Utah, and we happened to pass through Cedar City. We drove 15 miles farther on before we decided to turn around for another look. It was the university atmosphere that convinced us.

—Mr. and Mrs. Gale Waite

This small university town of 17,000 offers many advantages for retirement living. Sheltered in the foothills, just a few miles from some of the most spectacular landscapes in the world, Cedar City combines the cultural atmosphere of an active university with some of the best skiing and outdoor sports to be found anywhere. The 5,800-foot altitude guarantees a vigorous, four-season climate. According to residents, there are usually four good snowfalls every winter, but warm afternoons and plenty of sunshine make quick work at melting it away.

Cedar City is located on Interstate 15, which gives it easy access to St. George, 52 miles south, and to Salt Lake City, 270 miles north. Las Vegas is little more than a three-hour drive. You might expect a small city like Cedar City to be safe, and it is, exceptionally so. According to our calculations, only eight cities in the United States have lower crime rates than Cedar City.

Because of an exciting variety of cultural presentations, Cedar City calls itself the "Festival City." Now in its 24th season, the Shakespeare Festival is famous throughout the West and draws fans from far and wide. Running from the last week in June through Labor Day, each year Southern Utah University presents four Shakespeare plays plus another stage play and a musical. Another interesting festival is the yearly Jedediah Smith High Mountain Rendezvous. This follows an old-time Western theme, assembling trappers, traders and mountain men for a nostalgic festival of frontier contests and camaraderie. Southern Utah University's campus is the focus of many other community events like music festivals, ballet and the Utah Summer Games.

Even though a large majority of Cedar City residents are members of the Latter Day Saints church, Cedar City also has a comparatively large percentage of non-Mormons as well (there are 13 other churches in town). This is partly due to workers moving into the community with manufacturing companies which have relocated here.

Recreation and Culture A major attraction here is some of the West's best skiing at Brian Head, about 30 miles from Cedar City—close enough for easy day trips. With 400 inches annually of Utah powder and 53 spectacular ski trails through red rock scenery, Brian Head attracts downhillers from as far away as Los Angeles. The facilities are also used as a summer resort, with chairlift rides and community events such as the Fourth of July celebration, an Octoberfest and an annual kite flying contest.

For golfers, there's Cedar Ridge, a public 18-hole course. Its par 71 layout is enhanced by its surroundings of red cliffs and foothills. The city also has two tennis courts and a municipal pool.

In addition to the cultural opportunities already mentioned, continuing education at the university is encouraged. Retirees may audit any university class on a space-available basis for $10 (non-credit). The continuing-education department also offers a wide variety of evening courses.

Living Costs and Real Estate Cedar City has a low cost of living, about 12 percent below nearby St. George. Housing costs are dramatically lower as well, about 36 percent less. According to local realtors, a lower-cost home in an acceptable neighborhood would sell for $79,500 and a high end home for $157,000. As a comparison, the average selling price was $46,100 less than in nearby St. George.

Medical Care Valley View Medical Center is a 48-bed, full-service facility with some secondary level services and an Intensive Care/Cardiac Care unit. The city has 18 doctors, 15 dentists and four chiropractors. Four home health agencies and one nursing home are located in Cedar City.

When Grandkids Visit Take a 21-mile drive to Cedar Breaks National Monument. A miniature version of Bryce Canyon, many people consider Cedar Breaks even more colorful. The abrupt cliffs and fantastic formations are described as looking like a watercolor palette left in the rain, with ribbons of lavender and purple running into creamy gold and pink. Get there early, because every morning park rangers conduct nature walks. You can also do it yourself with hikes, picnicking and camping.

Important Addresses and Connections

Chamber of Commerce: 286 N. Main, Cedar City, UT 84720

Senior Services: Cedar City Senior Citizens, 489 E 200 S. Cedar City, UT 84720

Daily Newspaper: *The Daily Spectrum,* 66 W. Harding, Cedar City, UT 84720; weekly newspaper: *Iron County Advocate,* 195 West 650 South, Cedar City, UT 84720

Real Estate Agent: Era Realty, 259 West 200 North, Cedar City, UT 84720

Airport: Cedar City Municipal, with commuter service

Bus: while there are no public transportation services, there is a senior bus for trips to the doctor, shopping, etc., and Greyhound and Trailways both pass through town

CEDAR CITY	Jan.	Apr.	July	Oct.	Rain	Snow
Daily Highs	47	72	89	77	10	40
Daily Lows	28	44	66	48	in.	in.

St. George

We thoroughly enjoy the quiet and peacefulness of the living environment here and the warm and friendly nature of the residents. I even enjoy driving again, away from the rush and congestion of California.

—Ray and Betty Barney

The largest city in southern Utah, St. George works hard to attract retirees and has acquired a strong reputation as a retirement community. It consistently receives top recommendations from national magazines and retirement guides as a place to retire, often ranking number one in the West. Success has its price, however, because living costs in St. George are 5 percent above national averages, pushed up by real estate prices 17 percent above average.

Conveniently located on Interstate 15, a little more than two hour's drive from Las Vegas, St. George isn't as isolated as it might seem. The city's population of about 30,000 is large enough to provide adequate services, and the community stands on its own commercially.

St. George's picturesque surroundings are some of the more dramatic of any retirement destination described in this book. Stark red cliffs loom over the town, sometimes rising vertically from resident's back yards. You get the feeling that you're living in a Western movie set. In its own way, St. George is as spectacular as Sedona, Arizona, although on a smaller scale.

A combination of beauty, relatively mild winters and great golfing draws more retirees from outside Utah than do other Utah communities. This is important for non-Mormons, because non-locals dilute the religious majority, and newcomers won't be so likely to feel like outsiders. As a matter of fact, St. George has 24 community churches besides those of the Mormon faith. These range from Catholic to Jehovah's Witness, with five Baptist churches, an Episcopal, Lutheran, Presbyterian, Methodist and several I've never heard of. Of course, the majority of the residents are Mormon, but it looks as if there's plenty of room for others.

Settled in 1861 by 309 Mormon families, St. George was transformed from a forbidding alkali flat into a livable town in the space of a decade. Some original homes survive and are treated with reverence by local residents. Included in the list of old homes is Brigham Young's house, where he spent a few of his last years. Streets are wide, tree-lined, and homes are as neat and orderly as Brigham Young would have wished.

St. George boosters like to refer to the area as Utah's "Dixie," out of respect for the area's relatively mild winters. The truth is, the designation "Dixie" derived partly from the town's southernmost location in the state, but more from the early day cotton fields which brought prosperity to the pioneer community. It's true that an elevation of 2,840 feet blesses St. George with warmer winters than its nearby retirement counterpart, Cedar City. The tradeoff is warmer summer temperatures, yet evenings are always cool enough to sleep under blankets.

The FBI ranks St. George as very safe. According to my figures, St. George is in the top third of the lowest crime areas for recommended retirement locations.

Recreation and Culture   St. George has more golf course facilities per capita than any place this side of Palm Springs. Eight great courses are open year-round within a 15-minute drive from town. There's even an 1,800-square-foot indoor golf facility to help you find out why your slice is so messed up.

Dixie College, founded in 1911, provides a year-round cultural setting with music and theatre productions, a Celebrity Concert

Series, the Jazz Ensemble and the Southwest Symphony Orchestra. The college serves the retired community with continuing education.

Real Estate A wide variety of properties and housing is available in this area. Homes sell from $80,000 to over $1.5 million. An older, more economical, three-bedroom home averages about $99,500, and the annual property tax on it would be about $1,000. The average selling price of all homes here was $147,500 in late 1994. I suspect the higher prices reflect sales in the newer, upscale developments which are sprouting up around the area.

Several small towns nearby extend lower home prices for cost-conscious folks. In the southern section of St. George, the Bloomington and Bloomington Hills developments offer exceptionally well-designed homes, reminiscent of those in Arizona's Sun City projects. Incidentally, the rental market is tight here, with few vacancies and high rents, all reflecting the popularity of St. George as a place to live.

Medical Care As the health care center for the surrounding area, St. George is noted for providing quality care, with top facilities at lower costs than the national average. The 130-bed Dixie Medical Center is a progressive, regional referral facility that serves the health care needs of nearly 100,000 in a tri-state area of southern Utah, southern Nevada and north-eastern Arizona. Owned and operated by Intermountain Health Care, a private non-profit system based in Salt Lake City, the hospital provides quality care to those with medical needs regardless of their ability to pay.

When Grandkids Visit An unforgettable place to visit would be Zion National Park. This is one of the most spectacular scenic wonders of all Utah's fantastic scenic marvels. Massive, multi-colored cliffs and deep canyons, hiking trails through a petrified forest, past waterfalls and desert wildlife make this a must visit.

Important Addresses and Connections
Chamber of Commerce: 97 E. St. George Blvd., St. George, UT 84770
Senior Services: 245 N. 200 West, St. George, UT 84770
Daily Newspaper: *The Spectrum*, 275 East St. George Blvd., St. George, UT 84770
Real Estate Agents: Mansell & Associates Realtors, 1086 So. Main #202, St. George, UT 84770; Realty Executives, Sandra Strobell, 590 East St. George Blvd., St. George, UT 84770

Airport: the local airport offers commuter flights
Bus: no local bus, but there is Greyhound service and the St. George
   Shuttle to Las Vegas airport

ST. GEORGE	Jan.	Apr.	July	Oct.		Rain	Snow
Daily Highs	54	77	101	81		11	15
Daily Lows	27	44	68	46		in.	in.

Salt Lake City

*I love living here, because there's so much to do out of doors, close
to national parks and all. Yet, there's plenty of cultural activities,
like the symphony, ballet, opera and, of course, classes at the university.*
                                                      —Pat Sexton

In 1847 Brigham Young led a band of Mormons westward
across the plains and mountains in search of a new home free from
religious persecution. When the travelers looked down from mountains overlooking the valley of the Great Salt Lake, Brigham Young
announced that this was the Promised Land where they would live.
They set to work that same day, tilling the soil and began trans-
forming the dry and desolate land into beautiful, well-planned Salt
Lake City.

The capital of Utah and one of the largest cities in the Rocky
Mountain region (pop. 170,000), Salt Lake City is also the world
capital of the Church of Jesus Christ of Latter-day Saints. It sits in a
valley bordered to the north and east by mountains, near the southeastern shore of the Great Salt Lake.

At first the city's growth depended on the inflow of Mormon
converts from Europe and America. Later, industrial and business
expansion attracted many "gentiles"—that is, non-Mormons—who
now make up almost half the population. This makes for a more
cosmopolitan community than is found in most areas of Utah.

In the center of the city, surrounded by beautiful grounds, are
the chief buildings of the Mormon church. Other buildings of note
in the city are those of the University of Utah, the State Capitol, the
city and county building, the museum, the exposition buildings,
and two former residences of Brigham Young. In Temple Square is
the Sea Gull Monument, and at this point the altitude is 4,400 feet.

Most neighborhoods are clean and well-kept, with reasonably safe conditions.

Recreation and Culture Skiing in Park City, home of the U.S. Ski Team, and other winter sorts, draws sportsmen in the winter. Golf can be played most of the year, and hiking in city parks is a popular recreational activity here. Salt Lake City is the home base of the Utah (formerly New Orleans) Jazz professional basketball team. Local residents often brag about having their own opera, symphony orchestra and ballet as well as regional and amateur theater groups. Five major universities are within an hour's drive from Salt Lake City, plus several community colleges.

Provo Located about 40 miles south of Salt Lake City is the city of Provo, which recently received top rating as a place to retire by *Money* magazine. Provo is also the home of Brigham Young University, one of the largest private universities in the country. Most towns with high ratings for personal safety and low crime rates are small places, with populations around 20,000 to 30,000. So with 92,000 inhabitants, Provo is unusually large to rank so high in personal safety. It came in 24th place on our survey. Salt Lake City, by the way, ranks quite low in personal safety. This is puzzling, because folks who live there claim it's exceptionally safe. There must be some factor that causes this anomaly, but I've been unable to discover it.

Living Costs and Real Estate The overall cost of living in Salt Lake City is slightly below average, helped in part by exceptionally low utility costs (almost 20 percent below average). Housing costs, however are above average. The average sales price of a three-bedroom home in the Salt Lake City area was $125,000. Fixer-uppers go for much less, and better homes commonly top $300,000. (You may find real estate in Provo for slightly less than in Salt Lake City.)

Medical Care Seven major medical facilities serve this area, making it one of the premier places for health care in the West. Altogether, Salt Lake City has 13 hospitals. Provo is currently served by two excellent hospitals, providing over 400 beds.

When Grandkids Visit You'll find most attractions have something to do with Mormon history, reflecting the religious emphasis by state and local governments. But there are also the

Hansen Planetarium and the Natural History Museum, with a nice collection of dinosaur skeletons, neither with any particular religious bias.

Important Addresses and Connections

Chamber of Commerce: 175 E. 400 S. #600, Salt Lake City, UT 84111. (You may have to work a bit to get information out of these folks; they were one of the least helpful chambers I've encountered.)

Senior Services: 1992 S 200 E, Salt Lake City, UT 84115

Daily Newspapers: *Salt Lake Tribune,* 143 S Main St., Salt Lake City, UT 84111; *Deseret News,* 30 E 100 S, Salt Lake City, UT 84111

Real Estate Agent: David Sampson, Century 21, 1385 Fort Union Blvd., Salt Lake City, UT 84121

Airport: Salt Lake International, a major airline junction

Bus: both a city bus system and Greyhound serve the area

SALT LAKE CITY	Jan.	Apr.	July	Oct.	Rain	Snow
Daily Highs	37	61	93	67	15	58
Daily Lows	20	37	62	39	in.	in.

Index to Places

Our books are available in most bookstores. However, if you have difficulty finding them, we will be happy to ship them to you directly. Just send your check or money order.

Retirement

Exploring the Travel/Retirement Option
ADVENTURES ABROAD $12.95 $_____

Wintering, Retiring or Investing
CHOOSE COSTA RICA $13.95   _____

Living Well on $800 a Month
CHOOSE MEXICO $11.95   _____

Retirement Discoveries for Every Budget
CHOOSE THE SOUTHWEST   NEW $12.95   _____

Strategies for Comfortable Retirement on Social Security
RETIREMENT ON A SHOESTRING $8.95   _____

America's Best and Most Affordable Places
WHERE TO RETIRE $14.95   _____

Travel

An Impromptu Travel Guide
FRANCE WITHOUT RESERVATIONS $12.95   _____

Hiking Guides for Active Adults
WALKING EASY IN THE SWISS ALPS $10.95   _____
WALKING EASY IN THE AUSTRIAN ALPS $10.95   _____
WALKING EASY IN THE FRENCH ALPS $11.95   _____
WALKING EASY IN THE ITALIAN ALPS $11.95   _____
WALKING EASY IN THE SAN FRANCISCO BAY AREA $11.95   _____

Postage & Handling
          First book...............................$1.90   _____
          Each additional book...........1.00   _____
California residents add 8% sales tax   _____

                                        Total $ _____

Please ship to:

Name _____

Address _____

City/State/Zip_____

Our books are shipped bookrate. Please allow 2 - 3 weeks for delivery. If you are not satisfied, the price of the book(s) will be refunded in full. (U. S. funds for all orders, please.)

Mail to: Gateway Books 2023 Clemens Road Oakland CA 94602